Research Partnerships in Early Childhood Education

Research Partnerships in Early Childhood Education

Teachers and Researchers in Collaboration

Edited by Judith Duncan and Lindsey Conner

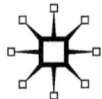

RESEARCH PARTNERSHIPS IN EARLY CHILDHOOD EDUCATION
Copyright © Judith Duncan and Lindsey Conner, 2013.

All rights reserved.

First published in 2013 by
PALGRAVE MACMILLAN®
in the United States—a division of St. Martin's Press LLC,
175 Fifth Avenue, New York, NY 10010.

Where this book is distributed in the UK, Europe and the rest of the World, this is by Palgrave Macmillan, a division of Macmillan Publishers Limited, registered in England, company number 785998, of Houndmills, Basingstoke, Hampshire RG21 6XS.

Palgrave Macmillan is the global academic imprint of the above companies and has companies and representatives throughout the world.

Palgrave® and Macmillan® are registered trademarks in the United States, the United Kingdom, Europe and other countries.

ISBN: 978–1–137–35067–1

Library of Congress Cataloging-in-Publication Data is available from the Library of Congress.

A catalogue record of the book is available from the British Library.

Design by Integra Software Services

First edition: November 2013

10 9 8 7 6 5 4 3 2 1

In acknowledgment and honor of Jeanette Rhedding-Jones (1943–2013), an internationally respected colleague in early childhood education and teacher education, and in reconceptualizing our taken-for-granted ways of understanding and knowing early childhood education and research. Jeanette gently and wisely guided us to a deeper awareness of our role and influence, particularly with regard to culturally inclusive pedagogies.

Contents

List of Tables ... ix

Acknowledgments ... xi

Foreword by Maggie MacLure ... xiii

Foreword by Richard Johnson ... xv

Notes on Contributors ... xxv

1 Introduction ... 1
   Lindsey Conner and Judith Duncan
2 Re-generating Research Partnerships in Early
   Childhood Education: A Non-idealized Vision ... 11
   Veronica Pacini-Ketchabaw and Fikile Nxumalo
3 Attunement of Knowledge Forms: The *Relational
   Agency* of Researchers, Policy Writers, and Early
   Childhood Educators ... 27
   Marilyn Fleer
4 Developing Effective Research–Practice Partnerships:
   Lessons from a Decade of Partnering with Schools in Poor
   Urban Communities ... 49
   Mei Lai and Stuart McNaughton
5 Partnership in Promoting Literacy: An Exploration of Two
   Studies in Low-Decile Early Childhood Settings
   in New Zealand ... 71
   Claire McLachlan, Alison Arrow and Judy Watson
6 Ko koe ki tēna, ko ahau ki tēnei kīwai o te kete: Exploring
   Collaboration across a Range of Recent Early
   Childhood Studies ... 93
   Jenny Ritchie, Janita Craw, Cheryl Rau, and Iris Duhn
7 An Ongoing Exploration of Uncertainty: Ethical
   Identities—Ours and Children's ... 115
   *Kim Atkinson and Enid Elliot, with input from
   the Victoria IQ group*

8 Teacher Reflection in Early Years Partnership Research
  Projects: But It's No Use Going Back to Yesterday, because
  I Was a Different Person Then (Says Alice from *Alice's
  Adventures in Wonderland*) 135
  Judith Duncan
9 Conclusion: Research Partnerships in Early Years Education 153
  Judith Duncan and Lindsey Conner

Index 167

Tables

5.1 Composition of participants from four early childhood centers 76

5.2 Mean Change from pretest to posttest for intervention and control groups 79

5.3 Pre, mid, and post scores of literacy abilities in kindergarten children ($n = 26$) 82

Acknowledgments

We wish to acknowledge all the teachers, children, and parents who have been partners and participants in the research discussed in this book. Without them this book could not have been written, nor the lessons learned and the *knowledges* gained.

We thank the funders of the research projects in this book and hope that they continue to fund such innovative projects in each country.

We thank Maggie Burgess (Dunedin, New Zealand), who assisted us with editing and formatting of this book, and survived our iterations with humor and goodwill.

And finally we thank our families, whose ongoing support makes everything possible for us.

Foreword by Maggie MacLure

If you are lucky, you will, like me, find this rich collection of work not only thought provoking but also slightly destabilizing. As a reader and researcher steeped in the UK contexts of early childhood education, many of the concerns that are addressed in the chapters, including of course the central notion underlying the book, of partnership itself. Yet at the same time, the distinctive geopolitical and historical locations of the contributions—Aotearoa New Zealand, Canada, and Australia—introduce a productive energy of difference and cultural complexity. The slight sense of disorientation induced by encountering the not-quite-familiar is particularly to be valued, I think, in a field such as early childhood education, where long-standing and deep-seated notions of *the child* and her development have proved resilient, even when their assumptions and effects have been challenged, and where there is a risk of continuing erasure of cultural difference as a result of the global travel of neoliberal education policies. Many of the chapters in this book allude to policy contexts that would, on the face of it at least, be deeply familiar to those who have been involved in early childhood education and research in England, and to some extent in other counties in the United Kingdom. For well over a decade, in the United Kingdom there has been significant state investment in young children and their families, serving the conviction that early intervention is needed to reduce inequality of opportunity and attainment, and ultimately to boost economic performance. This has resulted in reforms that are equally recognizable in the contexts described in this collection: the introduction of curricula for the under-fives; multi-agency support for children and families; accountability and quality assurance measures based on test scores and outcomes; and training and professional development programs for practitioners to underpin delivery and improve standards.

Partnership has become central under these contemporary conditions, not just as a buzz-word in policy rhetoric, but as a real and renewed challenge for researchers working with practitioners, children, and families. The contributors to the book offer a range of critical perspectives on what research partnership is and might be, drawing on diverse theoretical and methodological resources, and, importantly, putting these to work in their particular national and local settings. In many of the chapters, there is a real sense of an effort to push beyond rather idealized notions of partnership in the existing research literature in order to develop new conceptual frameworks for understanding and developing partnership. Thus, readers will find studies of partnership variously informed by cultural and historical activity theory, poststructuralism, Kaupapa Māori theorizing, and the new materialism of Barad and Deleuze among other approaches, using research methods ranging from quasi-experimental and mixed methods to case study and narrative. Equally importantly, many of the chapters acknowledge and address problems and tensions that often reside in the dynamics of research relationships, and in the struggle to develop *counter-colonial* research practices. It is this diversity of orientation and context that opens up concepts that may have become rather stale—partnership, collaboration, reflective practice—to new possibilities.

Ultimately the experience that the book offers, of moving back and forth between the familiar and the unfamiliar, does not depend on the reader's particular geographical location. Rather, it is a reflection of both continuities *and* fault-lines running through early childhood education and research, creating tensions between developmental, sociocultural, and reconceptualist approaches to young children's learning; between the cultures and practices of the global North and South; between competing models of professionalism; between different visions of practitioner–researcher relations, and between the desire for secure knowledge and outcomes, on the one hand, and the embrace of uncertainty and creative experimentation, on the other.

As the collection amply demonstrates, the notion of partnership is complex and shifting, and there is no attempt to bring all the accounts under one overarching framework. The chapters are, however, united by a common passion for and commitment to making a positive difference to young children's lives and educational experiences, and to the search for ways of working ethically and productively with their partners in this shared endeavor.

Foreword by Richard Johnson

Too often, professional learning is structured by a top-down model where educational knowledge is generated outside the classroom and transmitted to teachers, who must then implement the required program or content. Practitioner inquiry disrupts such prevalent arrangements, providing opportunities for teachers to theorize their practice and investigate issues they identify as important (Ghiso, 2012, p. 7).

Introduction

In some of my recent work, I've been attempting to focus on my particular notions of the over-standardization of teaching and learning in today's educational contexts and have presented critiques of these ideas and issues (Johnson, 2010a, 2010b). This content, based mostly on the context of where I work, in the United States, has been met with head-nodding affirmation(s) and confirmation(s) of said practices on a global scale (e.g., Norway, England, Australia, New Zealand, and Canada) from the diverse locales of conference participants present at international conference venues where I've discussed this. Some of the US issues I address in my initial brief critiques (Johnson, 2010c) included the current overblown educational focus on standards, accountability (rubrics), testing, curriculum, instruction, pedagogy, push-down curriculum, the gaze, surveillance, fit, conform, accreditation, "No Child Left Behind" (NCLB), "Race to the Top," constraints, confinement and containment, teacher education, syllabi construction, et cetera. Some of the related discourses apparent and felt in these deliberations included issues like deskilling, undoing, dumbing down, demystifying, and regimentation (Johnson, 2011, 2009).

My review of the personal contributions presented here in this larger text illustrates how so many other early childhood educators are interested in professionally and personally pursuing further collective critiques of these and many other related issues by contributing to this teacher-education book that critically engages this content on a more global level. I'm quite intrigued by the presented work in this text as a multitude of educators in this narrative share personalized critical accounts of innovative critiques of research as they critically deliberate about *research partnerships* in the early childhood education field of studies. A quick review of the content alone, presented in titles such as "Re-generating Research Partnerships," "Attunement of Knowledge Forms," "Lessons from a Decade of Partnering with Schools," "Partnership in Promoting Literacy," "Exploring the Enablers and Constraints of Research Collaboration," "Exploration of Uncertainty," and "Teacher Reflection in Early Years Partnership Research" illustrate the critical nature of the diverse content these authors intellectually pursue in this text.

The presented collection of original papers in this book, *Research Partnerships in Early Childhood Education*, brings together critical educational, postmodern, sociological, and cultural/postcolonial studies perspectives to bear on rethinking the origins of partnering with others to engage teacher educators and researchers and exploring new collaboration implications. A central concern running through all of these chapters is the emergence of embodied empowerment in the teacher and researcher(s) teams and the complexity of conceptualizing the relationship between external cultural and social forces, and the internal sense of agency that we aspire for our professional field(s) to possess. While considerable advances have been made theoretically in moving away from a simplistic notion of a human being as a person of absolute free will toward an acknowledgment of the social, linguistic, and cultural situatedness of human subjectivity, these insights have been slow to percolate down into everyday understandings of collaborative partnership research, as evidenced, for example, in conventional texts in early childhood education, curriculum studies, teacher education, and research methodology.

In the early childhood field of study, is it possible to conceptualize critical theoretical ways that acknowledge the powerful cultural situatedness of research traditional formations, yet also allows us to tease out the potential for agency and imaginative action in each individual's life? The works presented here challenge us to question "Is there a *space in between*—a space beyond what Lacan would call the symbolic—in which researchers and teachers might expand the opportunities for children to come to be in ways that are agentic and imaginative?" (O'Loughlin, 2010, p. 4). Psychoanalysts would argue that such a space exists in the realm of the unsymbolized—that part of our unconscious beyond reach of the symbolic. Others invoke theories of cultural memory, hauntology, et cetera, assisting us in articulating this *in-between space* as a place where productive work can be done to articulate individual agency, imaginative possibilities, and political awareness (Venn, 2004).

It is precisely this space—and the radical potential it contains for partnership research, embodied theorizing, and collaborative empowerment—that this book aims to address. The chapter reflections reveal that it is possible to bring together influential thinkers who are forthright in their refusal to be seduced by simplistic binaries and who are willing to address the notion of research partnerships in ways that are complex and critical, yet that also offer practical advances in our thinking about research partnerships, collaboration, shared theorizing, and ways of being as researchers and teachers.

Intentions

This work intentionally interrogates much of the age-old static teacher education formulae, which typically anticipates and adheres to a linear trajectory for each candidate, notions of the *best practices* and *best fit*, learning proper research form, and the now-inherent desire(s) of meeting the needs of an outside teacher education accrediting body, first and foremost. This work, this collection of life narratives and ongoing learning narratives, is intentionally meant to counter the above-mentioned "traps of individualization, scripting, and de-contextualization" (Goodson, 2006). This ongoing, intentional narrative critique through the storying of one's self relates closely with Cherednichenko, Hooley, Kruger, and Moore's (2001) ideas about *authentic learning* whereby these graduate teacher education students are authentically learning about and continuously reflecting upon a set of "social practices enabling students to act knowledgeably and powerfully in the classroom and world" (p. 10).

Narrative, too, has potential power for those who have been silenced, as the expression of their own voices can lead to new theories and ways of applying these new theories to practice in the classroom (Carr, 1985). When I (re)read the vast amount of teacher and researchers stories over the years, I see how empowering they are and how much potential weight they have as high-quality practice(s) indicators as these future and novice teachers make sense of their own lives as teachers, parents, partners, and community members. Through stories, I feel that individuals have a greater likelihood of rediscovering their own selves—and the interconnectedness among the many aspects of their selves (Johnson, 2010c). Through this powerful personalized knowledge acquisition and recognition technique, I believe our students will continue to creatively gain self-knowledge, as well as create new knowledge about themselves and about teaching and schooling, knowledge that will be assistive to these individual teachers and to larger professional teacher education collectives.

After the brief introductory chapter, the collection opens with Veronica Pacini-Ketchabaw and Fikile Nxumalo's work in which they immediately note that they "do not have definitive answers regarding enablers and barriers for effective relations in research partnerships" (p. 17). They go on to note that their work deeply involves "entanglements" as they purposely seek out to study and critique the partnership relationships that need ongoing, collaborative attention as researchers dutifully "regenerate change and relationality." Going back to my earlier comments on questioning the normative educational practices that are dominating our respective fields, Veronica and Fikile discuss movements *away from linearity* as they discuss how "re-generation embraces mutuality, mess, multiplicity and contradictions" (p. 18). They are actively seeking out alternative frameworks for pursuing collective and individual research work as we *disrupt* the normative practices that dominate our field. This work pushes us to think outside the normative structures and beyond the established borders as we consider unknown issues that are tentative, transformative, and experimental, instead of simply fixed and known. Their theoretical work urges us to creatively pursue collaborative research partnership engagements as we collectively pursue *becoming* instead of assuming traditional practices under the guise of *being* experts.

In Chapter 3, Marilyn Fleer explores the realm of researchers, policy writers, and early childhood educators coming together to collectively define and study their partnership practices in an open, engaging process. Unlike the currently popular top-down educational approaches, in this project, teams of experts brought their expertise together in collective meetings where they jointly analyzed video observations and then produced their own literacy- and numeracy-related learning resources. These findings were based on their knowledge production via dialogical interpretations of what they viewed and discussed as a professional intellectual team who brought different theories and personal practices to the table as they deliberated on and interrogated their viewings. Marilyn's work illustrates how teams of diverse experts (e.g., from family childcare workers, preschool teachers, and maternal health professionals, to school principals and university professors) engaged in and critiqued policies and current common procedures as they collaboratively analyzed different sets of data common to their individual and collective daily practices. Her work exemplifies the power of team generations of knowledge production as they worked through their individual and joint notions of child development and how those notions were opened up and made visible to their intellectual team and thereby had an impact on their daily professional practices.

Mei Lai and Stuart McNaughton focus their attention in Chapter 4 on how to effectively build research–school partnership models as the intellectual partners individually and collectively move toward improving student outcome measures. The chapter reviews the key principles for partnerships and highlights the importance of focusing on enduring collaborative enterprises between the researchers and school personnel. This work involves the research teams and school practitioners actively engaging in data gathering and research analyses as they work together while designing, engaging, and evaluating effective instructional practices. These practices involve bringing shared intellectual practices together while collaboratively being involved in identifying and solving urgent problems of current practice. These team practices recognize and honor different current educational communities of learners as these diverse teams bring their shared expertise together and work collectively as larger communities of practice. They expand their discussion to include the importance of cultural beliefs and content into these deliberations as much of their work involves Māori (indigenous New Zealanders) educators in Aotearoa New Zealand. From this cultural perspective they discuss the importance of establishing long-term relationships over a long period of time (e.g., 13 years), which is quite different from the well-established historical model whereby the outside researcher comes into a community(s) and collects data over a brief time period, and typically is never to be seen again.

In a chapter that engages the promotion of literacy development in early childhood centers, Claire McLachlan, Alison Arrow, and Judy Watson explore the impact of professional development on young children's literacy development. The authors note the global awareness of literacy experiences of young children before school entry and relate that to the relationship with effective teaching practices, especially those in their homeland of Aotearoa New Zealand. Noting how the new national curriculum addresses literacy development at school, they thoroughly review and present current research findings that illustrate how the early childhood field needs increased professional development activities to increase their knowledge of the most effective research-based practices for enhancing literacy development in young children. McLachlan, Arrow, and Watson then share the results of two different studies that they conducted, which were focused on enhancing the literacy development of preschool children in Aotearoa New Zealand. Their culminating findings from each of the literacy-based research studies speak to the importance of enabling teachers via effective professional development interventions focused on the literacy development of young children.

In Chapter 6, Jenny Ritchie, Janita Craw, Cheryl Rau, and Iris Duhn explore a wide range of different early childhood studies that focus on the importance of collaborative partnerships between academic researchers, teachers, and other community members invested in educational projects. Their work makes an open, honest pledge to approach partnerships with a critical, reflexive understanding of teaching, learning, early childhood care and education, and research. Beginning with the classical interview part of research, this chapter focuses on helping to provide voice for those *others* in research (i.e., teachers, children, parents) who typically remain mostly invisible in these procedural settings. This notion of voice included active listening strategies and deeper reflection around *truth* embedded in interview reflections and ongoing discussions about findings as teams make continuous reflective meanings about the layered content in the stories that unfold in these procedures. This work is not without tension of all the participatory parties as they negotiate meaning between the different individuals and groups participating in these projects while they are working toward continual change processes throughout their collaborative partnering experiences. They mention the tensions that exist in normative institutional hierarchies that we all participate in as teachers, researchers, parents, and community members. We must push and prod and challenge each other in different ways as we creatively move forward in these collaborative, ongoing intellectual and personal relationships that recognize the complicated research conversations embedded in this joint work.

Cheryl Rau illustrates the importance of incorporating indigenous ways of being into our work as she illustrates how the *Māori* worldview on responsibility and respectfulness to the collective is important to recognize and implement in collaborative partnerships. Each project recognizes and embodies the importance of *whanaungatanga* (relationships) whereby collective notions of each contributing person(s) empower the project from beginning to end, instilling a sense of cohesion throughout the project. In the closing part of this chapter, Jenny Ritchie discusses the long history of colonialism, racism, and cultural and economic inequities that have impacted the objectification of indigenous peoples the world over. She shares the importance of this recognition and the *counter-colonial* approach, which is ever more inclusive as it embodies the voices and spirits of all party members, from infants to elders, in the grand narrative portrayed in different project approaches.

Chapter 7 includes Kim Atkinson and Enid Elliot's theoretical pursuit of early childhood practices as a pedagogy of uncertainty. Here the authors pursue, among other issues, the personalized role of our ongoing self-examination of our ethical responsibility(s) as we continuously reflect on our practices and search deep inside our subjective selves as practitioners, colleagues, researchers, and community members. As researchers who began collaborative relationships with teachers and others, their shared verbal deliberations opened up spaces for further collaborative engagement, which may not have been pursued without these more formal partnerships. These established relationships then opened up space for enhanced critical, reflective dialogue about issues that may not have been discussed without these trusting relationships, such as gender, racialization, sexuality and politics, and violence. This closely knit dialogical space allowed these groups of researchers and practitioners to further pursue their personalized vulnerability as they intellectually critiqued their own developmental backgrounds and openly reconsidered their core values as they participated in *open listening* (Davies, 2011). These practices allowed for more risk taking as the authors noted that they allowed more critical space(s) for open, honest sharing, listening, and critically thinking through the many complexities of daily educational practices. Their work provides a wonderful critique of how to navigate our experiences with our *ghosts and fears* as we become vulnerable by opening up our dialogue with other theorists, practitioners, and community members.

Judith Duncan focuses her attention in Chapter 8 on how teacher reflection in early years partnership research projects can critically engage historical mindsets and expand the thinking on how we creatively expand our collaborative partnerships work(s). She interrogates the importance of validating starting points for effective reflection(s) as she questions the centrality of issues like the *now, then, before,* and the *after* in these important processes. Like the other authors present here, she brings to mind the importance of locating ourselves within these established reflective practices as we partner with professional colleagues in different educational venues. This work illustrates the importance of recognizing whether our so-called innovative work simply recycles dated assumptions or pushes beyond those established boundaries in professional and personal collaboration with other colleagues. The keen focus on Foucault's work (1977, 1980) in her research is highly assistive in illustrating how we continue to control ourselves and others through limiting processes and procedures (e.g., written records and reflective writing), how surveillance impacts our professional and personal work, and how self-control limits our individual and collaborative interactive work. Duncan illustrates how the increased accountability in educational practices impacts teachers and their subjective ways of being in the classroom and in deliberation with research partners. She creatively closes off with Deleuze and Guattari's (1987) notions of continuously *becoming* in the multitude of different, diverse encounters we participate in, especially as we, as researchers, engaged in collaborative research partnerships and are continuously *becoming*.

In the closing chapter, Judith Duncan and Lindsey Conner review the innovative findings presented in each chapter, while highlighting the seen and unseen presence of different creative theorizing embedded within the larger collective narrative. They note the central importance of our need to continually challenge traditions (i.e., what counts as knowledge; what is certainty, diversity, research methodologies, etc.) as we rethink our roles in educational collaborations. The ever-changing professional and personal identity of teachers is highlighted as they discuss empowered, embodied individuals and the diverse practices within the educational field at large. Highlighting the important nature of collaboration is a key aspect of this closing chapter as Duncan and Conner illustrate how each of the chapters discussed research partnerships, the traditional nature of these relationships, and how they have changed over time.

The contributors of this book creatively pull from many different innovative theoretical perspectives and infuse these critical ideas into their own and their partners' mindsets. The work presented here enhances the greater early childhood educational field with the deconstruction of historical practices and rethinking current and future creative, collaborative partnership practices. These collective works are of central importance to current and future education venues as the increase of internal and external surveillance and auditing of our various research projects will limit us if we do not collaborate with research and professional partners in innovative, restructured formats, just as these authors have.

References

Carr, D. (1985). Life and the narrator's art. In H. J. Silverman, & D. Ihde (Eds.), *Hermeneutics & deconstruction* (pp. 108–121). Albany, NY: State University of New York Press.

Cherednichenko, B., Hooley, N., Kruger, T., & Moore, R. (2001, December). Longitudinal study of school restructuring. Paper presented at the Annual Conference of the *Australian Association for Research in Education*, Fremantle, Australia.

Davies, B. (2011). Open listening: Creative evolution in early childhood settings. *International Journal of Early Childhood, 43*(2), 119–132. Doi: 10/10007/s13158-011-0030-1.

Deleuze, G., & Guattari, F. (1987). *A thousand plateaus: Capitalism and schizophrenia* (B. Massumi, Trans.). Minneapolis, MN: University of Minnesota Press.

Foucault, M. (1977). *Discipline and punish* (Alan Sheridan, Trans.). London, UK: Penguin Books.

Foucault, M. (1980). The eye of power. In C. Gordon (Ed.), *Power/knowledge: Selected interviews and other writings, 1972-1977: Michel Foucault* (pp. 194–228). Hemel Hempstead, U.K.: The Harvester Press.

Ghiso, M. (2012). Supporting teacher voices through inquiry and collaboration in professional development courses. *Voices of Practitioners, 7*(1), 1–6.

Goodson, I. (2006). The rise of the life narrative. *Teacher Education Quarterly, 33*(4), 7–21.

Johnson, R. (2009, April). *Analyzing curricular perspectives in early childhood settings.* Paper presented at the *Annual Meeting of the American Educational Research Association*, San Diego, CA.

Johnson, R. (2010a). Afterward. In M. O'Loughlin & R. Johnson (Eds.), *Imagining children otherwise: Theoretical and critical perspectives on childhood subjectivity* (pp. 229–232). New York, NY: Peter Lang Press.

Johnson, R. (2010b). Putting myself in the picture: Oppositional looks as sites of resistance. In M. O'Loughlin & R. Johnson (Eds.), *Imagining children otherwise: Theoretical and critical perspectives on childhood subjectivity* (pp. 111–134). New York, NY: Peter Lang Press.

Johnson, R. (2010c, May). *Working the space in between: Pedagogical possibilities in rethinking teacher identity(s)*. Paper presented at the Annual Narrative Matters Conference, New Brunswick, Canada.

Johnson, R. (2011, October). *Body representations in early childhood education: Interrogating teacher education through collective story constellations*. Paper presented at the Annual Conference on *Reconceptualizing Research in Early Schooling: Research, Theory and Practice*, London, UK.

O'Loughlin, M. (2010). Ghostly presences in children's lives: Toward a psychoanalysis of the social. In M. O'Loughlin & R. Johnson (Eds.), *Imagining children otherwise: Theoretical and critical perspectives on childhood subjectivity* (pp. 49–74). New York, NY: Peter Lang Publishing.

Venn, C. (2004). Post-affective Lacanian economy, being-in-the-world, and the critique of the present. *Theory, Culture, & Society, 21*(1), 149–158.

Contributors

Alison Arrow Dr. Alison Arrow is a senior lecturer in Literacy Education, Massey University, New Zealand. Alison's specific research interests include the study of early literacy development in preschool children and beginning readers. Her research is aimed at the prediction and prevention of literacy difficulties at the beginning of learning literacy instruction. Alison completed PhD in Psychology on kindergarten children's literacy skills at the University of Auckland in 2007, where she was the recipient of a University of Auckland doctoral scholarship. In 2012 she was awarded a Massey University Emerging Researcher Award for her contributions to educational research.

Kim Atkinson Kim Atkinson is an early childhood educator and pedagogista with the Unit for Early Years Research and Development at the University of Victoria, British Columbia, Canada. She is also the co-creator of *The Images of Learning Project* (imagesoflearningproject.com) an exhibit, blog, and presentations that highlight a powerful image of the child and the value of the work of early childhood educators. With the *Images of Learning Project*, Kim has travelled the province presenting to students, early childhood educators, teachers, and administrators, engaging them to reflect on ideas and practice. She has been a member of the Victoria Investigating Quality Project (IQ) since 2007.

Lindsey Conner Dr. Lindsey Conner is an associate professor in the School of Educational Studies and Leadership at the College of Education, *Te Whare Wānanga O Waitaha*/University of Canterbury, Christchurch, New Zealand. She is the director of the Science and Technology Education Research Lab, which lays an emphasis on researching pedagogy associated with the use of technology for teaching. Her varied teaching roles have included early years education, secondary teaching, and teacher education, while her research interests span partnership projects with schools, and Ministries. She has a strong interest in futures education and research that leads to educational change.

Janita Craw Janita Craw teaches across a range of undergraduate and postgraduate programs in Auckland University of Technology (AUT) School of Education/*Te Kura Mātauranga*, New Zealand. Her research interests include a range of areas relevant to early childhood, childhood generically, and research in education, and beyond, in the world of visual art. An interest in critical philosophy and theory is fundamental to her interests in researching—for example, mathematics, images of childhood, ecological sustainability, visual art, infant and toddler pedagogy—in early childhood education. Yet at heart, her interests lie in an interdisciplinary arts-based research project that continues to explore thinking in, through, and with visual art/artist's works as alternative (to philosophy and science) but valuable research methodology, one that contributes something valuable to our understandings of the world in early childhood, education, and research, and beyond.

Iris Duhn Dr. Iris Duhn lectures in the Faculty of Education, at Monash University, Australia. Her teaching and research focuses on critical childhood studies, in particular globalization, ecological sustainability, and governmentality studies. Her publications and research projects contribute a critical childhood studies perspective to early childhood education in New Zealand, Australia, and internationally.

Judith Duncan Dr. Judith Duncan is an associate professor of Education, School of Educational Studies and Leadership, College of Education at *Te Whare Wānanga O Waitaha*/ University of Canterbury, Christchurch, New Zealand. Judith is an established researcher with over 20 years of research experience, predominantly using qualitative research methods in a range of education settings. She has been involved in a range of projects that examine early childhood, from multiple and interdisciplinary perspectives, placing central to each research project the perspectives of children and their families. Judith is a co-editor of the Palgrave publication *Comparative Early Childhood Services: International Perspectives* (2012).

Enid Elliot Dr. Enid Elliot has been an early childhood educator for many years now. Over that time she has worked in Turkey, California, New York, and British Columbia in a variety of contexts and programs. She is continually surprised, intrigued, and delighted by the children, families, and early childhood educators with whom she is engaged. Babies and toddlers have been a particular source of interest, inspiration, and joy for her. Doing doctoral work helped her to develop different perspectives on that inspiration and her dissertation resulted in a book, *We're Not Robots: Listening to the Voices of Daycare Providers*. Recently she has begun to investigate the influence of outdoor natural settings on children's experiences. Currently she is an adjunct professor at University of Victoria, British Columbia, and on faculty at Camosun College, Victoria, BC, Canada.

Marilyn Fleer Dr. Marilyn Fleer holds the Professorial Foundation Chair of Early Childhood Education at Monash University, Australia, and is the president of the International Society for Cultural Activity Research (ISCAR). Her research interests focus on early years learning and development, with special attention on pedagogy, culture, science, and technology.

Richard Johnson Dr. Richard Johnson is a professor in Education at the University of Hawaii, Hawaii. Johnson's interests are focused on critiquing the normative practices in the field of early childhood.

Mei Kuin Lai Dr. Mei Kuin Lai is the associate director of the Woolf Fisher Research Centre, Faculty of Education, University of Auckland, New Zealand. Her research interests are in: Schooling improvement, research and development collaborations to raise achievement, professional learning communities, evidence informed decision-making.

Maggie McLure Dr. Maggie MacLure is a professor of Education in the Educational and Social Research Institute, Manchester Metropolitan University, United Kingdom. She started her career as a researcher on the influential Bristol Language Development Project, and later moved to the National Foundation for Educational Research, where she helped to develop the national framework for the assessment of oracy, for the Assessment of Performance Unit. She has continued to carry out research on language and discourse, and is also interested in the development of theory and methodology in applied social research. She is a member (from September 2006) of the Executive Council of the British Educational Research Association. Her book, *Discourse in Educational and Social Research*, won the 2004 Critics' Choice Award from the American Educational Studies Association.

Claire McLachlan Dr. Claire McLachlan is a professor and the leader of the Early Years Programme at Massey University Institute of Education, New Zealand. Claire's interests in literacy stem from her doctoral research, completed in New Zealand kindergartens in 1995 and she has since completed two further major studies of literacy in the early childhood setting. Claire is currently part of a large Health Research Council (HRC) funded project on "Healthy homework" in primary schools and has previous research on self-review; physical activity; and open, distance, and flexible learning. Claire is a co-editor of *Literacies in Childhood: Changing Views, Challenging Practices* (Elsevier, 2007), the lead author of two editions of *Early Childhood Curriculum: Planning, Assessment and Evaluation* (CUP, 2010, 2013) and *Literacy in Early Childhood and Primary Education: Issues, Challenges, Solutions* (CUP, 2012) and a lead author of the forthcoming book *Children's Learning and Development: Contemporary Assessment in the Early Years*

(Palgrave Macmillan, 2013). Claire was awarded an Individual Research Award for distinction in educational research in 2012.

Stuart McNaughton Dr. Stuart McNaughton is a professor and the Director of the Woolf Fisher Research Centre, Faculty of Education, University of Auckland, New Zealand. Stuart's research interests are: early literacy, schooling improvement, research and development collaborations to raise achievement, and literacy in families and communities.

Fikile Nxumalo Fikile Nxumalo was a caregiver for several years practicing in family child care. She is a participant in the *Investigating Quality* (IQ) project and a doctoral student at the University of Victoria, BC, Canada. Her research and pedagogical interests lie in issues of social justice and equity in early childhood education. Fikile has recently taken on a new role as a community facilitator working with early childhood educators in her community.

Veronica Pacini-Ketchabaw Dr. Veronica Pacini-Ketchabaw is a professor in the School of Child and Youth Care at the University of Victoria, British Columbia, Canada. She co-directs the School's Unit for Early Years Research and Development, the *Investigating Quality Project*, and the *British Columbia Early Learning Framework Implementation Project*. She is an active member of the international Reconceptualizing Early Childhood Education group and has contributed important insights into issues of racialization in early childhood. She has been practicing in the field since 1990.

Cheryl Rau Cheryl Rau is of *Tainui, Kahungungu,* and *Rangitane* descent. Her educational and research focus has centered on *Te Tiriti o Waitangi* (The Treaty of Waitangi) partnerships in Aotearoa New Zealand, *Māori* educators articulating strategies, which nurture *tamariki* (children) *Māori* potentiality across the early childhood community. From 2004 to 2008 she completed co-directing two research studies funded by the New Zealand Government's Teaching and Learning Research Initiative (TLRI), which centered on prioritizing *Māori* (indigenous to Aotearoa) ways of knowing, doing, and being and transformative praxis within the sector. She has recently completed co-directing a further two-year TLRI project, which explored *kaitiakitanga* (ecological sustainability) utilizing an ethic of caring for self, others, and the environment from both indigenous and Western perspectives. Cheryl's 30-year background in education has been across the range of sectors, including Primary, Secondary and Tertiary. During the past 13 years she has been an early childhood educator and coordinator/director of *Ngahihi* professional learning programs, a *Māori* organization facilitating professional learning programs funded by the

Ministry of Education. In 2009 she joined *Te Tari Puna Ora o Aotearoa*/The New Zealand Childcare Association, as the Central Regional Manager.

Jenny Ritchie Dr. Jenny Ritchie has a background as a childcare educator and kindergarten teacher, followed by 23 years' experience in early childhood teacher education. She is an associate professor in Early Childhood Teacher Education at *Te Whare Wānanga o Wairaka*/Unitec Institute of Technology, in Auckland, New Zealand. Her teaching, research, and writing has focused on supporting early childhood educators and teacher educators to enhance their praxis in terms of cultural, environmental, and social justice issues.

Judy Watson Judy Watson was a Senior Tutor in Early Years Education at Massey University College of Education, New Zealand, and collected data for Project Two reported in Chapter 5. Following restructuring of the College, Judy has become a kindergarten teacher for the Ruahine Kindergarten Association. Judy completed her MEd thesis on the topic of literacy in the early childhood setting.

1

Introduction

Lindsey Conner and Judith Duncan

Purpose of the Book

In many countries around the world, early childhood centers and schools are increasingly being given greater responsibility for determining their own future directions in professional learning (Schleicher, 2012). While this involves a political agenda (Nuttall, 2010), related to why we do things the way we do them, the challenge for practitioners in the early childhood sector is to find appropriate common objectives for collaborative activities. It seems that successful collaborative research has an element of common purpose, despite the various backgrounds and knowledge bases of the collaborative partners. When teachers bring forth what they intuitively know works and consider these situations from other alternative perspectives, they begin to reconceptualize practice in light of their new insights. Promisingly, there is a growing body of evidence that research partnerships within early years learning communities are leading to improved outcomes for children and, at the same time, are enabling the development of teachers as researchers of their own practice (Nuttall, 2010). Not only does this contribute to new knowledge about and for the sector, but it can also build the capability and capacity for teachers to contribute to their own learning and the learning of the early years education community more widely. As a result there seems to be a growing acceptance among early childhood teachers that involvement in such research projects, with support, can provide opportunities to consider practice from an informed base, rather than adopting a more intuitive approach or one that only perpetuates past practices.

The prospect that research might inform and reform practice is appealing to teachers, academics, policy makers, and curriculum developers. Such research may include multiple dimensions of what might be classed as professional development (Borko, 2004), even though this approach is not akin to more traditional models of professional development, such as taking a course or reading background information in isolation. Research based in practice and conducted collaboratively within a community of practitioners and academics can include combinations of investigating previous research and practices, the co-generation and iterative development of new knowledge, the opportunity to consider what changes in practice might enhance outcomes for young children, contributions to recommendations for policy, and contributions to teacher education. However, Pacini-Ketchabaw and Nxumalo in this volume caution us that research partnerships should not be seen as drivers of changes to practice, but rather as opportunities for possible changes in educators' practices. Lai and McNaughton indicate in this volume that establishing research partnerships as such does not necessarily guarantee improvement of teaching and learning. Success of these research projects has more to do with the way the partnerships are developed and sustained through relational appeasement throughout the research, where the research has a shared common purpose. As Bellacasa (2012) has pointed out, relationship building in partnership research is always multidimensional and complex, as well as far from being innocent. While the partners become complicit in the outcomes, there may be occasions for attribution that may or may not be warranted. We touch on the ethical concerns in this relational space in a separate section below and take these up again in the final chapter.

The potential outcomes of collaborative partnership research also reflect the shift in educational research on practice more generally, where teachers, rather than being *researched* by an external researcher, become an integral part of designing and conducting the research and analyzing the results, thus gaining a better insight into their own professional practice (Joseph, 2004). In the projects discussed in this volume, teachers had actively and purposefully given input into interventions, the evaluation of the outcomes, and their own learning. In other words, there were some choices about the level of reflective engagement and how they would then incorporate anything they learned into future practice.

Many of the contributions in this volume indicate that there was an inherent plasticity in the partnerships and the progress of the projects. That is, there was flexibility both in terms of the ways people contributed within the projects and in terms of relatively open outcomes, rather than predetermined ones. Through participation in these research projects, the partners are inevitably changed, but the change was not necessarily predictable as it was ongoing, through intra-action through time and space and was situated in thinking and actions (Barad, 2003).

All of the authors have indicated that insights gleaned from one project led to adjustments and adaptations that were incorporated into future projects. Each chapter describes these in detail. The summary elucidates the elements that contribute to the purpose of this book, including how partnership research in early years education can contribute to

a) building cumulative knowledge that links teaching to learning;
b) enhancing knowledge and generation of educational research on teaching practices;
c) enhancing connections between partners in research;
d) growing research capacity and its application to teaching practice (effectiveness of teaching on learning and effectiveness as a vehicle for teacher learning or professional development).

Overview of the Chapters

Each chapter discusses the challenges and insights that arise when working in research partnerships. Each chapter also considers the challenges for practice-based partnership research as set out by Joce Nuttall (2010):

a) the... challenge of knowledge, practice, and research—separated but deeply connected;
b) collaborations "demanding a level of relational expertise that must in itself be developed and enacted within the complex, social, political, cultural, environmental and economic agendas facing the education sector" (p. 3);
c) collaborations that must "result in a higher level of research consciousness amongst those practitioners adding yet another level of complexity" (p. 3).

Given that there are multiple uncertainties confronting contemporary human services professionals (Fook, Ryan & Hawkins, 2000), the research collaborations among these professionals demand complex forms of relational expertise (Edwards, 2010). The majority of collaborations described in the chapters herein were between teachers and research academics. Fleer, in her chapter, also describes multiagency projects that had to develop such relational expertise that she calls *relational agency*. In this sense, success depended on positive ongoing communication that checked the assumptions of the participants and included multiple activities that fostered reflection on and discussion about practice. Edwards (2010) indicates that successful research partnerships conceptualize themselves as a collective, with *collective expertise*. They do not rely only on their own expertise, but consider how they and others can collaborate to synergistically create new knowledge. Throughout the examples highlighted in each chapter, we see that valuing others' expertise and contributions forms a fundamental element of positive relations between partners in research.

If the co-evolution of activities that support changes (in thinking and practices) is an indicator of successful partnership research collaboration, then it follows that researchers must also develop more nuanced forms of expertise to create opportunities for developing new ways of generating knowledge (Nuttall, 2010). This may include developing new sensitivities and ways of finding out what assumptions and knowledge already exist, as well as pedagogical changes, developing new resources, artifacts, or events as potential sources or opportunities for collaborative discussion (Anderson & Shattuck, 2012). It may also involve developing new methodological strategies to sustain success (Mayo, Henson & Smith, 2008).

Ethical Responsibilities and Dilemmas as Researchers

As indicated in earlier sections of this chapter, when research is situated in educational practice, where professional development and research are intertwined, ethical concerns, dilemmas, and issues abound. The ethical dilemmas influenced how the partners operated and adjusted their approaches during the projects and how they reconceptualized subsequent projects. Within each chapter, the authors touch on how these ethical dilemmas related to each context in more detail. To varying extents, each set of authors grappled with the complex nature of partnership research and the ethical questions that were generated. For example:

a. How do we acknowledge existing expertise and enable educators to become empowered to make changes and experiment with their own practice, yet at the same time advocate for the children in their settings?
b. How are the risks of revealing practice negotiated?
c. What relational expertise enables groups to challenge their assumptions?
d. What strategies and tactics help communicate and sustain the community of researchers?
e. How do projects leverage the collective expertise of their participants and others?
f. How provocative can the participants be while maintaining ethical practice and professional relationships among the group?

The last question also relates to the complicity that researchers and teachers have in influencing each other's thoughts and actions during partnership arrangements. This is touched on in the chapter by Kim Atkinson and Enid Elliot in this volume, where a teacher chose to reveal how she challenged her own assumptions about the play *Bad Guy Beavers* and what was ethical in terms of her intervention in such a play. Understanding how the thoughts and actions of others are influenced by our contributions precludes setting up opportunities to discuss and understand others' perspectives and beliefs about practice and what is valued. The authors pose these questions and try to find out how they might be considered in the design of future approaches to partnership research in educational settings.

Contents of the Book

In Chapter 2, Veronica Pacini-Ketchabaw and Fikile Nxumalo use the concept of *regeneration* to reframe what is needed to interpret research partnerships. They argue that we need to move beyond models of progressive linear trajectories of change to embrace gestures aligned with growth. This seems to be a very useful concept given that regeneration, as a biological term, refers to new growth or replacement growth. Additionally, growth can be seasonal, occurring in spurts and varying depending on environmental conditions. Growth, if we consider a vine as an analogy, requires something to climb on, such as what is already known. The idea that growth can occur in three dimensions helps us to visualize that *regeneration* might support multiple solutions and trajectories for the future. That is, there is not necessarily one way of achieving a goal. *Regeneration* embraces mutuality, mess, multiplicity, and contradiction.

Marilyn Fleer reports on a research project related to the implementation of the first national early childhood curriculum in Australia in Chapter 3. The project drew on cultural-historical theory (Vygotsky, 1997) to assist the collaborators to consider how their different backgrounds and experiences contributed to different viewpoints. She argues that successful partnerships across these projects built *relational agency* (Edwards, 2010), where researchers and practitioners attuned themselves to the collective through activities that helped them to build common goals and understandings and clearly understood strategies for effective implementation. The chapter indicates that effective communication and challenging assumptions about each other's knowledge are important for sustaining partnerships, so that members can take the standpoint of others, be explicit about what matters, as well as recognize what matters to others. It is through the ability to attune one's actions with the action of others for *generating knowledge* in a project that *relational agency* of all members can be established. Fleer contends that it is the kind of knowledge valued by members that is worth paying attention to within a partnership, and that this must be explicitly discussed. The *agency* refers to how researchers, policy writers, and early childhood educators together raise the level of consciousness about constructing new ways of working with evidence. It is only then that *relational agency* can be genuinely established to realize in practice Australia's first national curriculum.

Researchers at the Woolf Fisher Research Institute have been conducting partnership research with schools in poor urban communities for the past decade or so. In Chapter 4, Mei Lai and Stuart McNaughton present an approach for partnering with schools that has been developed and successfully applied to improve teaching and learning in four New Zealand Teaching Learning and Research Initiative (TLRI) projects. They highlight key lessons learnt from applying a specific framework that addresses the challenges of partnership research. These included:

a. Research methodologies that require researchers to understand the reasons and beliefs for particular school practices so they are able to challenge these beliefs and cocreate ways of improving practice that will be accepted by school practitioners;
b. Building and maintaining a well-functioning community of practice with shared priorities and protocols (Wenger, 1998);
c. Recognizing the complementary and reciprocal nature of the expertise required to solve everyday problems (McNaughton, 2011);
d. Establishing mutual and reciprocal obligations (Snow, 2001). In the New Zealand context, this is represented by developing a whānau (family) of interest (Smith, 1999);
e. The research design needs to incorporate all of the above deliberately and systematically.

They argue that the development of effective partnerships does not necessarily happen naturally and requires support for researchers and practitioners in terms of time and skills development. The four projects discussed were partnerships between 13 schools in two urban, low socioeconomic communities serving primarily linguistically and culturally diverse students. The first two projects were three-year interventions using quasi-experimental designs to improve reading comprehension across the two communities. The third project examined the sustainability of achievement gains after the end of these interventions and the practices that led to sustainability. The final project built on findings from the sustainability project by adding a home–school partnership component to see how families could support school efforts in improving literacy achievement. When schools continued to partner with researchers and other external agents, there was a greater likelihood of sustainable outcomes.

Chapter 5, by Claire McLachlan, Alison Arrow, and Judy Watson, also focuses on literacy improvement in early years as an outcome focus. The authors discuss two different approaches to conducting research on literacy: one with a professional learning event and the other with a more intensive coaching and guiding strategy that helped teachers to reflect on their practices about how they might enhance children's literacy. Both of these projects were situated in early childhood low socioeconomic communities in New Zealand. The interesting aspect of this chapter is that what was learned from the first partnership project was directly incorporated into a new design for the second project. For example, the data collection period was extended over a much longer period of time in the second project, to capture changes in practice and outcomes as they occurred rather than a one-off event. They also discuss a methodological dilemma of setting up a *control* group that did not have the intervention similar to the groups of interest, only to find that the head teacher of the *control center* provided her own literacy intervention.

Jenny Ritchie, Janita Craw, Cheryl Rau, and Iris Duhn each provide in Chapter 6 examples of how their projects were situated in social and cultural contexts that provided opportunities and challenges for engaging in partnership research. All of these projects embraced research processes that embedded and valued relationships in line with *Te Tiriti o Waitangi* (The Treaty of Waitangi). They highlight some of the challenges and possibilities they encountered when there was an agenda to include the perspectives of children and extended family members (Pascal & Bertram, 2009). The common element across these cases was the importance of developing relational expertise, revolutionary thinking, co-theorizing as knowledge generation, and the valuing of expertise and knowledge that empowered all participants to contribute to social, cultural, and educational change.

In Chapter 7, Enid Elliot, Kim Atkinson, and the Victoria Investigating Quality (IQ) group also drew on children's and community's voices as part of the ongoing concern identified by them, that was turned into an opportunity to engage with the ethical issues involved. They also discuss the use of narrative as a tool for revealing problems and dilemmas of practice, describing how the use of narrative alongside critical reflection (MacNaughton, 2005) enabled a teacher to consider alternatives when grappling with a huge professional dilemma about ethical practice. Was it fair on other children for her to allow Bad Guy Beavers to shoot the girls and intimidate them? If she intervened, what life-learning skills was she denying the children? If she did not intervene, was she condoning their *unacceptable* behavior? This is a detailed example of a dilemma in practice and the thinking that underpinned the teacher's actions. But more than this, it provides an example of how narrative can be used as both a professional development and research tool.

Chapter 8 by Judith Duncan discusses several research dilemmas related to the power and expectations of the roles of both teachers and researchers. Partnership research is not always easy, and often requires the members to negotiate and communicate clearly about their expectations. She problematizes self-study and reflection, which are now commonly used tools within partnership projects, by questioning how professional learning journals and evidence of reflection (e.g., from conversations with researchers) can be used when teachers have already moved on or developed their thinking and practice since then. Using reflection and recordings of reflections tends to be used in partnership projects as though it is unproblematic despite the real possibilities for the teachers and researchers to have different intentions for the projects and the unequal risks related to revealing practice and thoughts about practice. Duncan asks how teachers are expected to know when the reflection starts and when it ends, and how the participation and contribution of this reflection to a research project influences what is written. The teachers in the two New Zealand TLRI projects discussed in the chapter considered reflective writing to be both a barrier and a support for their professional learning. What was usually silent was opened up and made explicit through the sharing processes, including the research meetings at the centers and public presentations as part of the requirements of the funding agency. Despite these limitations, there seems to be some hope for using reflection as a tool for teacher experimentation and as a source for opportunity to participate in ongoing development as a professional.

Conclusion

What is striking in all of the chapters of this book is the passionate commitment early childhood educators and researchers have for advancing knowledge about practice and its implications for positive learning and social outcomes for children in their early years. There are many instances of co-development of knowledge about both pedagogy and the methods for research as they iteratively co-evolve to reveal what children and teachers learned throughout the projects. The chapters in this book illustrate the elements mentioned above and how specific interventions or assumptions about practice were considered and incorporated into the design of the research. The examples are all situated in the local social, cultural, economic, and political contexts that provide rich accounts of practice. Each project has drawn on theory about practice and research. What is clear is that when there is a change or improvement agenda, there have to be actions that are likely to support that change.

The contribution that this edited volume makes is that it simultaneously addresses how early years education makes a difference and what early years teachers do to make this difference and the significance of researching this collaboratively. The acumens gained from each project provide a powerful resource for future projects, so that educational change, research, and professional development processes can potentially be accelerated and the barriers to making them successful can be minimized. Each chapter has its own locus and snapshots in time of how communities of practice worked on specific issues (Wenger, 1998). We hope that you find the examples in each chapter valuable for mobilizing future teacher activism (Sachs, 2003) and research/intervention collaborations.

References

Anderson, T., & Shattuck, J. (2012). Design-based research: A decade of progress in education research? *Educational Researcher, 41*(1), 16–25. doi: 10.3102/0013189x11428813.

Barad, K. (2003). Posthumanist performativity: Toward an understanding of how matter comes to matter. *Signs, 28*(3), 801–831.

Bellacasa, M. P. (2012). Nothing comes without its world: Thinking with care. *The Sociological Review, 60*(2), 197–216.

Borko, H. (2004). Professional development and teacher learning: Mapping the terrain. *Educational Researcher, 33*(8), 3–15. doi: 10.3102/0013189x033008003.

Edwards, A. (2010). *Being an expert professional practitioner: A relational turn in expertise*. Dordecht, the Netherlands: Springer.

Fook, J., Ryan, M., & Hawkins, L. (2000). *Professional expertise: Practice, theory and education for working in uncertainty*. Michigan, MA: Whiting & Birch.

Joseph, D. (2004). The practice of design-based research: Uncovering the interplay between design, research, and the real-world context. *Educational Psychologist, 39*(4), 235–242.

MacNaughton, G. (2005). *Doing Foucault in early childhood studies: Applying poststructural ideas*. Oxford, UK: Routledge.

Mayo, E., Henson, K., & Smith, H. (2008). Early childhood teachers as researchers: Story as innovation, one-pagers as methodology. In M. L. Heston, D. L. Tidwell, K. K. East & L. M. Fitzgerald (Eds.), *Pathways to change in teacher education: Dialogue, diversity and self-study. Proceedings of the seventh international conference on self-study in teacher education practices, Herstmonceux Castle, East Sussex, England* (pp. 239–242). Cedar Falls, IA: University of Northern Iowa.

McNaughton, S. (2011). *Designing better schools for culturally and linguistically diverse children*. New York, NY: Routledge.

Nuttall, J. (2010, November). The contribution of the Teaching and Learning Research Initiative to building knowledge about teaching and learning: A review of early years projects, 2004–2010. Paper presented to *TLRI Early Years Symposium*, Wellington, New Zealand.

Pascal, C., & Bertram, T. (2009). Listening to young citizens: The struggle to make real a participatory paradigm in research with young children. *European Early Childhood Education Research Journal, 17*(2), 249–262.

Sachs, J. (2003). *The activist teaching profession*. Sydney, Australia: McGraw-Hill.

Schleicher, A. (2012). (Ed.), *Preparing teachers and developing school leaders for the 21st century: Lessons from around the world*. Retrieved from http://www.oecd.org/site/eduistp2012/49850576.pdf.

Smith, L. (1999). *Decolonising methodologies: Research and indigenous peoples*. London, UK: Zed Books.

Snow, C. (2001). Knowing what we know: Children, teachers, researchers. *Educational Researcher, 30*(7), 3–9.

Vygotsky, L. S. (1997). *The history of the development of higher mental functions. The collected works of L.S. Vygotsky* (Vol. 4, M. J. Hall, trans.; R.W. Rieber, (Ed.); English trans.). New York, NY: Plenum. (Original work published 1931).

Wenger, E. (1998). *Communities of practice: Learning, meaning, and identity*. Cambridge, UK: Cambridge University Press.

2

Re-generating Research Partnerships in Early Childhood Education: A Non-idealized Vision

Veronica Pacini-Ketchabaw and Fikile Nxumalo

Non-idealized Vision of Partnerships

> A non-idealized vision of practices grounded on committed attachments needs a multi-layered, non-innocent, approach.... Relationality is all there is, but this does not mean a world without conflict nor dissension.
>
> *(Bellacasa, 2012, p. 204)*

We begin this chapter with a disclaimer. Although we have been working in collaboration with early childhood educators for many years now, we do not have definitive answers regarding enablers and barriers for effective relations in research partnerships, for transformations in educators' practices, and for advancement of educators' thinking and actions. Yet, since our research collaborations with educators began in 2006, we have dedicated much thinking about the *troubles* and *struggles* of research partnerships. It is precisely the troubles and struggles that are inherited in research partnerships that we want to address in this chapter. We do so by outlining challenging theoretical pathways. Using Bellacasa's (2012) words as our inspiration, we show how relational work in research partnerships is always multilayered and far from innocent. We also attempt to think-with *a non-idealized vision* of research partnerships that is based on entanglements. For example, we pay attention to research practices that entangle researchers with everything they encounter in their relations with educators. To engage with this non-idealized vision of research partnerships, we experiment with the notions of regenerating change (bringing Deleuze and Guattari (1987) into the discussion), and regenerating *relationality*. We write about the multilayered aspects of knowledge-in-the-making; about non-innocent relations; about difficulties of thinking change in research; and about the potentialities of conflict and dissension. Yet, there are not certainties and closures in our arguments about research partnerships.

We speak of re-generation as a way of displacing "development, fulfillment and containment" (Haraway, 1997, p. 12)—interrupting an all too easy move toward interpreting our work with educators' through progressive linear trajectories of change. Re-generation, through its gestures to growth, as consisting of complicated, entangled, and continually emergent past–present–futures, creates movement away from linearity. Re-generation embraces mutuality, mess, multiplicity, and contradiction.

> Regeneration is not about starting points. It is the always already—it is augmentation and fragmentation and building and deconstruction. Regeneration is nonchronological and is not only disinterested in origin, but is interested in being antagonistic to origin. The moment of replication and appropriation is along a trajectory that is nonlinear and messy. What do we know? What can we change? What did we used to do that was good? What has been lost and found and invented and fused? ... [Regeneration] is not situated along a chronology of time, a narrative of progress, or a framework of history. It is looking for new location.
>
> (Handlarski, 2010, p. 88)

We draw on re-generation as *ways of seeing* that produce mutual interferences to ordered narratives of our research. Haraway (1992) refers to these ways of seeing as "differential artifactualism" (p. 299), where research is relational, embraces difference and, and acts in disruptive ways. An important part of these disruptions has been to resist limiting our work to humanist relationships—to put differential artifactualism to work in order to inhabit *naturecultures* (Haraway, 2008) through located stories of place. Importantly, re-generation provides an entry with which to engage with the more-than-human relationalities that have inhabited our collaborative work with educators.

We bring forward selected stories from our research practices. These stories allow us to follow a feminist politics (Haraway, 1991) to which we are committed to in our work (e.g., see Nxumalo, Pacini-Ketchabaw & Rowan, 2011; Pacini-Ketchabaw, 2012a; Pacini-Ketchabaw, Nxumalo & Rowan, 2011). These are stories that grapple with troubles, but have no generalized moral teachings nor are finished stories of grandiose research practices. They do, however, have "consequences for response-ability" (Haraway, 2012, p. 312). The stories we tell about our research are not reflected upon, but they are linked to other stories. Stories become entangled without following a linear trajectory. The stories and encounters we write about are troubling to us. As *researchers* we struggle to understand what it entails to be in a research relationship, to respond to the troubles that these encounters bring, to acknowledge our own implication in these encounters, to care for the world we are in—to stay with the trouble itself.

We take seriously recent critiques of qualitative research practices (e.g., Battiste & Henderson, 2000; Law, 2004; MacLure, 2010; Mazzei & McCoy, 2010), and acknowledge research practices as non-innocent, as always embedded in and reproducing social relations of power (McWilliam, 2002). Therefore, we engage with the *details* of research accounts in the middle of mundane practices of research with educators and avoid generalizations. As Haraway (2012) says:

> The details link actual beings to actual response-abilities. Each time a story helps me remember what I thought I knew, or introduces me to new knowledge, a muscle critical for caring about flourishing gets some aerobic exercise. Such exercise enhances collective thinking and movement too. (p. 13)

We also attend to what Phelan (2011) refers to as an impoverishment in research pertaining to teacher education and practices. Phelan notes that what is needed are research approaches that "nurture thought and cultivate—different ways of understanding and imagining"; research approaches that are "non-consequentialist in character"; research approaches that enrich rather than improve; research approaches that "tolerate interminable questions"; research approaches that "do not try to resolve the difficulties that their explorations may surface" (p. 208). Therefore, we avoid thinking of research partnerships with early childhood educators as external interventions that can be measured, and instead focus on what these partnerships might bring to co-create new visions of relationality.

We begin by describing the context of the *stories* we use throughout the chapter. Then, we address the re-generation of change by interfering in a story of professional development. We propose the re-generation of relations by putting differential artifactualism to work and addressing human–nonhuman relations. Through these movements in our texts, we draft a vision of non-idealized research partnerships.

Collaborative Researching

The stories we write-with come from a research project involving early childhood educators and ourselves within the context of western Canada. We have been experimenting with what we call collaborative critically engaged communities to rethink practices in early childhood (Pacini-Ketchabaw, Nxumalo, Kocher, Elliot & Sanchez, in press). Since 2006 we have been working collaboratively with groups of early childhood educators using what we call pedagogical narrations (Berger, 2010) as a way to reconceptualize pedagogy. At the heart of these collaborations is political work *taking apart* and contesting some of the pedagogical understandings that underlie our practices in early childhood, as well as figuring out what is next after the contestation. In addition, we discuss how we might work with postfoundational theories (Pacini-Ketchabaw et al., in press) to shift our perspectives and inspire ethical action in response to everyday pedagogical encounters. We try to engage in research with educators from a position of ethical responsibility that does not mean transcending problems but engaging and situating ourselves and our own practices in such problems.

Postfoundational perspectives are very important in our work with educators (for a detailed description, see Pacini-Ketchabaw et al., in press). We work with ideas brought forward by postfoundational theories to broaden the lenses through which we view children, educators, learning, and teaching. We strive to move beyond dominant perspectives (as exemplified in this chapter) and make visible the political aspects of early childhood education. As we explore through examples of educators' pedagogical narrations, our readings of postfoundational literatures (e.g., post-humanist, postcolonial, antiracist, queer, feminist, and poststructural) lead us to new spaces of critical inquiry that complexify our practices in ways that would not be possible if we rely solely on dominant understandings of early childhood education. Postfoundational perspectives allow us to *contextualize* and *politicize* ideas about early childhood education that tend to be taken for granted.

By creating spaces for collaborative critical work in our research, we challenge each other and engage with a multiplicity of pedagogical possibilities. The process invites us to think differently about early childhood pedagogies, by making space for new connections between theory and practice. We view such research practices as incomplete, ongoing, messy processes filled with struggles, tensions, challenges, frustrations, unknowns, discomfort, and divergence. At the same time, we experience within these spaces deep connections with each other as well as *lines of flight* (Deleuze &

Guattari, 1987) that cracked open our pre-established modes of thinking and acting in research. This is not to say that we view our research as having a clear end goal that is easily reached. We do not necessarily resolve the tensions we encounter. But from new lines of thought, new possibilities emerge for rethinking practices and our implicated positions in these practices. Thus, our work with educators is ongoing, tentative, transformative, and experimental.

In the rest of this chapter, we engage with the troubles that partnership stories, outlined at the beginning of each section, bring to research. All of the stories told emerged when Fikile was working with one childcare center two years ago as part of our collaborative research project. As mentioned above, the aim was to bring in change to the educators' practices. The stories come from the same classroom, but took place at different times during the academic year. Although we feature only six stories here, similar stories could be taken from other childcare centers we worked with (however, our goal is not to generalize these moments). We selected these stories because they *spoke to us* and *troubled us* (Haraway, 2012). Our engagements with the stories are not solutions or explanations, but rather they are our way of grappling with what Bellacasa (2012) describes in the introductory quote: "A non-idealized vision of practices grounded on committed attachments needing a multi-layered, non-innocent approach" (p. 204). We follow the stories as non-innocent tales that implicate us—a diffractive rather than a representational approach (Barad, 2007; Haraway, 2008). In this understanding, research is a "critical practice of engagement, not a distance-learning practice of reflecting from afar" (Barad, 2007, p. 90).

Re-generating Discussions of *Change* in Research with Educators

An educator whispers to Fikile:

> We have four completely different philosophies in our team.... One thing that's frustrating to me is that we are still so fixed on meeting a daily schedule. Could you talk to the team, maybe if they hear it from you, they will see the problem and change?

> A child is sitting with me (Fikile) quietly creating an intricate arrangement of stones and sticks collected from a walk. An educator calls the child's name in a loud tone: "Come now, it's circle time." The child is led into the nap room for circle time where the other children are already sitting on square mats. The door closes shut as I sit and fidget with the stones at the table. I silently wonder when these practices will change...

Initially, we designed our project as action research because we wanted to actively engage educators in discussions and actions that relate to their current circumstances in early childhood (MacNaughton, 2005). An important goal of action research is to effect change through action by generating knowledge that people can then use in their everyday lived situations (Carr & Kemmis, 1986). One way we pursued this goal was by starting our conversations with educators and funders as doing *professional development*. Research and professional development blur in our work, as both relate to notions of change. We were interested in practical change, in how we could transform participants' theories and everyday actions in relation to equity and social justice. We focused on ways to enact an activist approach in our research practices, and we attempted to shift power relations by foregrounding voices (educators and children) that have been marginalized by particular knowledge/power structures.

> So too professional development must be acknowledged to be a flawed project that constructs new power/knowledge relationships... for better and worse. Academics and academic managers should bring to professional development the same systematic curiosity and capacity for skepticism that is the hallmark of good science and good scholarship whatever the object of analysis.
>
> (McWilliam, 2002, p. 298)

Professional development, with its assumed position toward change, is entangled in our research actions and assumptions. For example, when the educator whispered to Fikile that she could change the other educators' approach to daily schedules and when our research and pedagogical practices collided with circle time routines, we reminded ourselves of how professional development, as a material-discursive *actant* (Latour, 2004), creates certain worlds and excludes others. We wondered about the kinds of relationships between academic and educator research partnerships we had inherited and inhabited: What assumptions are embedded in these relationships? How do we inhabit or tease out these assumptions? What are the consequences of these inheritances?

Professional development programs for early childhood educators in North America and other parts of the world tend to aim at changing educators' knowledge, beliefs, skills, and practices to effect improvements in children's learning outcomes (Biesta, 2007; Phelan, 2011). The emphasis of professional development is on changing the educators and their practices by implementing a specific source of change, such as a research program (e.g., see Smith & Gillespie, 2007). There are three interrelated assumptions embedded in this idea of professional development. These assumptions are: that professional development is an innocent, passive event in educational processes; that the educator who participates in professional development is a stable, unchanging subject; and that change is something exceptional, while stability and order are the norm. In modern thought, representational thinking works through language to deem objects, concepts, and events as real and as having a concrete entity unto themselves. Underlying this view is "an unshakeable assumption that reality is essentially discrete, substantial and enduring" (Chia, 1999, p. 215). As the stories we relate suggest, professional development is filled with "tensions, resonances, transformations, resistances, and complicities" (Haraway, 1988, p. 588), which cannot be explained through a simple process of providing tools for change.

The term professional development is understood to accurately represent "an external world of discrete and identifiable objects, forces and generative mechanisms" (Chia, 1999, p. 215). Guskey (2002) acknowledges that professional development involves different processes at different levels, but he views them as purposeful endeavors that need to be carefully evaluated to determine whether they are achieving their purposes. This normative depiction of the effects of professional development assumes that the learning that takes place in professional development involves responding "to pre-formulated questions and eventually arriving at pre-existing answers" (Bogue, 2004, p. 333)—a passage from non-knowledge to knowledge, from ignorance to enlightenment. Reflected in this model is an individual who can be known, defined, and represented.

There are other images of change that would allow us to reconceptualize professional development and our conceptualizations of research partnerships, and, in turn, challenge us to create other worlds and other ways of caring for each other. By exploring the notion that change is both constant and intra-active (Barad, 2007), we hope that our work with educators can regenerate other worlds. What if we do not presuppose a static, knowable educator? Instead, could we view the educator "as an incomplete project" (Britzman, 2007, p. 3)? This alternative view shifts the focus of professional development from *being* to *becoming*. A focus on being—which is typical of professional development and research with educators in the North American context—concerns itself with the organized state of things—their unity, identity, essence, structure, and discreteness. In contrast, a focus on *becoming* allows for dissonance, plurality, constant change, transience, and disparity (Chia, 1999).

By giving priority to being—and consequently to representation—the transformation that is action research's primary goal is seen as something exceptional that takes place under specific circumstances with the help of certain people who are referred to as agents of change (Chia, 1999). This view privileges outcomes and end-states and does not acknowledge the dynamic nature of ongoing developmental processes. As an example of professional development that takes this view, Fullan (2001), a leading scholar on educational change, writes that real change "represents a serious personal and collective experience characterized by ambivalence and uncertainty; and if the change works out it can result in a sense of mastery, accomplishment, and professional growth" (p. 32). Fullan (2001) contends that people need pressure to change; he identifies "do's" and "don'ts" that support the view that change is an exceptional process through which individuals need to be led, and which must be carefully orchestrated (pp. 108–109). Phelan (2011) challenges this model:

> This view not only neglects that (teacher) education [and research] is a process of mutual interpretation by participants (academics, teacher mentors...), it also sidesteps the question of the very desirability of ends. Even if we can produce a certain type of teacher by means of a particular kind of teacher education programme it does not mean that that 'teacher' is desirable. Neither can we take recourse to any set of means to produce what might be considered desirable ends because the means are part and parcel of what is produced. (p. 210)

In contrast to this view, Tsoukas and Chia (2002) borrow from process-oriented philosophers such as Deleuze and Guattari (1987) to argue that change is not an exceptional capacity of individuals, but a pervasive state of life: "Individuals... are themselves tentative, and precariously balanced but relatively stabilized assemblages of actions and interactions" (Tsoukas & Chia, 2002, p. 592).

A *becoming* style of thinking invites us to see the early childhood educator as continuously produced rather than predefined. Semetsky (2004), also drawing on Deleuze's work, explains that "one's self is always already in a process of becoming-other" (p. 319). Thus there is no presupposed identity, but always novelty and something new. If we accept that we are in a process of *becoming*, of constant change, then we must abandon our idea of a static, knowable educator and move to a view of an educator in a state of constant becoming and change.

Change as *becoming* is conceptualized as the ultimate fact for every phenomenon, including individuals (Chia, 1999). Tsoukas and Chia (2002) use Deleuze and Guattari's concept of the rhizome to think about change:

> Change is subtle, agglomerative, often subterranean and heterogeneous. It spreads like a patch of oil. Change takes place by variations, restless expansion, opportunistic conquests, sudden ruptures and offshoots. Rhizomatic

change is anti-genealogical in the sense that it resists the linear retracting of a definite locatable originary point of initiation.
(Tsoukas & Chia, 2002, p. 580)

From a Deleuzian perspective, the world is constantly in a flux, thus it is "unrepresentable in any static sense" (Chia, 1995, p. 579). If we focus on becoming rather than being, we need to look at "the micro-organizing processes which enact and re-enact [professional development] into existence" (Chia, 1995, p. 587). This is to say that we need to look closely at the micro-practices involved in developing professionals.

Perhaps change in professional development and action research programs is constituted and reconstituted in intra-action (with educators, with practices, with children, with pedagogical narrations, and so on). Therefore, it is "perpetually open to rearrangements, rearticulations, and other re-workings" where none of these participants is fixed, mutually exclusive or independent (Barad, 2007, p. 203). The educator who participates in a professional development program or in a research program is always changing. The change materializes *through intra-action* through time and space; it is a *doing,* a *becoming* (Barad, 2003). Both the educator and the professional development and research program emerge from their intra-action. The change that takes place is constituted. It is not a static relationality, and it cannot be predicted in advance. These are "co-constitutive relationships in which none of the partners preexist the relating, and the relating is never done once and for all" (Haraway, 2003, p. 12).

We feel it is naïve to talk about research partnerships as opportunities that bring about change in educators' practices. This is what troubles us about the stories presented above. Following Tsoukas and Chia (2002), we suggest that research partnerships may be seen in terms of *possibilities.* If no single (predetermined) trajectory exists that educators take through professional development or in research, we need to work toward opening up to the multiple trajectories of the processes in which educators engage. The task is not to provide *do's* and *don'ts* to produce educational change, but to relax these instructions and attend to the surprising possibilities that emerge from the constant, undetermined nature of reality. How have the educators and the researchers been constituted in these events? What has emerged through these events?

Re-generating Discussions of *Relationality* in Research with Educators

Educators have been concerned about children's prolific use of paper at the center and have been thinking about how to engage in an inquiry with children on the ethics of caring for paper. One day during Fikile's visit to the center, she and the educators discussed possibilities for extending the inquiry beyond the *fact-based* approach educators have been engaging with (trees–pulp–papermaking). An educator mentions to Fikile that perhaps a First Nations person could come to the center to talk about taking care of trees and land.

> A white poster board titled "Nature Discovery" hangs on a wall outside the child care centre. Several red maple leaves are glued in rows on the poster. Beside each leaf, a child's name is neatly printed.
>
> The children are having a *music circle time*. The educator instructs the children to pretend to be trees; children's bodies bend, tangle, twirl into many tree-branch configurations as they dance to the music.
>
> It is a cold crisp morning as Fikile, the children and the educators begin a walk to the forest that is nearby to the childcare centre. They encounter a large hole where a tree once stood. It's a 'bear hole', one child says. They encounter many 'bear holes' and 'bear sprints' that morning as well as *other* possible inhabitants of the forests. Each hole they encounter is named by the children: 'rabbit-hole', 'bear-print', 'bear-hole', 'a giant's prints'.

As we noted above, by attending to the possible worlds enacted through these stories of place, rather than their interpretation and representation, we engage below with a diffractive approach. We are reminded of what Haraway (1992) explains: "Artifactualism is askew of productionism; the rays from my optical device diffract rather than reflect. These diffracting rays compose interference patterns, not reflecting images" (p. 299). We moved away from explaining and representing these stories as *problems* with the educator, that were then smoothly resolved through imparting of *knowledge* or providing solutions. We found that thinking about research as being relational practices that bring into view particular worlds (Haraway, 1991), generated more possibilities and brought our discussions to complex layers of participants beyond the individuals in the encounter.

In this conception, relationality is not about imparting expert knowledge but about taking seriously what ways of *relating* to social and material worlds are enacted through these stories and through our discussions of these encounters with educators—this is not to say that we have overcome or transformed the troubles that such encounters bring, but that we have attended to the multiple relationalities that they have brought into view, including the complex more-than-human relations that emerge and are already embedded in the work that we have done: attending to relationalities, "gaps and awkward encounters" (Choy et al., 2009, p. 382) simultaneously.

As Bellacasa (2012) notes, this is a non-innocent engagement with research practices that is relational, yet these connections are not without frictions and tensions (Tsing, 2005). For instance, when the educator speaks to us of bringing a First Nations individual into the childcare center, when we encounter and are troubled by representations of nature, of children in nature, and of children as naturally closer to nature, all of these encounters enact worlds that are affectively resonant with the colonial past–present histories in which our work is situated; worlds (Taylor, 2013) in which we as researchers are also implicated and embedded. That is to say, the relations we inhabit in this work are not limited to relations between us (educators and researchers), but also to the settler colonial past presents including the "colonial histories and neocolonial rhetorics that continue to infuse 'commonsense' categories and identities like 'nature'" (Willems-Braun, 1997, p. 3). How do we account for these colonial relations when engaged in research with educators? What is our responsibility? How do we respond?

We attempted and continue to attend to relationalities in our research with educators that go beyond human-centric relations. We want to locate our work within the *places* we inhabit as part of being/becoming human and more-than-human colonial *contact zones* filled with multiplicities, intensive power relations, and unresolved belongings (Taylor & Giugni, 2012). While we have not necessarily solved these tensions, they provided disruptions, such as in unsettling and resituating the static, representation, and familiarity underlying the so-called natural places (Taylor, 2013; Taylor & Giugni, 2012) as a site for children's experiences in early childhood settings within the specific context of what is now British Columbia. As van Doreen and Rose (2012) note, our approach has been relating to places as inherently vibrant and storied, enacting different questions and histories:

> [P]laces are understood and embedded in broader histories and systems of meaning. But stories and meanings are not just layered over a pre-existing landscape. Instead, stories emerge from and impact upon the way in which places come to be—the material and the discursive are all mixed up in the making of places, as with worlds more generally. If we accept this notion of place, however, an important question remains before us, namely, who stories these places? Whose stories come to matter in the emergence of a place? In particular, we are concerned to ask: What might it mean to take storied-places seriously as multispecies achievements?
>
> (pp. 2–3)

We see potential in rethinking the concept of relationality in research that attends to relations with place/land and colonial past–presents. Relations with place/land are always already present, as is exemplified in the stories above. Attending to these relations allows us to begin to trouble colonial anthropocentrism that privileges not only humans over other humans, but that are predicated on human mastery over *nature* and other more-than-human worlds (Tsing, 2012). Inhabiting relationality in our research practices is thereby an important move towards unsettling the nature/culture binary and towards research practices that "resituate the human within the environment, and to resituate nonhumans within cultural and ethical domains" (Rose et al., 2012, p. 3).

We also see ethical potentialities in relational research practices as creating interferences and disruptions to the exteriorities claimed by colonizing research practices that "teach that knowers are manipulators who have no reciprocal responsibilities to the things they manipulate" (Battiste & Henderson, 2000, p. 88). In our research with educators, by attending to materialized practices and their interrelated histories and discourses, we attempted to create openings toward making visible colonialisms as material-discursive assemblages of histories, place practices, bodies, things, materials, economies, discourses, affects, and memories among other constituents and processes. Importantly, regenerating relationality in our research practices was not an attempt to completely map or represent all the constituent parts of these stories, but, rather was an intentional politicized *noticing* of events and encounters (Tsing, 2012). A located and close "noticing the seams" (Tsing, 2012, p. 152) of colonialisms and anthropocentrisms is an important place to begin; where contradictions and troubles abound; "this is no place to search for utopia" (p. 152) but perhaps can be a productive site to seek out new potentialities, new ethical and affirmative possibilities for *living well with others* (Haraway, 2008), including more-than-human others (Tsing, 2012).

These stories entangle us in relations with place as a site of asymmetric power relations, as a relational place of conflict and friction; where place is not "as static or bounded but...mobile and in process...open to conditionality and emergence" (Anderson, 2012, p. 571). We continue to investigate how storying encounters with place in our research practices might make visible how "place is far from a static, stable, or fixed entity no longer reliable, consistent, or necessarily coherent; it is wholly provisional and unstable" (Anderson, 2012, p. 574), a relational *gathering* of things, bodies, and histories that require close attention to its enactments and socio-material multiplicities. In storying troubling encounters with and conceptions of nature, we have begun to explore with educators' possibilities for attending to situated entanglements with and their connections to the sticky materialities and histories of place, where humans are not necessarily the only actants and where their relations are not necessarily determined by human encounters (Tsing, 2005). For example, we began to think how to bring *big ideas/ethical questions* alive with young children, such as how to engage the political, environmental, and sustainability aspects of pedagogical inquiries, how to honor the lands in which the childcare centers we work with are located, and how we are entangled with nonhuman others (e.g., Nxumalo, 2012; Pacini-Ketchabaw, 2012a, 2012b). Veronica is currently working with a group of educators and children to rethink the pedagogical possibilities of *water*. Their goal is to go beyond the sensory experiences usually offered and, instead, view water through unfamiliar lenses. By concentrating on water for an extended period, many questions are beginning to arise: How do children/educators relate to water when it is seen as political? What are the risks involved as we think beyond our educational experiences with water? How has water been viewed historically? How will our view of water shift as we engage in thinking with the children? What are our pedagogical responsibilities when the notion of water as a *natural resource* covers up so much of our colonial histories and presents in Canada?

As Tsing (2005) explains, "our encounters are infused with other social histories-with humans in more or less important roles, depending. And there is nothing about social relations, per se, that requires human forms of consciousness or anatomy" (p. xx). We see regenerating relationality in research partnerships through *more-than-human* relations as creating openings to "speak beyond the boundaries of conquest and domination" (hooks, 1995, p. 297).

On Re-generating Research Partnerships in Early Childhood

Drawing on Haraway (2004), this chapter has not been a rebirth but regeneration of the concepts of change and relationality. This regeneration has involved "maintaining elements of past and present and reconstructing these with emerging and useful elements" (Bellacasa, 2012; Handlarsky, 2010, p. 97). This chapter has proposed a non-idealized vision of research practices that is based on close attachments to what we do and how we relate. This non-idealized vision of research practices has also been for us a way of engaging with the colonial anthropocentrism that permeates qualitative research that addresses partnerships with educators.

In this chapter we have only begun to explore ways of thinking about change and relationality in research partnerships. There are no doubts that further work needs to take place to articulate (but not restrict) non-idealized visions of research partnerships. Aspects such as relations to nonhuman others, relations to places, and entanglements with colonialisms might be worth emphasizing.

Our future endeavors related to this work are to continue to think about the ideas of partnership with early childhood educators. These kinds of dialogues are necessarily unpredictable and, of course, will escape our intentions.

References

Anderson, J. (2012). Relational places: The surfed wave as assemblage and convergence. *Environment & Planning D: Society & Space, 30*, 570–587.
Barad, K. (2003). Posthumanist performativity: Toward an understanding of how matter comes to matter. *Signs, 28*(3), 801–831.
Barad, K. (2007). *Meeting the universe halfway: Quantum physics and the entanglement of matter and meaning.* Durham, NC: Duke University Press.
Battiste, M., & Henderson, J. Y. (2000). *Protecting Indigenous knowledge and heritage: A global challenge.* Saskatoon, SK: Purish.
Bellacasa, M. P. (2012). Nothing comes without its world: Thinking with care. *The Sociological Review, 60*(2), 197–216.
Berger, I. (2010). Extending the notion of pedagogical narration through Hannah Arendt's political thought. In V. Pacini-Ketchabaw (Ed.), *Flows, rhythms and intensities of early childhood education curriculum* (pp. 57–76). New York, NY: Peter Lang.
Biesta, G. (2007). Why 'what works' won't work: Evidence-based practice and the democratic deficit in educational research. *Educational Theory, 57*(1), 1–22.
Bogue, R. (2004). Search, swim and see: Deleuze's apprenticeship in signs and pedagogy of images. *Educational Philosophy and Theory, 36*(3), 327–342.
Britzman, D. (2007). Teacher education as uneven development: Toward a psychology of uncertainty. *International Journal of Leadership in Education, 10*(1), 1–12.
Carr, W., & Kemmis, S. (1986). *Becoming critical: Education, knowledge and action research.* Basingstoke, UK: Falmer.
Chia, R. (1995). From modern to postmodern organizational analysis. *Organization Studies, 16*(4), 579.
Chia, R. (1999). A 'rhizomic' model of organizational change and transformation: Perspective from a metaphysics of change. *British Journal of Management, 10*, 209–227.
Choy, T., Lieba, F., Hathaway, M. J., Inoue, M., Satsuka, S., & Tsing, A. (2009). A new form of collaboration in cultural anthropology: Matsutake worlds. *American Ethnologist, 36*(2), 380–403.
Deleuze, G., & Guattari, F. (1987). *A thousand plateaus: Capitalism and schizophrenia*, (Brian Massumi, Trans.). Minneapolis, MN: University of Minnesota Press.
Fullan, M. (2001). *The new meaning of educational change.* New York, NY: Teachers College Press.

Guskey, T. R. (2002). Professional development and teacher change. *Teachers & Teaching, 8*(3/4), 381–391.
Handlarski, D. (2010). Pro-creation: Haraway's "regeneration" and the postcolonial cyborg body. *Women's Studies, 39*(2), 73–99.
Haraway, D. (1988). Situated knowledge: The science question in feminism and the privilege of partial perspective. *Feminist Studies, 14*(3), 575–599.
Haraway, D. (1991). *Simians, Cyborgs and women: The reinvention of nature.* New York, NY: Routledge.
Haraway, D. (1992). The promises of monsters: A regenerative politics for inappropriate/d others. In L. Grossberg, C. Nelson, & P. A. Treichler (Eds.), *Cultural studies* (pp. 295–337). New York, NY: Routledge.
Haraway, D. (2004). *The Haraway reader.* New York & London: Routledge.
Haraway, D. (1997). *Modest_witness@second_millenium. FemaleMan©_meets_OncoMouse TM: Feminism and technoscience.* London, UK: Routledge.
Haraway, D. (2003). *The companion species manifesto: Dogs, people, and significant otherness.* Chicago, IL: Prickly Paradigm.
Haraway, D. (2008). *When species meet.* Minneapolis, MN: University of Minnesota Press.
Haraway, D. (2012). Awash in urine: DES and Premarin®in multispecies responseability. *WSQ: Women's Studies Quarterly 40*(1 & 2), 301–316.
hooks, B. (1995). "This is the oppressor's language/yet I need it to talk to you": Language, a place of struggle. In A. Dingwaney & C. Maier (Eds.), *Between languages and cultures: Translation and cross-cultural texts* (pp. 295–302). Pittsburgh, PA.: University of Pittsburgh Press.
Latour, B. (2004). Why has critique run out of steam? From matters of fact to matters of concern. *Critical Inquiry, 30,* 225–248.
Law, J. (2004). *After method: Mess in social science research.* London, UK: Routledge.
MacLure, M. (2010). The offence of theory. *Journal of Education Policy, 25*(2), 277–286.
MacNaughton, G. (2005). *Doing Foucault in early childhood studies: Applying poststructural ideas.* New York, NY: RoutledgeFalmer.
Mazzei, L. A., & McCoy, K. (2010). Thinking with Deleuze in qualitative research. *International Journal of Qualitative Studies in Education, 23*(5), 503–509.
McWilliam, E. (2002). Against professional development. *Educational Philosophy and Theory, 34*(3), 289–299.
Nxumalo, F. (2012). Unsettling representational practices: Inhabiting relational becomings in early childhood education. *Child & Youth Services Journal, 33*(3–4), 281–302.
Nxumalo, F., Pacini-Ketchabaw, V., & Rowan, C. (2011). Lunch time at the child care centre: Neoliberal assemblages in early childhood education. *Journal of Pedagogy, 2*(2), 195–223.
Pacini-Ketchabaw, V. (2012a). Postcolonial entanglements: Unruling stories. *Child & Youth Services, 33*(3–4), 303–316.
Pacini-Ketchabaw, V. (2012b). Acting with the clock: Clocking practices in early childhood. *Contemporary Issues in Early Childhood, 13*(2), 154–160.

Pacini-Ketchabaw, V., Nxumalo, F., & Rowan, C. (2011). Nomadic research practices in early childhood: Interrupting racisms and colonialisms. *Reconceptualizing Educational Research Methodology, 2*(1), 19–33.
Pacini-Ketchabaw, V., Nxumalo, F., Kocher, L., Elliot, E., & Sanchez, A. (in press). *Journeys in Curriculum: Complexifying Early Childhood Education Practices.* Toronto, ONT: University of Toronto Press.
Phelan, A. (2011). Towards a complicated conversation: Teacher education and the curriculum turn. *Pedagogy, Culture & Society, 19*(2), 207–220.
Rose, D. B., van Dooren, T., Chrulew, M., Cooke, S., Kearnes, M., & O'Gorman, E. (2012). Thinking through the environment, unsettling the humanities. *Environmental Humanities 1,* 1–5.
Semetsky, I. (2004). Becoming-language/becoming-other: Whence ethics? *Educational Philosophy and Theory, 36*(3), *313–325.*
Smith, C., & Gillespie, M. (2007). Research on professional development and teacher change: Implications for adult basic education. In J. Comings, B. Garner, & C. Smith (Eds.), *Review of adult learning and literacy: Connecting research, policy, and practice* (pp. 205–244). New York, NY: Routledge.
Taylor, A. (2013). *Contesting childhood beyond nature.* London, UK: Taylor & Francis.
Taylor, A., & Giugni, M. (2012). Common worlds: Reconceptualising inclusion in early childhood communities. *Contemporary Issues in Early Childhood, 13*(2), 108–119.
Tsing, A. (2005). *Friction: An ethnography of global connection.* Princeton, NJ: Princeton University Press.
Tsing, A. (2012). Unruly edges: Mushrooms as companion species. *Environmental Humanities, 1,* 141–154.
Tsoukas, H., & Chia, R. (2002). On organizational becoming: Rethinking organizational change. *Organization Science, 13,* 567–582.
van Dooren, T., & Rose, D. B. (2012). Storied-places in a multispecies city. *Humanimalia: A Journal of Human/Animal Interface Studies, 3*(2). Retrieved from http://www.depauw.edu/humanimalia/issue%206/rose-van%20dooren.html.
Willems-Braun, B. (1997). Buried epistemologies: The politics of nature in (post)colonial British Columbia. *Annals of the Association of American Geographers, 8*(1), 3–31.

3

Attunement of Knowledge Forms: The *Relational Agency* of Researchers, Policy Writers, and Early Childhood Educators

Marilyn Fleer

Introduction

There is a growing trend toward forming multidisciplinary research teams in order to address the complex and challenging problems that now face education (Cummings & Wong, 2012). The field of early childhood education and development has traditionally brought together early childhood academics, early childhood educators, psychologists, speech pathologists, infant health nurses, midwives, and the like (Atkinson, Jones & Lomat, 2007; Tomlinson, 2003). However, as more funding is directed toward early childhood education, we are also seeing how research within this area has caught the attention of neuroscientists, pediatricians, and even economists (Fleer, 2010). Yet there is robust evidence that inter-agency collaborations struggle to produce the desired outcomes they profess to deliver (e.g., Edwards et al., 2009). The literature suggests that there are fundamental reasons why partnerships struggle to form and be effective (Cheminais, 2009; Edwards et al., 2009). Most of the problems center on how collaborators within partnerships view themselves in relation to their role and in relation to others. Challenges arise when professionals have to talk across professional boundaries where different knowledge traditions intersect.

The focus of this chapter is on examining the enablers for effective relationships, barriers, and the knowledges that are generated through collaborations in research contexts between educators, policy writers, and academics. *Educators*, in this chapter, refer to all staff, regardless of qualifications, who interact directly with young children for the purposes of supporting their learning and development (Australian Government Department of Education, Employment and Workplace Relations, 2013a). In drawing upon cultural-historical theory (Vygotsky, 1997), this chapter seeks to unpack how the different members of partnerships have different ways of framing their goals, communicating their intentions, and looking for different kinds of evidence for change, which may not easily coalesce with other views. Specifically, the chapter reports upon a project that built new knowledge and resources for building understandings and capacity of educators as one aspect of realizing the quality agenda in Australia (Australian Government Department of Education, Employment and Workplace Relations, 2013a). In this chapter it will be argued that successful partnerships build *relational agency* (Edwards, 2004, 2010; Edwards & Apostolov, 2007), where researchers, policy writers, resource developers, and educators attune themselves to the collective, building common knowledge across the partnership, agreed goals, and clearly understood strategies for effective implementation (Edwards et al., 2009).

In drawing upon the literature, it will be argued that effective partnerships have members who are able to take the standpoint of the other, are able to be explicit about what matters, as well as recognize what matters to others (Edwards, 2010). However, this chapter will go one step further, arguing that the kinds of knowledges (e.g., empirical, narrative, or theoretical) (Davydov, 2008) that people build and use are central to enabling or challenging partnership collaboration. This perspective on knowledge-building and sharing within partnerships has not been adequately brought to light and is worthy of serious study. It will be argued that being able to attune one's actions with the actions of others for generating knowledge in a project will support *relational agency* of all members. It is more than what kind of evidence that one looks for in ascertaining change. It is the kind of knowledge that is valued by its members, worthy of paying attention to, or worthy of building within a partnership, that must be made explicit. It is only then that *relational agency* can be genuinely established so that researchers, policy writers, and early childhood educators can work together to enable Australia's first national curriculum to be realized in practice.

Relational Agency

In the context of a worldwide recognition of the impact that quality early childhood experiences can have on children's development, both in the short term (Sylva, Melhuish, Sammons, Siraj-Blatchford, & Taggart, 2010) and in the long term (Sammons, 2010a, 2010b), governments have put more resources into supporting early childhood education and development (OECD, 2006). With increased resourcing has come increased responsibility for agencies to deliver greater outcomes for children and their families (Hannon & Fox, 2005). In response to communities managing the increase in services, there has been the need for better interagency collaboration (Rowe, 2005). Evaluations of the outcomes of these services are broadly based across family support (Croft, 2005; Drake, Weinberger & Hannon, 2005; Weinberger, 2005), health generally (Carlisle, 2005; Ford, 2005; Rowe, 2005), breastfeeding specifically (Batterby, 2005), education (Pickstone, 2005; Marsh & Forde, 2005; Martinez, 2005; Morgan, 2005), and strengthening communities (Hale, 2005; Lomas & Hannon, 2005). The international context of early childhood education and development has increasingly moved away from the boundary of specific institutions, such as preschools or maternal health clinics, and has become framed as multidisciplinary professional work teams (Wong, Sumsion, & Press, 2012). In this changing landscape (Cummings & Wong, 2012; Woodrow, 2012), how do different partnerships collaborate to generate new knowledge to inform practices, particularly in the area of teaching?

In the context of multiagency collaboration, Edwards (2005) introduced the concept of *relational agency* to conceptualize how successful partnerships are formed and maintained for increased outcomes for children at risk. It is thought that the concept of *relational agency* (Edwards & Apostolov, 2007) is useful for examining how policy writers, researchers, curriculum developers, and educators work together to realize greater educational outcomes for children.

The concept of *relational agency* captures a whole host of practices and thinking that are enacted in successful collaborations. Research by Edwards (2004, 2005, 2010) and colleagues (Edwards & Apostolov, 2007; Edwards, Daniels, Gallagher, Leadbetter, & Warmington, 2009) indicates that successful partnerships conceptualize themselves as a collective, with *collective expertise*. They do not simply focus on their own expertise, but consider their contributions in relation to others within the partnerships. In addition, successful interagency collaborations where relational agency features, identify that members of the partnerships pay ongoing attention to building their partnership. Edwards and Apostolov (2007) argue that relational agency is the ability to recognize and draw upon the distributed expertise that is brought together in multidisciplinary teams. This means being able to "align one's own interpretations of a problem of practice with those of others, and in so doing expand the object of professional activity" (Edwards & Apostolov, 2007, p. 73).

Taken together, *relational agency* can be defined as

> an enhanced form of professional practice in part because working with others on complex problems is likely to prevent an over-simplification of the problems; and in part because it involves being explicit about one's own expertise as one aligns and realigns one's actions in response to the strengths and needs of others. (p. 73)

We now draw upon this concept to discuss an example of a partnership that was formed in Australia, to build educator capacity for supporting the then pending Government agenda for improving the learning experiences of those children attending early childhood centers, family day care, and playgroups. Specifically, we draw attention to one major political imperative—the development and implementation of the national Early Years Learning Framework (EYLF), (Australian Government Department of Education, Employment and Workplace Relations, 2009), the first Australian curriculum for the birth-to-five sector. This document explicitly invites educators and those that support them to draw upon a broad suite of child development theories (Sumsion et al., 2009). This introduces a new need or challenge for the field to engage with less familiar or even completely unknown theories in the context of existing practices and beliefs about child development (Fleer & May, 2011). We use the concept of *relational agency* to explore knowledge generation as a result of how the emerging partnerships (policy writers, educators, and researchers) realized their common research goal to implement the EYLF locally, statewide, and nationally. Specifically we examine one major project: "Development of early learning resources to support the practices of the least qualified educators" (see Australian Government Department of Education, Employment and Workplace Relations, 2013b; Fleer & Raban, 2007a).

Even though the project preceded the publication of the EYLF, the project itself is conceptually linked to the national context in Australia for realizing the uptake of the EYLF across all states and territories and within all service types who have responsibility for children aged from birth to five years (see Australian Government Department of Education, Employment and Workplace Relations, 2013a).

Contextual Influences of the Project

One of the traditional theoretical perspectives guiding early childhood education in Australia and elsewhere has been developmentally appropriate practice (DAP). Longstanding critiques (e.g., Blaise, 2009) of the foundations of this perspective have shown the limitations of this ethnocentric and reductionist view of child development for practice. Despite these established understandings, developmental theories are still named within the EYLF as one view of child development from a range of theoretical perspectives advocated. What is important here is that while a broad range of theories are advocated to guide practice, only two theories of child development exist to support educators—a developmental or maturational theory of child development (i.e. ages and stages), and a cultural-historical theory of child development (sometimes called sociocultural theory). Poststructuralist theories, critical theories, and colonial theories, like cultural-historical theory, are part of the post-developmental paradigm guiding early childhood education (Fleer, 2013). But poststructuralist theories, critical theories, and colonial theories are not specifically theories of child development per se (Peers, 2011), but rather are powerful tools for problematizing practices and thinking, and as such they are important for educators when planning and teaching (Ailwood, 2004, 2010). For example, poststructuralist theories help with reflecting upon dualisms that are loaded with discourses of power, as we may see at centers where gendered interactions are left unchallenged by educators, who may hear, for example, boys directing girls out of the block corner. Cultural-historical theory with its focus on social practices and mediation as the source of children's development is different from views of child development that focus on milestones where age is the criterion for framing development. Maturational (developmental) and cultural-historical theories (post-developmental) of child development are the foundational theories named in the EYLF. Only having two theories of child development to guide educators has set up a dramatic context for practice, as educators move from a developmental to a post-developmental perspective of practice.

By advocating multiple theoretical perspectives, and by taking the position that there is no theoretical truth, the EYLF by default foregrounds a poststructuralist stance (Fleer, 2013). This is both a strength and a limitation for educators. It is a strength because educators have at their disposal a broad range of powerful tools to inform their work. They can ask questions about practices, critique by using their knowledge of a range of inclusive perspectives, and they can think in an informed way about how some practices and interactions could be exclusionary, gendered, and full of power relations that they would want to actively contest (see Giugni, 2011). But it is a limitation when it comes to child development, because only two theories of child development are currently available to support educators—developmental and cultural-historical. Introducing the EYLF with its range of theories (rather than just one theory) created the need for educators, policy writers, and curriculum developers to re-engage with theory, and to understand that child development is contested. That is, development is not a universal construct. Given that taken-for-granted beliefs about development following ages and stages have been normalized against middle class, mostly European heritage or North American children, developmental stages must be problematized in communities such as Australia, where cultural and linguistic diversity is the norm.

To transition the field into using contemporary theories to guide practice, the Australia Government was mindful of the need to build the capacity of its workforce. The project described in the following section is but one early initiative to support the profession following a positive model of practice where high levels of conceptual engagement are expected (Goodfellow & Hedges, 2007).

The Project: Development of Early Learning Resources for Educators

In this section it will be shown how researchers, policy writers, and early childhood educators worked together to develop new resources for supporting the professional knowledge of the field, particularly those who have either no qualifications or who are the least qualified staff to work in the field. The concept of *relational agency* will be used alongside Vygotsky's (1997) concept of *everyday concepts and scientific concepts* (sometimes called spontaneous and non-spontaneous concepts) to show how partner members draw upon their distributed expertise and align and realign their beliefs about child development as they research and develop a set of early learning resources for supporting the field.

Early Learning Resources

The *Early Learning Resources* project was commissioned by the Australian Government Department of Education, Employment and Workplace Relations (2013b) to produce a set of early learning resources that would support the practices of the least qualified educators working with young children, and would at the same time be suitable for families to support them in engaging in literacy and numeracy interactions in everyday life. Monash University as the lead organization partnered with Melbourne

University, Early Childhood Australia, and the Curriculum Corporation to develop these resources for the Australian Government. This national project ran for over two years, involving a panel of 12 early childhood professionals, made up of educators, policy developers, advisors, mathematics education experts, professional associations, directors of centers, and university academics from different parts of Australia. The goal was to develop resources that were informed by cultural-historical theory for supporting the learning of early literacy and numeracy. The resources that were developed were a series of postcard-sized resources; a professional development booklet for center directors to use with their own staff; and a website from which these resources could be downloaded, and which also offered a brief literature review explaining the evidence base around literacy and numeracy development. See the website for the Australian Government Department of Education, Employment and Workplace Relations http://deewr.gov.au/early-childhood-learning-resources-project.

Process of Resource Production and Worldview Changes

To achieve the project goal, the project directors (university partners) sought to slowly introduce cultural-historical theory to the partner members as a source of development for the whole group, including the academics. This was done because maturational theories were well understood, but little was known about how a cultural-historical conception of child development could be realized in practice. Each of the members of the partnership involved in researching and producing early learning resources came with their own beliefs and practices about child development and how literacy and numeracy learning are culturally constructed for young children (i.e. as a cultural form of knowledge invented by society). To create a common context for discussion, Monash University researchers gathered a series of six video observations of everyday family practices, such as feeding the chickens, wiping tables, serving meals, and gardening. These video clips were progressively used with the partners over time. Through the capturing and analyzing of everyday practices in families as part of the research phase, partners sought to understand the possibilities for literacy and numeracy learning occurring in everyday interactions. At each meeting, a segment of data with numeracy and literacy possibilities would be shown in the context of introducing concepts from cultural-historical theory to explain how development might progress from the everyday situation to abstract concepts in literacy and numeracy. Over time, all the partners focused on using the lenses of cultural-historical theory to make the learning visible. That is, they identified in the video clips the everyday mathematics and numeracy, as well as the possibilities for extending the interactions with children in families at home for more learning. What this would mean for resource production had to be co-created with the group, and through this, new knowledge was collectively developed. The distributed expertise of the group was important for realizing theory into practice, as well as practice into theory. Partner expertise was needed for generating the new knowledge that was to sit under the early learning resources.

National meetings for all the partners (one person from each of the major populated states of Australia) were held approximately every four months. The team deliberately drew upon the dialectical relations of *practice-informed theory* and *theory-informed practice* (Chaiklin, 2011). What drove all the partners was the need to produce early learning resources that were transformative of everyday practice—that is, with a higher level of consciousness of concepts of literacy and numeracy by educators and family for thinking about practice in new ways, and where children's new thinking transformed what they could do in everyday life. For example, in everyday practice, such as wiping the table at home or at a center, the early learning resources needed to support educators to interact in new ways in these everyday situations. That is, with greater knowledge of numeracy in these everyday situations (e.g., where children experience surface area and a sense of boundary as they "wipe the whole surface, and wipe to the edge of the table"), educators introduce terms such as *edge* and *surface* in situ in order to build foundational knowledge in mathematics. This was a new way of thinking about practice, as up until then partners discussed notions of free play and the need for children to discover the concepts for themselves. For example, educators suggest that: "Well, I kind of know that these experiences lead to thinking mathematically, but I wouldn't necessarily say or do anything special here. The children will discover it". In this traditional maturational view of child development, children's role is to discover while the educator's role is to observe. That is, their role as teachers is de-emphasized. To think explicitly with concepts and to take an active role required what one partner said early on: "Throwing out the baby *and* the bath water."

Partners not only discussed the everyday language that features in home interactions in families, but made comments early on about how cultural-historical theory could be misunderstood, such as, "We have to be careful that we don't turn every interaction into a maths or literacy lesson. This could put too much pressure on families and children"; "What is the key concept here that is being learned when the grandfather says 'put half of the grain for the chickens over here, and the other half over there', is it fractions"?; or "We need to make the language on the cards accessible to all families, so they are empowered to take a more active role when interacting with their child." These examples give an insight into the dialogue that featured during the analysis of the video observations, while also illuminating the theoretical lenses being used and the agency that gradually become established as discourses around concepts became understood and slowly aligned. One partner said: "I have come to trust that what we are creating is iterative, we get better at talking about our practice and professional knowledge with each version of the resource drafts that form, from one iteration to the next."

In the example of wiping the table, partners came to see that this (and other examples) is an *everyday concept* enacted in everyday practice (Vygotsky, 1997). Knowing about surface area and measurement would constitute a *scientific concept* that represents a cultural form of knowledge that gives new meaning to everyday practices (Vygotsky, 1997). Everyday practices build the foundational experiential learning needed to make sense of scientific concepts, such as the geometrical concept of area. This is a dialectical relationship because everyday concepts are transformed in practice when children work with scientific concepts to think about everyday practices in new ways. This was also relevant for the members of the partnership. When someone works with professional tacit knowledge of everyday early childhood practice, using theories to think differently can be transformative, as the concepts and theories allow a new level of consciousness about the everyday tacit ways of doing things to be made visible. For example, partners talked more explicitly about concepts: "I know a lot about interacting with children, but I have never thought so consciously about the professional knowledge I have, as scientific concepts that I bring to my everyday interactions."

In these four monthly sessions, the partners built understandings about the importance of identifying and naming concepts for developing children's understandings in literacy and numeracy. The partners identified that children needed to engage with concepts for transformative thinking. Transformative thinking was understood in this partnership as children moving from working intuitively to thinking with concepts. Partners also had transformative moments. For instance, knowing that children need to have a sense of an area (table surface) and a boundary (edge of the table), before they can think about the fact that surfaces with a boundary can be measured, represented for them a shift in thinking that was directly applied to practice. Partners began to share transformative moments from their own lives. For example, one partner gave the example of how her husband was helping their daughter to learn to ride a bike, and it was only when the daughter was instructed to look in the direction of where she wanted to go (beyond the immediate) that she stopped falling off her bike. That is, the specific instruction given (as a new way of thinking about bike riding) during the everyday practice of learning to ride a bike, was a key transformative moment for the child. Identifying these everyday concepts as opportunities for transformative interactions was important for the partners to consider while developing the resources.

The partnership also developed ideas related to applications of concept knowledge. That is, knowing about measurement, and measuring a table can be useful for everyday practice when buying a table cloth or when wanting to move the table through the door into another room (Willis, 2007). By measuring the table, children do not need to physically move the table in a trial-and-error fashion through the door, or take it to the shopping center when buying a tablecloth. By discussing applications of concepts, all partners identified situations where using mathematical concepts is useful for a child's everyday life. But these concepts are always built into practice. Identifying the transformative moments was something that needed to be led by the educators, as they were the ones with the greatest professional knowledge of practice. The video observations and collective analysis by the members of the partnership allowed for this theoretical knowledge to be co-created. For example, in group analysis, the maths expert commented on the mathematical moments in the video clips, the university academics often discussed the conceptual possibilities for transformation of thinking, and the early childhood educators gave insights and exact wording of the sentences needed for the cards, so they were expressed better and more accessible to family members and other educators who might be using the cards. The expert and professional knowledge that were held by each partner member were used together to create the resources with partners regularly commenting: "I now think more deliberately about the role of the teacher" (Early Childhood Australia partner); "I now have greater insights into why working concepts matter for preschool aged children" (Educator); and "I now have a better way of talking about cultural-historical concepts, such as, everyday and scientific concepts as being about concepts and contexts" (University Academic).

Theoretical knowledge was being developed across the group through bringing distributed expertise to the process of developing early learning resources, which used cultural-historical theory. High levels of dialectical thinking evolved as everyone discussed the relations between the everyday and the literacy and numeracy concepts in the video clips. Davydov (2008) has defined theoretical knowledge and dialectical thinking as building mental models, engaging in thought experiments, and in ascertaining relational connections between many different elements within a system. Davydov (1972/1990) argues that "mental experimentation forms the basis of theoretical thought, which operates by *scientific* concept" (p. 249).

Thinking dialectically involves the consideration of both a general view and a particular view—that is, thinking about the particular table being wiped, while at the same time thinking about the knowledge tradition of measurement (general view). Here historically formed knowledge traditions, such as mathematics, can be understood as part of everyday cultural practice. Concepts have been invented by humans so that we can understand our world and solve a particular need. To deeply understand these concepts, the learner must come to know both the context in which the need was created for inventing a new concept (e.g., importance of a common measurement system to support trade), and the purpose of the concept for current practice. That is, it is important that practice and the concept be studied together, even if the traditional view is that young children appear not ready to understand concepts such as measurement (as a maturational view of development would suggest). The general concept must also be viewed in the context of a historically located knowledge tradition (named by Davydov (2008) as rising to the concrete) or a culturally constructed knowledge system. Theoretical knowledge of this kind is different from narrative knowledge, which seeks to provide the most convincing case for the listener (i.e. best story), or empirical knowledge which is about causal relations that build blocks of knowledge that stack one on top of the other as cumulative evidence.

Theoretical Concepts Driving Knowledge Construction and Transformation of Thinking

Specifically the partners used everyday concepts and scientific concepts, and through this they not only generated new theoretical knowledge, but also gained deep insights into learning about the central concepts of cultural-historical theory. This is easy to write, but to undertake such a worldview change required significant investment in facing what is already well understood (i.e. everyday practice) and thinking about it in a completely new way. That is, to move away from bundling up learning into what has traditionally been considered appropriate for infants, toddlers, and preschoolers, where age is the central criterion for marking development, to examining concepts and contexts in social relations (Fleer, 2010). In a developmental worldview, initially common among partners, children do not engage explicitly with concepts, but rather learn them indirectly and in a roundabout way (Fleer, 2009). A cultural-historical conception of child development sees the social and material environment, and the child's active engagement and contribution to it (child's agency), mediated by an educator. The use of contexts provides a rich learning vehicle for children to experience and learn about a range of concepts. These contexts become the source of a child's development (rather than the unfolding of a biological process). All children experience things, but not all experiences lead to a child's development (Veresov, 2010). Through analyzing the everyday practices (everyday concepts), while also considering important literacy and numeracy concepts (scientific concepts), the members of the partnership came to the view that children build knowledge of concepts by means of educators taking a more active role in children's everyday interactions with their culturally framed material and social world. That is, a child together with an adult can wipe the table until the child is ten years of age, and never think consciously about surface area, boundary, or the possibility of how measurement can transform how she or he does things in everyday life. These latter ideas are part of the cultural knowledge of mathematics. Transforming an everyday practice into the concept of measurement is representative of a cultural practice, and this cultural practice needs to be introduced to children by those who already have these practices as part of their culture. This constituted the conceptual product that was actively being co-created by members of the partnership. To achieve this, the distributed nature of the expertise of the group was brought to bear on the common problem, which, as Edwards et al. (2009) have argued, is important in a multiagency partnership. By collectively analyzing the video observations of everyday practices, this allowed all partners to turn discussions about practice and theory into resources that supported new directions in pedagogy and allowed for a new understanding of child development. What was created was a photograph on one side of a card that showed an everyday interaction, like wiping the table. On the back of the card were three discrete sentences. The first sentence on the card represented the everyday conversation that the educator or parent could have with a child such as "Let's wipe the table together." This is followed by the introduced scientific concepts in context in the second sentence: "Did you wipe to the edge? We covered the whole area." The final third statement discusses explicitly what the concepts lead to later on in schooling, for example: "When we talk about *edge, side, top* or *bottom*, children are learning about area. Children often don't think about area. Helping children pay attention to it helps them later on when they will measure these surfaces and make comparisons." This cultural-historical framework of three elements constituted how the partners developed all of the cards. Later, after the resources were formally piloted with families and educators (see Fleer & Raban, 2007b), and the results were examined by the partners, one member said, "The head-banging was all worth it, when you can see the resources work." The statement "It works!" is the equivalent of Archimedes' "Eureka!"

A paradigm shift from developmentalism to post-developmentalism resulted for partner educators, and a deeper understanding of cultural-historical theory in practice took place for the university academic partners and policy writer partners. Through the alignment and realignment of one's own interpretations of both practice and theory, partners came up with ways to make practices more deliberate.

Enablers

There were several key enablers that provided the space for the partners to create their new resources and to research this process. These were the situational opportunity provided by the dramatic tension created by different beliefs and knowledge of the partners, the discussions that resulted from viewing the video observations, as well as discussions about the resources being developed to support educators, and how a cultural-historical lens allowed us to refocus on the underlying purpose and human needs that contributed to the main concepts. The collaborative approach allowed for combining and extending collective expertise, while simultaneously learning from each other. As a result, the resources created were based on richly theorized understandings that could be adapted by educators into their practice.

In line with Edwards et al. (2009), a common language about both theory and practice was developed by all partners through the shared lens of cultural-historical theory. Through the process of viewing and talking about the video clips, all the partners were able to express insights that were drawing upon professional knowledge of their area (i.e. policy perspective, educator perspective, academic perspective, mathematics, literacy), which Edwards et al. (2009) argues is critical for deepening understandings of the others' professional knowledge. The valuing of professional knowledge resulted and a real sense of relational agency was realized as partners brought their expertise to bear on the common goal of the project.

Challenges

Because the partners collectively analyzed the video observations of children and adults engaged in everyday practices, they each articulated the theories (tacit or otherwise) they were working with to interpret what they saw. For example, an initial comment made was, "We have to make cards for babies, toddlers and preschoolers, why are we only working with examples from the preschool aged children in the garden in this video clip?" (maturational perspective). The partners discussed what kinds of pedagogical practices might allow children to notice the literacy or numeracy concepts in everyday situations. For example:

> The video clips of everyday numeracy are very different to the sorting and classifying tasks given to children in preschools, where they sort beads. This has nothing to do with their everyday life. Sorting toys to put them away is far more meaningful and brings together everyday concepts with scientific concepts of classification.

A sense of the professional knowledge that individuals brought to bear on the problem was made visible and conscious to all listening. Each of the partners discovered that there was a need to explain different concepts drawn from specific professions in relation to the concrete examples, so that it was possible to identify the kinds of evidence in the videos that provided examples of how to draw out the literacy and numeracy of the everyday situations. As a result, the challenges identified by Edwards et al. (2009) that occur in many multiagency partnerships were dealt with because it was understood that the whole process was iterative. That is, the group continued to collectively interrogate the video observations until all the conceptual tools and terms being used were understood and a consensus was reached, ready for piloting in the field. In the lead up to the piloting, and as a result of the piloting, final wording on the cards and in the booklet continued to change to reflect what worked best for families and educators.

Knowledge Generation and Transformation of Thinking

In bringing together the cumulative learning of the partner members for this project, it is possible to realize new insights into what are enablers and barriers for effective relations, what forms of knowledge are generated, and how multiagency partnerships can lead to transformative thinking and practice. Much of this has already been touched upon in the discussions and analyses in the previous sections. However, in the context of Hedegaard's (2008) model of learning and development in which personal, institutional, and societal perspectives are dialectically related, Hedegaard foregrounds how the motives and needs of individuals are directly linked to how institutions support particular kinds of practices, which in turn are legislated into societies through governing agencies, such as government departments. It is not possible to think about an individual partnership without considering the influences of institutional and societal perspectives.

The complexity of the *relational agency* that emerged in the project discussed in this chapter was associated with the different background knowledge contributed by the different partners that was brought to bear on the problem, and the political imperatives that the Australian Government is seeking to achieve. The implementation of the EYLF was one contributor to quality reform in early years education in Australia. Underpinning this was the imperative to develop the knowledge base of the field. That is, the existing field was being supported through professional learning, through access to resources to support contemporary thinking about child development, and through structures to upgrade qualifications (see Australian Government Department of Education, Employment and Workplace Relations, 2013a, 2013b). Simultaneously, the Government changed legislation for mandating qualified four-year degree staff in early childhood settings, provided more funded places in universities and scholarship programs to support upgrading qualifications for existing educators, plus more (see Australian Government Department of Education, Employment and Workplace Relations, 2013a; Fleet & Patterson, 2009; Georgeson, 2009). A suite of programs and funding was put in place to achieve the goal of developing more knowledgeable early childhood educators, who could in turn support greater outcomes for individual children. The Australian Government had used the best available research evidence to support building professional knowledge of the field as a whole (i.e. more of highly qualified educators interacting with children will qualitatively improve outcomes for children). In putting in place quality reform, Government also ensured that base line evidence would be generated about the existing field (Fleer & May, 2011), so that future evaluations could determine if the sector had been successful in building professional knowledge.

Relational agency was achieved in the partnership project because the quality agenda that underpinned the project was commonly viewed as an important process and was valued by educators, policy writers, and academics alike. While there was a *demand* made upon the sector to communicate across institutions (discourses and knowledge systems), the common *motive* (Hedegaard, 2008) for a more knowledgeable profession was valued by the partner members. Like Government, the partnership was already well informed about the research evidence of quality early childhood experience—a need for a more knowledgeable workforce that is able to support higher outcomes and higher quality learning contexts for children.

The knowledge created through the project was hard won because it required considerable time and a great deal of intellectual engagement of the partner members. That is, it required a major intellectual commitment and willingness to engage in a new way of thinking about the nature of child development. What was achieved in the project moved beyond just knowing about contemporary theories or practices, to examining taken-for-granted beliefs about development and using a new theory to think differently about child development. Knowledge was collectively generated. It was not an accumulation of empirical facts, such as building blocks, but rather knowledge was formed relationally in the context of practice while making video observations and in the creation of cards that drew upon different worldviews and lenses, that had to iteratively be applied and discussed. New concepts and new practices were directly related to each other—practice was grounded in theoretical knowledge, and theory was conceptualized as practice. The potential for *institutional* change was being enacted through the project.

In Hedegaard's (2008) model the concept of crisis is a central feature for understanding how development is activated. This concept comes from Vygotsky's (1987) theory of child development, as a revolutionary process. In the project discussed in this chapter, it was also noted that a crisis emerged. The university researchers, educators, policy writers, and curriculum developers focused on the success that resulted from the dramatic situations that arose and were used to work toward new conceptualizations of practice and theory. The project indicated the power of collectively analyzing everyday practices as shown in the video observations. The discussions allowed beliefs about child development to emerge. As the partners worked hard to understand each other's perspectives, their own beliefs and assumptions about child development emerged. Whether it is a crisis, dramatic tension, or a contested space, the importance of having a common focus (i.e. analyzing video observations or creation of resources) where different beliefs, discourses, and practices can be made visible created a productive zone for the collective transformation of thinking.

Knowledge generation resulted from a partnership that was engaged in collaboratively thinking about development in new ways. Here dialectical thinking and theoretical knowledge emerged as an outcome (Davydov, 2008) that was additional to the resources produced. While narrative knowledge was used to make visible aspects of the data being shared, and empirical knowledge was what drove the data-gathering process, it was the theoretical knowledge that was created collectively by the participants, that was transformative. By seeing the data holistically and relationally, members of the partnership were able to consider how practice informed theory, and how theory informed practice. Stetsenko and Vianna (2009) have argued that there is nothing more practical than a good theory, and nothing more theoretical than good practice.

Conclusion

It can be argued that successful partnerships build *relational agency* (Edwards, 2010), that is, they attune themselves to the collective, building common knowledge across the partnership, set agreed goals, and use agreed strategies for effective implementation. Members of the partnership are able to take the standpoint of the other, are able to be explicit about what matters, as well as recognize what matters to others, and can attune one's actions with those of others.

Being able to attune one's actions with the action of others for generating knowledge in a project was an important feature of the project described in this chapter. It was through the process of using new theories and concepts (scientific concepts) to analyze everyday practices (everyday concepts) that enabled individuals to think in new ways about practice and about theory. This resulted in higher levels of discussions about pedagogical practices, and supported a transformation of thinking.

What was realized in the analysis of the project was that successful partnerships pay simultaneous attention to societal goals and values, institutional discourse and practice, and individual motives and demands, in the creation of new knowledge and practice. Where there exists a common vision, such as a quality reform agenda (as identified through developing education expertise), among the intersecting institutions, and the personal goals and motives of individuals to realize this vision through the production of a set of resources, we find attunement and the valuing of distributed expertise. Together this expertise can be harnessed for supporting dialectical thinking and building new theoretical knowledge to improve practice and theory and thereby better serve society as a whole.

Acknowledgment

Project Leaders were Bridie Raban and the author.

References

Ailwood, J. (2004). Genealogies of governmentality: Producing and managing young children and their education. *The Australian Educational Researcher, 31*(3), 19–33.

Ailwood, J. (2010). Playing with some tensions. Poststructuralism, Foucault and early childhood education. In L. Brooker, & S. Edwards (Eds.), *Engaging play* (pp. 210–222). London, UK: Open University Press: McGraw-Hill Education.

Atkinson, M., Jones, M., & Lamont, E. (2007). *Multi-agency working and its implications for practice: A review of the literature*. Reading, UK: Centre for British Teachers (CfBT).

Australian Government Department of Education, Employment and Workplace Relations. (2009). *Early Years Learning Framework*. ACT, Australia: Commonwealth of Australia.

Australian Government Department of Education, Employment and Workplace Relations. (2013a). *Early childhood*. Retrieved from http://deewr.gov.au/early-childhood

Australian Government Department of Education, Employment and Workplace Relations. (2013b). *Early Childhood Learning Resources Project*. Retrieved from http://deewr.gov.au/early-childhood-learning-resources-project

Battersby, S. (2005). Supporting breastfeeding mothers. In J. Weinberger, C. Pickstone, C. Hannon, & P. Hannon (Eds.), *Learning from Sure Start: Working with young children and their families* (pp. 86–102). London, UK: Open University Press.

Blaise, M. (2009). Revolutionising practice by doing early childhood politically. The revolutionary planning group. In S. Edwards, & J. Nuttall (Eds.), *Professional learning in early childhood settings* (pp. 27–48). Rotterdam, Netherlands: Sense Publishers.

Carlisle, R. (2005). Child safety scheme. In J. Weinberger, C. Pickstone, C. Hannon, & P. Hannon (Eds.), *Learning from Sure Start: Working with young children and their families* (pp. 115–130). London, UK: Open University Press.

Chaiklin, S. (2011). The role of practice in cultural-historical science. In M. Kontopodis, C. Wulf, & B. Fichtner (Eds.), *Children, development and education: Cultural, historical, anthropological perspectives* (pp. 227–246). Dordrecht, The Netherlands: Springer.

Cheminais, R. (2009). *Effective multi-agency partnerships: Putting every child matters into practice*. London, UK: Sage.

Croft, D. (2005). Meeting the needs of teenage parents. In J. Weinberger, C. Pickstone, C. Hannon, & P. Hannon (Eds.), *Learning from Sure Start. Working with young children and their families* (pp. 55–70). London, UK: Open University Press.

Cummings, T., & Wong, S. (2012). Professionals don't play: Challenges for early childhood educators working in a transdisciplinary early intervention team. *Australasian Journal of Early Childhood*, *32*(20), 127–135.

Davydov, V. V. (1972/1990). *Types of generalization in instruction: Logical and psychological problems in the structuring of school curricula. Soviet studies in mathematics education* (Vol. 2, trans. J. Teller). Reston, VA: National Council of Teachers of Mathematics.

Davydov, V. V. (2008). *Problems of developmental instruction. A theoretical and experimental psychological study* (Trans. P. Moxhay). New York, NY: Nova Science Publishers.

Drake, M., Weinberger, J., & Hannon, P. (2005). "Connecting with our kids" parenting programme. In J. Weinberger, C. Pickstone, C. Hannon, & P. Hannon

(Eds.), *Learning from Sure Start. Working with young children and their families* (pp. 43–54). London, UK: Open University Press.

Edwards, A. (2004). The new multi-agency working: Collaborating to prevent the social exclusion of children and families. *Journal of Integrated Care, 12*(5), 3–9.

Edwards, A. (2005). Relational agency: Learning to be a resourceful practitioner. *International Journal of Educational Research, 43*(3), 168–182.

Edwards, A. (2010). *Being an expert professional practitioner: A relational turn in expertise*. Dordrecht, The Netherlands: Springer.

Edwards, A., & Apostolov, A. (2007). A cultural-historical interpretation of resilience: The implications for practice. *Outlines, 9*(1), 70–84.

Edwards, A., Daniels, H., Gallagher, T., Leadbetter, J., & Warmington, P. (2009). *Improving inter-professional collaborations. Multi-agency working for children's wellbeing*. London, UK: Routledge.

Fleer, M., (2009). Supporting conceptual consciousness or learning in a roundabout way. *International Journal of Science Education, 31*(8), 1069–1090.

Fleer, M. (2010). *Early learning and development: Cultural-historical concepts in play*. New York, NY: Cambridge University Press.

Fleer, M. (2013). *Play in the early years*. New York, NY: Cambridge University Press.

Fleer, M., & May, W. (2011). *Professional development program. Contemporary child development theories for early childhood educators, Progress Report 1*. Melbourne, Australia: Monash University.

Fleer, M., & Raban, B. (2007a). *Early childhood literacy and numeracy: Building good practice*. Canberra, Australia: Early Childhood Australia.

Fleer, M., & Raban, B. (2007b). Constructing cultural-historical tools for supporting young children's concept formation in early literacy and numeracy. *Early Years: An International Journal of Research and Development, 27*(2), 103–118.

Fleet, A., & Patterson, C. (2009). A timescape. In S. Edwards, & J. Nuttall (Eds.), *Professional learning in early childhood settings* (pp. 9–26). Rotterdam, The Netherlands: Sense Publishers.

Ford, F. (2005). Low birth weight—exploring the contribution of nutrition. In J. Weinberger, C. Pickstone, C. Hannon, & P. Hannon (Eds.), *Learning from Sure Start: Working with young children and their families* (pp. 71–85). London, UK: Open University Press.

Georgeson, J. (2009). The professionalization of the early years workforce. In S. Edwards, & J. Nuttall (Eds.), *Professional learning in early childhood settings* (pp. 115–130). Rotterdam, The Netherlands: Sense Publishers.

Giugni, M. (2011). "Becoming worldly with": An encounter with the Early Years Learning Framework. *Contemporary Issues in Early Childhood, 12*(1), 11–27.

Goodfellow, J., & Hedges, H. (2007). Practitioner research "centre stage": Contexts, contributions and challenges. In L. Keasing-Styles, & H. Hedges (Eds.), *Theorising early childhood practice: Emerging dialogues* (pp. 187–210). New South Wales, Australia: Pademelon Press.

Hale, I. (2005). The young families' advice service. In J. Weinberger, C. Pickstone, C. Hannon, & P. Hannon (Eds.), *Learning from Sure Start: Working with young children and their families* (pp. 205–216). London, UK: Open University Press.

Hannon, P., & Fox, L. (2005). Why we should learn from Sure Start. In J. Weinberger, C. Pickstone, C. Hannon, & P. Hannon (Eds.), *Learning from Sure Start: Working with young children and their families* (pp. 3–12). London, UK: Open University Press.

Hedegaard, M. (2008). A cultural—historical theory of children's development. In M. Hedegaard, & M. Fleer (Eds.), *Studying children: A cultural—historical approach* (pp. 10–29). Berkshire, UK: Open University Press.

Lomas, H., & Hannon, P. (2005). Community involvement. In J. Weinberger, C. Pickstone, C. Hannon, & P. Hannon (Eds.), *Learning from Sure Start: Working with young children and their families* (pp. 193–204). London, UK: Open University Press.

Marsh, J., & Forde, J. (2005). Community teaching in a Sure Start. In J. Weinberger, C. Pickstone, C. Hannon, & P. Hannon (Eds.), *Learning from Sure Start: Working with young children and their families* (pp. 141–153). London, UK: Open University Press.

Martinez, S. (2005). Quality of play and learning opportunities. In J. Weinberger, C. Pickstone, C. Hannon, & P. Hannon (Eds.), *Learning from Sure Start: Working with young children and their families* (pp. 131–140). London, UK: Open University Press.

Morgan, A. (2005). A dialogic reading intervention programme for parents and preschoolers. In J. Weinberger, C. Pickstone, C. Hannon, & P. Hannon (Eds.), *Learning from Sure Start: Working with young children and their families* (pp. 177–192). London, UK: Open University Press.

OECD. (2006). *Starting strong II. Early childhood education and care*. Paris, France: Organization for Economic Co-operation and Development.

Peers, C. (2011, August). *Developmental and post developmental theories. Presentation at Professional development program. Contemporary child development theories for early childhood educators*. Melbourne, Australia: Monash University.

Pickstone, C. (2005). Screening and language development. In J. Weinberger, C. Pickstone, C. Hannon,& P. Hannon (Eds.), *Learning from Sure Start: Working with young children and their families* (pp. 154–165). London, UK: Open University Press.

Rowe, A. (2005). The impact of Sure Start on health visiting. In J. Weinberger, C. Pickstone, C. Hannon, & P. Hannon (Eds.), *Learning from Sure Start: Working with young children and their families* (pp. 102–114). London, UK: Open University Press.

Sammons, P. (2010a). Does pre-school make a difference? Identifying the impact of pre-school on children's cognitive and social behavioural development at different ages. In K. Sylva, E. Melhuish, P. Sammons, I. Siraj-Blathford, & B. Taggart (Eds.), *Early childhood matters: Evidence from the effective pre-school and primary education project* (pp. 92–113). Oxon, UK: Routledge.

Sammons, P. (2010b). Do the benefits of pre-school last? Investigating pupil outcomes to the end of Key Stage 2 (aged 11). In K. Sylva, E. Melhuish, P. Sammons, I. Siraj-Blathford, & B. Taggart (Eds.), *Early childhood matters: Evidence from the effective pre-school and primary education project* (pp. 114–148). Oxon, UK: Routledge.

Stetsenko, A., & Vianna, E. (2009). Bridging developmental theory and educational practice. Lessons from the Vygotskian project. In O. A. Barbarin & B. H. Wasik (Eds.), *Handbook of Child Development and Early Education. Research to practice* (pp. 38–54). New York, NY: The Guilford Press.

Sumsion, J., Barnes, S., Cheeseman, S., Harrison, L., Kennedy, A. M., & Stonehouse, A. (2009). Insider perspectives on developing belonging, being and becoming: The Early Years Learning Framework for Australia. *Australasian Journal of Early Childhood, 34*(4), 4–13.

Sylva, K., Melhuish, E., Sammons, P., Siraj-Blatchford, I., & Taggart, B. (2010). (Eds.), *Early childhood matter: Evidence from the effective pre-school and primary education project.* Oxon, UK: Routledge.

Tomlinson, K. (2003). *Effective interagency working: A review of the literature and examples from practice.* LGA Research Report 40. Slough, UK: National Foundation for Educational Research.

Veresov, N. (2010). Introducing cultural historical theory: Main concepts and principles of genetic research methodology. *Journal of Cultural-Historical Psychology, 4,* 83–90.

Vygotsky, L. S. (1987). *Problems of general psychology. The collected works of L.S. Vygotsky* (Vol. 5, N. Minick, trans.; R. W. Rieber & A. S. Carton, Eds.; English trans.). New York, NY: Plenum. (Original work published 1934)

Vygotsky, L. S. (1997). *The history of the development of higher mental functions. The collected works of L.S. Vygotsky* (Vol. 4, M. J. Hall, trans.; R. W. Rieber, Ed.; English trans.). New York, NY: Plenum. (Original work published 1931)

Weinberger, J. (2005). Community research. In J. Weinberger, C. Pickstone, C. Hannon, & P. Hannon (Eds.), *Learning from Sure Start: Working with young children and their families* (pp. 217–230). London, UK: Open University Press.

Willis, S. (2007, July). *Mathematics in early childhood education.* Keynote presentation. Professional development program for the *"Catch the Future"* research project. Melbourne, Australia: Monash University.

Wong, S., Sumsion, S., & Press, F. (2012). Early childhood professionals and inter-professional work in integrated early childhood services in Australia. *Australasian Journal of Early Childhood, 37*(1), 81–88.

Woodrow, C. (2012). Relationships, reflexivity and renewal: Professional practice in action in an Australian children's centre. In L. Miller, C. Dalli, & M. Urban (Eds.), *Early childhood grows up: Towards a critical ecology of the profession* (pp. 21–36). Dordrecht, The Netherlands: Springer.

4

Developing Effective Research–Practice Partnerships: Lessons from a Decade of Partnering with Schools in Poor Urban Communities

Mei Lai and Stuart McNaughton

Introduction

In recent years, partnerships between researchers and schools have been promoted as a way to advance knowledge about teaching and learning, and improve student outcomes. This emphasis is due in part to emerging empirical evidence that demonstrates improvements in achievement when partnerships between schools and researchers are an integral part of interventions (McNaughton, Lai & Hsiao, 2012). Although the effects of partnerships cannot be disentangled from other components of these interventions, they provide some evidence that partnerships are important.

However, partnering with schools in and of itself is no guarantee for improving teaching and learning as it is possible for partners to work together in ways that are not educative. For example, an early evaluation of a schooling improvement initiative found that partnerships between local communities, schools, and government were highly problematic for reasons such as blaming another partner for the educational *failures*, rather than attempting to learn together how best to raise achievement (Timperley, Robinson, & Bullard, 1999). It is also possible for partnerships to focus on the building of relationships between partners, rather than the task of jointly improving teaching and learning. For example, a research–school partnership might focus on building trust and friendships, but not progress the task of improving the teaching and learning problems the partnership was meant to solve, as partners are too afraid of offending other partners to critique ineffective practices. As such, it is how these partnerships are developed and sustained through the research that is critical.

There are many types of research–school partnership models proposed in literature. Recent partnership models share core features but vary for the responsibility of defining research questions, designing intervention, and the analytic capability (Bryk, Sebring, Allensworth, Luppescu, & Easton, 2010). In this chapter, we present an approach to partnering with schools that has been developed and successfully applied to improve literacy teaching and learning in three government-sponsored Teaching and Learning Research Initiative (TLRI)[1] projects that we have led. The partnership model we used (*The Learning Schools Model*) adopted principles similar to those of the *Strategic Research Partnership* model (Snow & Donovan, 2012) with an added focus on schools developing their evaluative capability. These principles will be explained in detail later in the chapter.

The three projects discussed here were partnerships between the Woolf Fisher Research Centre[2], The University of Auckland, and two clusters of schools ($n = 7$ and $n = 6$ schools) in two urban, poor (i.e., low socioeconomic) communities serving primarily linguistically and culturally diverse students. These projects, representing part of our decade-long work involving partnerships, were conducted from 2003 to 2010 and built cumulative knowledge about how to work with such schools. The first two projects were three-year interventions using quasi-experimental research designs to improve reading comprehension across the two communities. The third, a mixed-method project, examined the sustainability of achievement gains after the end of these interventions and the practices that led to sustainability (or not) of these achievement gains. The chapter begins by describing the interventions and their successes in improving outcomes for students, followed by a discussion of the key principles underpinning our approach for partnering with schools, which was integral to the interventions.

The Interventions and Their Success

New Zealand is described as a high-quality but low-equity education system (OECD, 2010). Students have high levels of reading comprehension, as shown by international comparisons, but there are large disparities within the distribution of achievement. These are between children from both *Māori* (indigenous) and *Pasifika* (immigrants from the Pacific Islands) communities in urban schools with the lowest employment and income levels, and other children. *Māori* and *Pasifika* children generally score lower in achievement measures than children from other ethnic groups (McNaughton, 2011a). The goal of the TLRI projects was to raise and sustain reading achievement over a five-year period (three years for intervention, and two years for sustainability). We have previously described these interventions in detail (Lai, McNaughton, Amituanai-Toloa, Turner, & Hsiao, 2009); so we will only briefly summarize them here.

The interventions to improve reading comprehension comprised three phases, each phase lasting approximately a school year. First, a profiling phase in which researchers, school leaders, and teachers formed Professional Learning Communities (PLC) to examine the nature of the achievement problem collaboratively (students were on average two years behind their peers in reading comprehension), and to analyze how to solve the achievement problem. The PLC examined reading comprehension data from standardized tests, data from other teacher-administered assessments (formal such as standardized assessments and informal such as reading tasks given during class), and observations of teachers' instructional practices in their classrooms. The discussions with teachers consisted of analyzing these different data sources to uncover the patterns of achievement (i.e., students' strengths and learning needs) and matching those patterns to observations of classroom teaching to find out what specific teaching practices might be improved to address students' learning needs[3].

At this juncture, we need to emphasize that this problem-solving process is *not* about teaching to the test, in that teachers learn how to teach particular test items or how to address the narrow range of test skills. Rather the process is about formative assessment, where teachers learn about the specific learning needs of students that are identified through assessments, reflect on their current practices in relation to the specific learning needs, and design better teaching practices to address the learning needs.

In the second phase, problem-solving using achievement data continued, but teacher knowledge of how to address the patterns of student learning was increased through professional development workshops with researchers. The content of these workshops was based on the teaching and learning needs identified in Phase I, and covered aspects of literacy instruction such as vocabulary instruction and increasing students' awareness of the goals and formats of classroom activities and the relevance of their skills and knowledge to these activities[4]. For example, in Phase I, students' performance on the reading assessments showed that students did not have the breadth of vocabulary of other children in New Zealand. When observing classrooms we noticed that the rate of interactions between teacher and child around building vocabulary may have been lower than what was needed; the focus on any one particular word occurred typically once and there was little evidence of repeated opportunities to use or elaborate words; and that meanings of words were seldom checked in ways that elaborated specific connotations in context. So the workshops focused on strategies to increase teacher–child interactions around vocabulary, including developing multiple opportunities to elaborate words; and strategies to check the meanings of words in context. As part of the workshops, teachers designed how they would use the workshop content, trialed the changes to their practice in their classes, examined the impact on students through formative assessment in the classrooms (e.g., feedback from students, homework), and reported back to the PLC. The PLC comprised of teachers from other schools, researchers, and at least one school leader from each school. The report back to the PLC included discussions on how to modify the practices so that they become more effective. For example, one teacher used song lyrics to teach language features, but reported that the activity would have been more effective had she picked a song that students were more familiar with.

In the final phase of the intervention, problem-solving using data continued, but we added interschool teacher-led conferences to strengthen the problem-solving capability in schools (i.e., teachers determined a problem they wished to solve, investigated it and presented their findings for discussion with teachers from other schools). Other measures for sustainability of the intervention included working with school leaders to develop school-wide strategies for sustainability such as induction for new teachers.

Results from these projects indicated that students made about one year's worth of progress in reading comprehension *in addition to* nationally expected progress over a three-year period (Lai, McNaughton, Amituanai-Toloa, Turner, & Hsiao, 2009; McNaughton & Lai, 2009). Prior to the intervention, the average student scored in the *below average* achievement band, but after the intervention, the average student scored in the *average* band of achievement. There was a reduction of students in the *low* or *below average* achievement bands from about 60 percent to about 30 percent by the end of the intervention. The improvements in achievement, when measured using the statistical test of effect sizes, were comparable or higher than those reported internationally for similar schooling improvement initiatives (Borman, 2005). Our intervention effect sizes for clusters were in the order of $d = 0.60$ and 0.62, respectively, whereas Borman reported effect sizes of less than 0.2 for interventions of similar length.

One year after the interventions, gains in achievement were sustained, as statistical tests (hierachical linear modelling) showed that students continued to make yearly gains that were comparable to those made during the interventions (Lai, McNaughton, Timperley, & Hsiao, 2009). During and after the intervention, students on average improved by about three to four months *in addition to* expected yearly progress.

In other words, schools were able to improve achievement at the same rate as during the intervention without the intensive support and resources that were available during the intervention. This is significant because a recent synthesis of professional learning found only seven studies that were able to show continued improvements in achievement after the end of interventions (Timperley, Wilson, Barrar, & Fung, 2007). In addition, results from the sustainability study indicated that schools continued to partner with the same researchers and other external agents, placing considerable emphasis on the importance of partnerships for ongoing sustainability. The nature of these partnerships after the intervention varied according to the different schools in the projects. The types of partnerships ranged from the same researchers becoming critical friends of the school (e.g., answer ad hoc email queries) to the same researchers working together with some schools to seek further funding[5].

Key Principles for Partnerships

Contemporary partnerships between researchers, schools, and their communities come in different forms. While they share core features such as a joint focus on a major educational change project, and a commitment to advance scientific understanding of effective educational processes, they do vary. Specifically, they vary in situations in which the responsibility lies for defining research questions, for the design of the intervention, design of the research methods, and the analytic capability.

A basic model is provided by the Consortium on Chicago School Research (CCSR) (Bryk et al., 2010). The CCSR is a long-standing partnership network, which has set the benchmark for enduring partnerships. The consortium comprised of researchers, policy advocates, community activists, school system, and professional organization leaders as well as civic and philanthropic leaders. The shared mission was to inform the major reforms taking place in the Chicago public schools using evidence from high-quality research. Researchers treated the major reforms as a natural experiment but stood aside from direct involvement in designing the reforms to understand the process and outcomes. Like other partnerships, systematic feedback by researchers to schools was provided, and researchers' data and theory building have informed the ongoing policy and reform design. An example is the development of their theoretical framework of *essential supports* for school change with school leaders as drivers for establishing *program coherence*. The concepts evolved through the partnership and were fed back to the schools through the CCSR steering committee. The direct impact on schools is not known. Traditional views of the *gold standard* for experimental design were judged as inappropriate and the CCSR methods have used variability (e.g., within and between schools) as a source for developing and testing model components.

A partnership model with more of a direct involvement with the leaders within the schools, and which has a deliberate goal to design and test the changes in literacy instruction, is the Strategic Education Research Partnership (SERP) involving Boston schools (Snow & Donovan, 2012). In the SERP model the research team is involved directly in the design of change processes using the local school and community context as the site for shared problem definition. Their model proposes a shift in authority from researchers to a partnership with shared authority, to capitalize on the shared skills and knowledge of educational professionals, researchers, and designers. An example is the response to teachers' and administrators' concerns about vocabulary instruction. The SERP team developed and tested with the schools an intervention called *word generation* and the partnership acted to embed the redesign of classroom instruction into everyday practice.

In essence the SERP model adopts what has come to be called a design-based research approach (Anderson & Shattuck, 2012). The design-based approach has key features of being situated in a real educational context, and focusing on the design and testing of a significant intervention using mixed methods with multiple iterations in an enduring collaborative enterprise between researchers and schools. By multiple iterations we mean iterative cycles of data collection, analysis, and feedback that are used by both researchers and school practitioners to design more effective instruction. The design principles are distinctly different from action or practitioner research in that rigorous design formats (e.g., quasi-experimental) are deemed critical and like the CCSR, systematic analysis of variation is a central analytic strategy. But it shares with action research a commitment to an educationally significant impact on practice. Cobb and Smith's (2008) research group focused on improving middle school mathematics in partnership with clusters of schools is another example of this design-based approach. The Learning Schools Model (LSM) shares aspects of these features. The key operating principles in the LSM, and other school and research partnerships, draw on two interrelated dimensions.

One concerns the properties of educational science that are needed to ensure that the partnership can impact on valued outcomes, for example, improvements in student achievement or improvements in student engagement. Effective partnerships use methodologically robust methods in order to advance teaching and learning, and this includes design principles and analytic rigor. Research methodologies with which researchers can understand the reasons and beliefs for particular school practices are also required. This means there is a need for greater capability to identify the beliefs and assumptions that lead to the continuation of these practices and this in turn increases the likelihood of co-creating ways of improving practice that will be accepted by school, that is, teachers, senior managers, and principals (e.g., Robinson & Lai, 2006).

These properties of a methodologically robust educational science are dependent on, and provide conditions for, the second dimension—the social and cultural processes needed for the partnership to function effectively to meet goals. This dimension includes the importance of building and maintaining a well-functioning community of practice in which shared foci and shared protocols are established to meld together diverse cognitions and personalities (Wenger, 1998).

In addition, there are two further dimensions in the LSM that may be more context-specific to New Zealand. Common to the more collaborative partnership models is the need to treat partners in ways that recognize the complementary and reciprocal nature of the expertise required to solve everyday problems (McNaughton, 2011b). In the applications of the LSM this has meant viewing the PLCs in schools as having basic evaluative capability, and seeing teachers in general as having properties that Darling-Hammond and Bransford (2005) term "adaptive expertise" (p. 49). The fourth dimension involves an ethical imperative. Ethical treatment of those working in a collective problem-solving process requires a set of mutual and reciprocal obligations. The latter has a cultural dimension in the context of New Zealand based research. It comes from *Kaupapa Māori* theorizing (theorizing from *Māori* principles), which requires researchers and educators with their local communities to become joined in a *whānau* (extended family) of interest (Smith, 1999). The metaphor draws attention to the reciprocal obligations, rights, and roles that are similar to those operating in an extended family.

Partnerships Based on Robust Research Methods

It is taken for granted that as researchers our methods should be robust, in the usual sense of methodologically robust science. But in the context of research, development, and design partnerships between schools and researchers, there are several specific meanings of being robust. Robust models for partnering with schools are those that focus on shared and urgent problems of practice, involve an iterative process of collaborative problem-solving using evidence that can include, but are not limited to, quasi-experimental and replication research designs that can systematically incorporate these iterative processes, and use methodologies that take into account practitioner's theories of action[6].

A Focus on Shared and Urgent Problems of Practice

One such meaning of *robust* is that the research provides what the SERP model calls a focus on shared and urgent problems of practice. Effective partnerships are designed to solve real-world problems of concern in the local context. It could be argued that this focus interferes with or might even be antagonistic to the traditional assumptions about good science, especially ideas of dispassionate objectivity, and the need to address theoretical concerns rather than immediate practical needs. But we argue, like the proponents of design-based approaches and the other partnership models, that such a focus can contribute to scientific knowledge of teaching and learning. In the LSM, solving the community problem of low literacy achievement also accomplished the goals of generating scientific knowledge about the nature of effective instruction for comprehension. It contributed to the research literature by demonstrating, for example, that collaborative analysis and use of data by researchers and teachers can be powerful tools for improving achievement. The intervention, of which a key component was collaborative analysis and use of data, was associated with improvements in achievement that were greater than those reported internationally (McNaughton, Lai, & Hsiao, 2012). These improvements have been described earlier in the chapter. In fact, the LSM is one of the few empirical studies internationally that can demonstrate links between collaborative data use and achievement outcomes (Schildkamp, Ehren, & Lai, 2012).

An Iterative Process of Problem-Solving Using Evidence

Solving local problems requires a collaborative iterative process for collectively analyzing and using data to design and refine teaching and school practices, and to evaluate the impact of these practices on student learning. This in turn means the partnership gets better and better at understanding which practices are more likely to lead to improvements in student learning. Why do we need an iterative process? Should we not know the *solution* from the start of an intervention? Schools are open systems and constantly changing in the demographic characteristics of their students and teachers; in the retention and transience of students; and in instructional resources, professional capabilities, and curricula (McNaughton et al., 2012). As such, intervention practices that have raised achievement in previous years may no longer be effective in raising achievement. For example, if the school's intake changes to include larger proportions of students who speak English as a second language, it may need new teaching approaches to meet the needs of these students. Moreover, little is known about how these changes interact with the characteristics of specific models of intervention generally; for example, how staff turnover impacts on intervention success (McCall, 2009) or specifically in the area of school improvement (Borman, 2005), for example, what teaching practices are most effective for indigenous communities.

The LSM has built in iterative processes for each phase of the intervention to collectively analyze and use data to design and refine teaching, school, and researcher practices, and to examine the impact of these modified practices on achievement outcomes. Each phase had a formal beginning and end-of-year examination of achievement alongside other data, which was used to refine the subsequent intervention strategies. As part of the intervention, teachers and school leaders continually analyzed and examined the impact of their teaching practices in professional learning communities, which met regularly (sometimes fortnightly in teams of teachers teaching similar year levels). For example, in one school, teachers identified a small group of target students who needed greater support in reading. During the year, they met in small teams to design teaching methods to support these students, and discussed the effectiveness of teaching methods for which they were trialing to support the target students.

Quasi-Experimental and Replication Research Designs

It is often necessary to have research designs adapted to the context that support an iterative data analysis process and these include quasi-experimental formats. The need to employ quasi-experimental research designs, certainly in the early stages of a partnership to develop new teaching practices, is appropriate to the iterative nature of a research–school partnership, as it allows greater flexibility in testing and refining theories of teaching and learning. Consistent with this, McCall and Green (2004) argue that in applied research contexts, evaluation of program effects requires a variety of designs, including quasi-experimental. They also argue that robust knowledge is dependent on systematic across-site analyses, that is, the analysis of the impact of an intervention across different sites such as across different schools. The argument is that an intervention can be judged as having more robust and generalizable findings if the findings can be replicated across different contexts. Replication across sites can also add to our evaluation of intervention effects, particularly when it is inappropriate or premature to conduct experimental randomized designs. The need to systematically replicate effects and processes is heightened with these designs because of the reduced experimental control gained with a quasi-experimental design (Borko, 2004; Chatterji, 2006; Raudenbush, 2005) and the substantial variability associated with schools as open systems.

The research design of the LSM used a quasi-experimental design to demonstrate improvements in achievement at the end of the intervention (McNaughton et al., 2012). Quasi-experimental designs are similar to experimental designs in that both use treatment and control groups. However, they differ in one key point—random assignment to treatment and control groups. It compared the achievement of students who participated in the intervention against a projected baseline of student achievement, had the intervention not occurred, and in the case of one cluster of schools, against a comparison group of similar students who did not receive the intervention. Replications were also undertaken in terms of replications of intervention effects across schools, gender, ethnicity, year levels, et cetera, to show that the interventions had made an impact across different groups of students and schools. These analyses of student achievement collectively provided strong evidence that the students in the intervention performed better than others that did not receive the intervention and that student performance replicated across sites (see chapter section "The interventions and their successes" for details).

Methodologies That Take into Account Practitioner's Theories of Action

Research often fails to impact the very teaching practices it is intended to improve, even when the research is relevant to teaching and is undertaken rigorously. Take for example, the research on tracking (or streaming), which is of high academic quality with findings that are consistent over time (Robinson, 1993). Tracking students, for example, is associated with achievement inequalities where ethnic minorities and indigenous groups are overrepresented in lower tracks (Oakes, 1992). There are multiple reasons proposed for the *gap* between research and practice that relate to dissemination (research is written for an academic, rather than school audience); for example, parental pressure to continue tracking. Although these factors are important, perhaps a more fundamental reason is that researchers and school leaders are trying to solve different problems. School leaders could track students for reasons such as pressure from vocal parents to continue tracking, and teachers that are unable to teach groups with different levels of achievement in their classes. By contrast, researchers focus on different issues with tracking, such as inequitable outcomes for particular groups as a consequence of tracking. Consequently, research on tracking does not address the reasons why the school tracks students, and thus the research is more likely to be ignored by schools who find that the research does not address the reasons (or even belittles the school's reasons) that led to tracking.

In other words, research methodologies, such as problem-based methodology (Robinson & Lai, 2006) which require researchers to understand the reasons and beliefs for particular school practices, are better able to identify the beliefs and assumptions that lead to the continuation of these practices. In short, it is easier to understand the theories of action that have led to the particular school practice. This increases the likelihood of challenging and modifying misplaced assumptions and ineffective practices, and co-creating ways of improving practice that will be accepted by school practitioners (e.g., Robinson & Lai, 2006). As the focus is on understanding school practice, these methodologies also highlight a respectful and empathetic stance to partnering with schools, in that it is respectful of school expertise and empathetic to the problems they are trying to solve.

In our interventions to improve reading comprehension with indigenous and ethnic minority students from low socioeconomic communities, we based our partnership model on problem-based methodology, a methodology that has been used to improve practice through examining teachers' beliefs and assumptions using evidence (Robinson, 1993). In particular, we used the methodology to design the collaborative problem-solving process between researchers and schools. That is, we (researchers, school leaders, and teachers) collectively developed a shared understanding of the problem to be solved, including the reasons and assumptions for the existence of the problem from the teachers' and our perspectives, and co-created new ways of improving practices using evidence. For example, at the start of the intervention, researchers, school leaders, and teachers identified and agreed on a problem that both researchers and schools wanted to solve, in this case, improving reading comprehension of students reading two years behind their peers. Then researchers and schools examined both the researchers' and school's theories for why the problem existed, treated any different theories as theory competition (Robinson & Lai, 2006), and used evidence to adjudicate competing theories. Theories were raised such as whether the poor reading comprehension scores were due to a lack of decoding skills (the skill of reading words), and whether there was sufficient direct instruction of reading. Both teacher and researcher theories were tested against evidence; for example, was there evidence of a decoding problem? Finally, once the problem and the theories of the problem were established, we co-constructed the professional development to improve the identified teaching and learning needs (see Robinson and Lai (2006) for more detailed descriptions of how the methodology was used in the intervention). The co-construction process was as follows: the researchers used relevant research-based evidence to develop the content of the professional development based on identified needs. Teachers worked collectively (with teachers within their school, and with teachers across schools in the cluster) to develop ways of incorporating the new research-based knowledge into their classroom teaching. They designed how they would use the workshop content, trialed the changes to their practice in their classes, examined the impact on students through formative assessment in the classrooms (e.g., feedback from students, homework), and reported back to the PLC.

Building a Community of Practice—Shared Cognition and Collective Efficacy

The second principle is that partnerships need to involve building a community of practice focused on learning from each other to solve agreed problems, and members of the partnership need to commit to a durable partnership to meet the shared objectives (Snow & Donovan, 2012). While it is possible to employ a robust methodology for partnerships with individuals (e.g., a mentoring relationship between a researcher and a teacher), we argue that partnerships are strengthened when they involve a community of practice or professional learning community, ideally involving all key members of schools and researchers. That is, building a community of students, parents, teachers, school leaders, and researchers where shared foci and shared protocols are established to meld together diverse cognitions and personalities (Wenger, 1998). This is based on a Vygotskian notion of learning as socially constructed (Vygotsky, 1978), and in this chapter, we focus on the advantages of shared cognition and collective efficacy resulting from this type of partnership.

A community of practice has numerous advantages in advancing knowledge about teaching and learning through the shared cognition developed in the community, that is, the notion that the sum is greater than the parts. This shared cognition can be in the form of complementary knowledge where each community member draws on a different knowledge base to enhance the understanding of the problem and how to solve it. Such knowledge can be gained from collective reflection from within a community (Seashore-Louis, 2006), or external to it in order to extend the pool of expertise (Annan, 2007). In other words, learning for all parties can be sped up if they each use their respective expertise to collectively solve the pressing educational issues.

In our intervention, the PLC drew on multiple diverse knowledge bases such as research knowledge about using data for improvement, research expertise in data warehousing (collecting and storing school data), data analysis, literacy acquisition, and intervention design; teacher knowledge of their students and what practices might be more effective; the curriculum and how to turn the research ideas into classroom practice; and school leader knowledge on how to turn the research and teacher ideas into a coherent whole-school teaching program and support teachers learn new literacy and problem-solving skills. This is best illustrated in Phase II of our model, where we focused on advancing teacher knowledge through professional development. In this phase, researchers presented research knowledge on aspects of literacy acquisition in professional development workshops. After each workshop, teachers were responsible for developing teaching practices based on the research knowledge from the workshops, implementing those practices in their classrooms and monitoring the impact on student learning through formative assessment (e.g., through talking to students to ascertain student understanding or through tasks given to students to complete during class). In the next workshop, teachers presented the impact of their modified teaching practices to researchers and peers and critiqued what each other did. School leaders supported teachers by providing time for teachers to participate in the workshops, and by developing structures within the school (such as reflection time in syndicate meetings) for teachers to support each other to learn these new practices. At least one school leader also participated in the workshops and contributed to the group critique. Thus, while researchers had extensive literacy knowledge, they did not necessarily know how best to apply the research knowledge to the specific context of each teacher's class. Conversely, while teachers knew their classes and what might work best, they did not necessarily have the research-based knowledge of how to teach some aspects of literacy more effectively. Moreover, without school leader expertise in organizing time and resources for teachers to learn from the workshops, the new practices would not have been supported by the school and therefore would have been less likely to succeed. As such, each community member's expertise was respected and utilized in a way that advanced teaching and learning.

Diverse knowledge was not just used in our intervention for creating new practices, but also in the critique of both new and existing practices.

In PLCs, particularly when problem-solving using data, members of the community made their thinking about the nature of students' learning needs explicit. The different members' diverse knowledge was then used to critique each member's thinking. For example, researchers proposed that fluent and accurate decoding might be an issue, but the teachers, using their knowledge of their students and their achievement data (e.g., running records), showed the researchers that decoding was not the issue for the majority of their students. This knowledge was then used to focus the intervention on other aspects of reading comprehension that students were struggling with.

A community of practice also serves to develop the collective efficacy of the community (Bandura, 1995). Self-efficacy is the belief in one's own ability to produce the desired outcome and collective efficacy is the collective's belief in its ability to produce the desired outcome. Strong collective efficacy in schools is important because it is a predictor of student achievement (Bandura, 1995). Bandura (1995) describes a depressing cycle in which a sense of unsolvable problems lowers beliefs in personal effectiveness, which in turn results in a decreased commitment to teaching and innovating. The resulting impact on students further reduces teachers' sense of being effective. By contrast, a high sense of collective efficacy, where teachers collectively share a sense of solving difficulties and of making a difference and have the evidence to support these beliefs, enhances personal efficacy. Teachers who feel more efficacious tend to be more willing to experiment to meet the needs of students, are more resilient and have greater persistence (McNaughton, 2002).

The need for collective efficacy is heightened in contexts such as the one we worked in, where achievement problems with culturally and linguistically diverse students in poor communities appear to be entrenched and intractable and there are multiple external forces (e.g., high unemployment) that threaten the interventions. In our interventions, collective efficacy was developed in the communities through several ways. First, the project evidence revealed to the community that they can successfully improve achievement. We did this initially by showing that achievement gains were made by some schools and some classrooms. When the teachers saw that other schools and teachers in similar situations could make improvements, a sense of efficacy was created, and this created the impetus for learning from each other's successes and failures. The sense of collective efficacy was further enhanced when the intervention was successful across schools in its first year.

A related strategy was to focus the schools on what they can do for their students, rather than what they cannot do. For example, it was important that teachers focused on improving teaching in the classroom (which is under their control), rather than on the factors beyond their control, such as poverty. Allied to that was the idea of reframing issues as problems to be solved, rather than leaving them as explanations of the current situation. For example, rather than treating teacher turnover as the reason for the achievement problems, schools examined what could be done to redress the turnover (Lai et al., 2009). The idea of collective efficacy is best summed up in the following extract from a conversation between a school leader who believed that his chances of being efficacious were reduced by the profile of students in his school and another school leader who challenged his perception of efficacy by pointing out what he could control.

School Leader: If a teacher has 28 kids and eight scored at stanine one (the lowest achievement band), we cannot get gains from them.
School Leader 2: Some teachers are making high gains and they have the same 28 kids. The point is about making gains.

Teachers as Adaptive Experts

Contemporary partnership models commonly treat partners in ways that recognize the complementary and reciprocal nature of the expertise required to solve everyday problems (Snow & Donovan, 2012). In the applications of the LSM this has meant viewing the PLCs in schools as having basic evaluative capability, and researchers are community members who bring particular forms of expertise. However, it also means seeing teachers in general as having the properties that Darling-Hammond and Bransford (2005) term "adaptive expertise" (p. 49). This view of teaching is that a highly effective teacher cannot be like a technician following a largely prescribed set of procedures. Rather, teachers need to be deeply knowledgeable about what they do, how they do it, and why they do it; and to be flexible and adaptable in their practices (McNaughton, 2011b).

The general psychological definition of an expert is they are very goal focused and intentional; they are strategic, being able to adapt to circumstances and to modify their tools or even develop new tools and ways of performing (Darling-Hammond & Bransford, 2005). They know the medium within which they act very well. Experts are keenly aware of the effectiveness of their performances in the sense of being in control by being able to monitor, check, and modify. There are other more social aspects of being an expert. An expert is immersed in the traditions and practices of their community including the standards, rules, and procedures. The combination of these attributes give experts the twin features of being technically adept as well as innovative and adaptable.

In the context of a partnership, recognizing and promoting these attributes of experts means researchers have two roles. One is that researchers focus on understanding how teachers on the ground create solutions and how their pedagogical content knowledge influences valued student outcomes, rather than focus on ensuring that teachers implement a closely scripted program that researchers have designed. This is because researchers are limited in how they might contribute to ongoing instructional design and testing redesigns without understanding how the variability in teacher practices and teacher knowledge influence student outcomes. It may be that some teaching practices for improving literacy only work if teachers have a high degree of literacy knowledge. In addition, the nature of the learning and teaching challenges with culturally and linguistically diverse students, who traditionally have not been well served by schools, requires the sort of adaptive expertise identified by Darling-Hammond and Bransford (2005).

As such, in our LSM, we treated teachers as adaptive experts who could innovate and adapt their practices to improve valued student outcomes within a research design that continually assesses the impact of these adaptations on student learning. Our focus, in every phase of the intervention (described previously), was on developing teachers' capabilities to collaboratively analyze and use data to improve teaching and learning, and to assess the impact of these changes on student outcomes.

An Ethical Imperative

The fourth dimension is the ethical and moral stance taken in the partnership, to each other, and to the enterprise to *do good*, in the manner proposed by Gawande (2007) for medicine. In the context of New Zealand, this includes how outcomes for students are rationalized and judged in the partnership. Although each of the applications of the LSM has had a powerful focus on students' achievement, it has been within a more general commitment to educationally significant outcomes for students. What is educationally significant is a deeply cultural and political question, as much as it is a developmental one (McNaughton, 2011b). For example, in the context of New Zealand, the cultural aspirations of *Māori* communities for educational success have been couched in the strategic goal for education to be "*Māori* enjoying education success as *Māori*" (Ministry of Education, 2009, p. 11), meaning to lift up or step up performance. It proposes principles of a "*Māori* potential approach" (p. 19) to educational change and innovation in which success includes enhancing one's identity as *Māori*. The *Māori* potential approach emphasizes partnership, working together, and sharing power and seeing *Māori* children as culturally advantaged by virtue of who they are and having the potential to achieve at the highest levels. In the applications of the LSM, which have involved significant numbers of *Māori* students, the concern to accelerate achievement and to achieve equitable distributions of achievement has been in service of this broader concern.

Like the other partnership models, the ethical stance also means jointly developing ways of using and sharing evidence for evaluative, design, and development purposes that meet principles of professional and research ethics and quality. This commitment can be seen from *Kaupapa Māori* theorizing (theorizing from *Māori* principles) that requires researchers and educators with their local communities to become joined in a *whānau* (family) of interest (Smith, 1999); the reciprocal obligations, rights, and roles similar to those operating in an extended family. Many of these reciprocal obligations, rights, and roles have been discussed previously (e.g., the problem-solving process using mutual critique of researcher and school leaders and teachers' theories). So in this final section, we present two examples to further illustrate what this looks like.

First, in the application of the LSM, researchers and schools were committed to work together with educators and their local communities to solve pressing local problems, in this case, improving literacy achievement to achieve parity with national norms and distributions. The researchers did not *force* a goal on the school or community; rather at the start of the intervention, the goal was discussed and agreed to as a pressing concern we could solve collectively. Or as one community leader put it: "There is no reason why our children cannot perform as well as other children. So, we want our children to perform as well as other children nationally."

Second, *whānau* implies an ongoing relationship over time, rather than a *project relationship*, where researchers enter a research site, conduct research for a finite set of time, deliver some findings, and then have little (if anything) to do with the school and communities again. In the LSM, this relationship has endured over 13 years and is continuing to evolve. At the beginning, the relationship was established through working together on Ministry of Education Schooling Improvement Initiatives, which were initiatives set up by the New Zealand Ministry of Education to improve student achievement (Timperley, Robinson, & Bullard, 1999). Then the researchers and schools jointly sought contestable funding from TLRI to conduct further interventions in reading comprehension, which led to another TLRI-funded project examining the sustainability of their interventions. More recently, the relationship has taken the form of critical friendships, rather than a formal research project. For example, the school leaders in one community met with researchers for a day to discuss their achievement data and what they can do to address the problems.

Conclusion

In this chapter, we have described the features of partnerships between researchers and schools in interventions that were successful in raising achievement for students from poor, urban schools serving culturally and linguistically diverse communities. These partnerships were deliberately developed as part of the intervention design to enhance both teacher and research knowledge of how to teach students more effectively, and were based on robust empirical research. Partnerships with schools were not an *add on* to the intervention or viewed as simply an enabler of the intervention. Rather, we systematically and deliberately designed the intervention with partnerships at its core. In our LSM partnership model, partnerships were embedded in the intervention through the use of collaborative problem-solving in each phase of the intervention; in how the professional development was integrated into classroom practice in the second phase through co-construction by school leaders, teachers, and researchers; and in how the development of teacher-led action research conferences were designed to confirm and build ongoing evaluative capability to solve further problems. An implication of our work is that effective research–school partnerships cannot be left to chance. Rather, these partnerships need to be developed systematically from the start of any intervention, and with appropriate support to both schools and researchers to understand how to effectively learn from each other. A useful avenue for strengthening research–school partnerships is supporting researchers to understand and implement effective approaches for partnering with schools.

Notes

1. The Teaching and Learning Research Initiative (TLRI) was established by the New Zealand government in 2003 to enhance the links between educational research and teaching practices, and to improve outcomes for learners. It funds a number of projects focused on partnerships between schools and researchers each year.
2. Established in 1998 with funds from the Woolf Fisher Trust, the Woolf Fisher Research Center is an internationally recognized research center for the development of education and schooling success for diverse communities within New Zealand, with a particular focus on *Māori* and *Pasifika* communities. The Center

has spent 12 years developing a model to raise and extend student achievement, working in more than 50 schools and with more than 10,000 children.
3. For further information on how we matched the teaching practices to students' needs, please see Lai & McNaughton, 2009.
4. Details of the workshops can be found in Lai, McNaughton, Amituanai-Toloa et al. (2009).
5. Details of these partnerships are given in Lai, McNaughton, Timperley & Hsiao (2009).
6. Theories of action are the beliefs, values, and understandings (theories) that explain why a practitioner does what she or he does (action) (Robinson & Lai, 2006).

References

Anderson, T., & Shattuck, J. (2012). Design-based research: A decade of progress in education research? *Educational Researcher, 41*(1), 16–25. doi: 10.3102/0013189x11428813.

Annan, B. (2007). *A theory for schooling improvement: Consistency and connectivity to improve instructional practice.* Doctor of Philosophy Thesis, University of Auckland, Auckland, New Zealand.

Bandura, A. (Ed.). (1995). *Exercise of personal and collective efficacy in changing societies.* Cambridge, UK: Cambridge University Press.

Borko, H. (2004). Professional development and teacher learning: Mapping the terrain. *Educational Researcher, 33*(8), 3–15. doi: 10.3102/0013189x033008003.

Borman, G. (2005). National efforts to bring reform to scale in high-poverty schools: Outcomes and implications. In L. Parker (Ed.), *Review of research in education* (Vol. 29, pp. 1–28). Washington, DC: American Educational Research Association.

Bryk, A. S., Sebring, P. B., Allensworth, E., Luppescu, S., & Easton, J. Q. (2010). *Organizing schools for improvement: Lessons from Chicago.* Chicago, Ill.: University of Chicago Press.

Chatterji, M. (2006). Reading achievement gaps, correlates, and moderators of early reading achievement: Evidence from the Early Childhood Longitudinal Study (ECLS) kindergarten to first grade sample. *Journal of Educational Psychology, 98*(3), 489–507. doi: 10.1037/0022-0663.98.3.489.

Cobb, P., & Smith, T. (2008). The challenge of scale: Designing schools and districts as learning organizations for instructional improvement in mathematics. In T. Wood, B. Jaworski, K. Krainer, P. Sullivan, & D. Tirosh (Eds.), *International handbook of mathematics teacher education* (Vol. 3, pp. 231–254). Rotterdam, The Netherlands: Sense Publishers.

Darling-Hammond, L., & Bransford, J. (Eds) (2005). *Preparing teachers for a changing world: What teachers should learn and be able to do.* San Francisco, CA: Jossey-Bass/Wiley.

Gawande, A. (2007). *Better: A surgeon's notes on performance.* London, UK: Profile Books Limited.

Lai, M. K., & McNaughton. S. (2009). Not by achievement analysis alone: How inquiry needs to be informed by evidence from classrooms. *New Zealand Journal of Educational Studies, 44*(2), 93–108.

Lai, M. K., McNaughton, S., Amituanai-Toloa, M., Turner, R., & Hsiao, S. (2009). Sustained acceleration of achievement in reading comprehension: The New Zealand experience. *Reading Research Quarterly, 44*(1), 30–56. doi: 10.1598/RRQ.44.1.2.

Lai, M. K., McNaughton, S., Timperley, H., & Hsiao, S. (2009). Sustaining continued acceleration in reading comprehension achievement following an intervention. *Educational Assessment, Evaluation and Accountability, 21*(1), 81–100. doi: 10.1007/s11092-009-9071-5.

Levin, B. (2012). *More high school graduates.* Toronto, Canada: Thousand Oaks Corwin and Ontario Principals Council.

McCall, R. B. (2009). Evidence-based programming in the context of practice and policy. In L. Sherod (Ed.), *Social policy report. Giving child and youth development knowledge away,* XXIII (III, pp. 3–20). Retrieved April 17, 2013 from http://www.eric.ed.gov/ERICWebPortal/search/detailmini.jsp?_nfpb=true&_& ERICExtSearch_SearchValue_0=ED509748&ERICExtSearch_SearchType_0= no&accno=ED509748.

McCall, R. B., & Green, B. L. (2004). Beyond the methodological gold standards of behavioral research: Considerations for practice and policy. *SRCD Social Policy Report, 18*(2), 3–19.

McNaughton, S. (2002). *Meeting of minds.* Wellington, NZ: Learning Media.

McNaughton, S. (2011a). Educational outcome in adolescence for Māori and Pasifika students. In P. G. Gluckman (Ed.), *Improving the transition: Reducing social and psychological morbidity during adolescence* (pp. 99–110). Wellington, NZ: Office of the Prime Minister's Science Advisory Committee.

McNaughton, S. (2011b). *Designing better schools for culturally and linguistically civerse children: A science of performance model for research.* New York, NY: Routledge.

McNaughton, S., & Lai, M. K. (2009). A model of school change for culturally and linguistically diverse students in New Zealand: A summary and evidence from systematic replication. *Teaching Education, 20*(1), 55–75. doi: 10.1080/10476210802681733.

McNaughton, S., Lai, M. K., & Hsiao, S. (2012). Testing the effectiveness of an intervention model based on data use: A replication series across clusters of schools. *School Effectiveness and School Improvement, 23*(2), 203–228. doi: 10.1080/09243453.2011.652126.

Ministry of Education. (2009). *Ka Hikitia—Managing for Success: The Māori Education Strategy 2008–2012.* Wellington, NZ: Ministry of Education.

Oakes, J. (1992). Can tracking research inform practice: Technical, normative, and political considerations. *Educational Researcher, 21*(4), 12–21.

OECD. (2010). *PISA 2009 results: What students know and can do* (Vol. 1). Retrieved from dx.doi.org/10.1787/9789264091450-en.

Raudenbush, S. W. (2005). Learning from attempts to improve schooling: The contribution of methodological diversity. *Educational Researcher, 34*(5), 25–31. doi: 10.3102/0013189x034005025.
Robinson, V. M. J. (1993). *Problem-based methodology: Research for the improvement of practice.* Oxford, UK, Pergamon Press.
Robinson, V. M. J., & Lai, M. K. (2006). *Practitioner research for educators: A guide to improving classrooms and schools.* Thousand Oaks, CA: Corwin Press.
Schildkamp, K., Ehren, M., & Lai, M. K. (2012). Editorial article for the special issue on data-based decision making around the world: From policy to practice to results. *School Effectiveness and School Improvement, 23*(2), 123–131. doi: http://dx.doi.org/10.1080/09243453.2011.652122.
Seashore-Louis, K. (2006). Changing the culture of schools: Professional community, organizational learning and trust. *Journal of School Leadership, 16*, 477–489.
Smith, L. T. (1999). *Decolonizing methodologies: Research and indigenous peoples.* New York, NY: St: Martins Press.
Snow, C. E., & Donovan, M. S. (2012). *The strategic education research partnership: A new approach to educational research.* 1–24. Retrieved from April 17, 2013 from http://www.serpinstitute.org/downloads/SERP%20Singapore.pdf.
Timperley, H., Robinson, V., & Bullard, T. (1999). *Strengthening education in Mangere and Otara: Final evaluation report.* Wellington, NZ: Auckland Uniservices Ltd for the Ministry of Education.
Timperley, H., Wilson, A., Barrar, H., & Fung, I. (2007). *Best evidence synthesis iterations (BES) on professional learning and development.* Wellington, NZ: Ministry of Education.
Vygotsky, L. (1978). Interaction between learning and development. In M. Cole (Ed.), *Mind in society: The development of higher psychological processes* (pp. 79–91). Cambridge, MA: Harvard University Press.
Wenger, E. (1998). *Communities of practice: Learning, meaning, and identity.* Cambridge, UK: Cambridge University Press.

5

Partnership in Promoting Literacy: An Exploration of Two Studies in Low-Decile Early Childhood Settings in New Zealand

Claire McLachlan, Alison Arrow and Judy Watson

Introduction

Reading and writing skills serve as the major avenue for achieving the essential learning areas of the "New Zealand Curriculum" (Ministry of Education, 2007a) and are the foundation for learning in all subjects studied at school. If children do not learn to read, their general knowledge, spelling, writing, and vocabulary development suffer (Stanovich, 2000). The National Early Literacy Panel Report (NELP) (2009) identified some critical understandings that children need to develop in early childhood in order to become literate at school, which include knowledge of the alphabet, phonological awareness (being aware of sounds in words), the ability to rapidly name letters, numbers, objects, and colors, the ability to write their own name and to be able to remember spoken information for a short period of time. In addition, children need to understand print conventions and concepts, have strong oral language and the ability to match and discriminate between visual symbols. It is not surprising then that many countries have looked at what experiences children should have to develop literacy before school entry and the implications for teaching practice (McLachlan & Arrow, 2011).

Most young children develop an intuitive knowledge of sounds and can recognize rhyme and alliteration and learn alphabet and vocabulary through their interactions at homes and community settings (Whitehurst & Lonigan, 1998), but approximately 25 percent of children in New Zealand do not (Nicholson, 2005). Intervention studies that have taught phonological awareness skills to children prior to school entry show that it helps children with formal literacy learning on school entry (Phillips, Clancy-Menchetti, & Lonigan, 2008). Many intervention studies use a structured curriculum along with strong reading readiness programs (O'Connor, Notari-Syverson, & Vadasy, 1996), although recent studies show that literacy knowledge and skills can also be promoted within more naturalistic settings (Justice, Kaderavek, Fan, Sofka, & Hunt, 2009; Piasta & Wagner, 2010; Phillips et al., 2008). The studies reported in this chapter provide two different models for partnership approaches to professional learning and research on literacy teaching.

Literacy Research in Early Childhood Settings in New Zealand

There is limited research in New Zealand on how children develop literacy prior to school entry and most studies are small-scale and qualitative. McLachlan-Smith (1996) examined the policies and practices concerning emergent literacy in 12 New Zealand kindergartens in the early 1990s, prior to the advent of *Te Whāriki* (the national early childhood curriculum) (Ministry of Education, 1996). Kindergartens in New Zealand are primarily for children aged 3–5 years.

Findings revealed that teachers espoused eclectic understandings of literacy and the amount and type of literacy experiences that children received differed according to teachers' beliefs about their role. More recent research (McLachlan, Carvalho, de Lautour, & Kumar, 2006) found that although most teachers report providing literacy-rich environments, fewer than 50 percent used *Te Whāriki* to support literacy at their centers and teachers reported diverse understandings of literacy, how to promote it, or how to identify and support children *at risk*.

Similar findings are reported by Hedges (2003) and Foote, Smith and Ellis (2004). Hedges (2003) found that teachers could not decide whether or not their role was to foster literacy. Foote, Smith and Ellis (2004) found that although teachers were providing rich learning experiences, when it came to literacy development, they tended toward formal skills-based instruction, without being able to articulate why they did this. These findings are of concern since other research has found that teaching phonemic awareness and simple phonics around school entry can reduce the incidence of reading difficulties during primary schooling (Nicholson, 2005; Tunmer, Chapman, & Prochnow, 2004). Phillips, Clancy-Menchetti and Lonigan (2008) state that early childhood teachers can support the development of early literacy knowledge and skills, but not necessarily through formal instruction. A literacy-rich environment, where teachers take any opportunity to promote literacy knowledge and skills, is of greater benefit.

Arrow's (2007, 2010) research on the development of phonological awareness in kindergarten children found that children with good alphabetic knowledge have multiple pathways to reading and spelling. Arrow's research supported incorporating teaching of phonological awareness, alphabetic knowledge, and vocabulary development. Phillips, McNaughton and MacDonald (2002) found that many early childhood teachers had limited knowledge of literacy development and that therefore there was scope to improve literacy outcomes for children through professional development. Research by Tagoilelagi-Leota, McNaughton, MacDonald and Ferry (2005) also indicated that young Samoan and Tongan children were supported to gain literacy skills in both their home language and English when they experienced high-quality literacy teaching in both early childhood and primary school settings.

An Education Review Office (ERO) (2011) report on literacy illuminates the current effectiveness of literacy teaching in early childhood in New Zealand. In the review of 353 early childhood services in 2009, most services provided an appropriate range of literacy opportunities for children. However, the following concerns were identified: inappropriate use of commercial phonics packages with very young children, large formal mat times that did not cater to the diverse abilities of children, and formal and teacher-led literacy *transition to school* programs that tended to limit children's engagement with meaningful literacy activities.

"The New Zealand Curriculum" (Ministry of Education, 2007a) is quite explicit about how children will develop literacy at school. It highlights that children need to make connections between letters and sounds, and will slowly develop a sight-word reading vocabulary and knowledge of text conventions (Ministry of Education, 2007a). The Literacy Learning Progressions (Ministry of Education, 2007b) provide further information for teachers, stating expectations of children's knowledge and skills at school entry, and milestones after one year at school, and so on. However, there is a mismatch between the Ministry of Education's expectations of children at school entry and the early childhood curriculum document's aspirations for literacy (McLachlan & Arrow, 2011) as well as the much less specific guidance available to early childhood teachers. *Te Whāriki* (Ministry of Education, 1996) is open to diverse interpretation and it does not clearly align to the more recent national curriculum (Ministry of Education, 2007a) or the Literacy Learning Progressions (Ministry of Education, 2007b). The major link for literacy in *Te Whāriki* is the Communication Strand, in which children develop verbal and non-verbal communication for range of purposes, experience the stories and symbols of their own and other cultures and discover and develop different ways to be creative and expressive.

Nuttall (2005) argues teachers do not simply apply a curriculum document, rather they interpret and enact curriculum in different ways. Nuttall contends there is no empirical evidence that *Te Whāriki* makes a difference to children's learning but there is evidence from *Kei tua o te pae* (the early childhood assessment exemplars) (Ministry of Education, 2005) that teachers are overlooking children's literacy practices in their learning stories, instead they are interpreting their observations in terms of dispositions such as collaboration and exploration. For our studies, we wanted to investigate children's emergent literacy, as well as whether teachers were able to "notice, recognise and respond" as advocated in *Kei tua o te pae* (Ministry of Education, 2005). Increasing teacher awareness of components of literacy was key to both studies.

In-Service Professional Learning

McGill-Franzen (2010) argues that early childhood teachers have the most marginalized knowledge and skills in how to develop literacy of all teachers and there are few opportunities for professional learning. She proposes teachers need professional learning to increase knowledge of literacy acquisition for diverse learners using a range of appropriate pedagogies. Wong, Fillmore and Snow (2000) similarly argue that teachers need intensive preparation in "educational linguistics," as they gain inadequate preparation in teacher education programs.

Cunningham, Perry, Stanovich and Stanovich (2004) proposed literacy domain knowledge to be crucial for teachers of young children. They found in their study of 722 North American kindergarten to third grade teachers that the knowledge base of teachers did not align with current research on the role of phoneme awareness and the alphabet principle in developing literacy. There is little evidence that early childhood teachers in New Zealand have this knowledge either (McLachlan et al., 2006; Mitchell & Cubey, 2003).

Cullen (2006) states that many New Zealand early childhood teachers have not considered teaching literacy to be part of their role and suggests that the "lack of attention to literacy competencies and meanings could reflect a gap in initial teacher education and professional development" (p. 5). Cullen (2006, pp. 5–6) proposes three major responsibilities for teachers: to monitor gaps in children's literacy competencies as well as strengths and interests; to provide curriculum that supports skills and meanings; and to engage in ongoing professional learning. In-service professional learning or postgraduate study is the only real options for practicing teachers to gain skills in supporting literacy learning.

Doubek and Cooper (2007) identify some critical variables for professional learning for literacy: time; the importance of the role of the leader and their awareness of obstacles to effecting change; understanding of what constitutes an effective literacy environment; and receptiveness to change. Mitchell and Cubey (2003) identified key features of effective professional learning: it builds on teachers' existing knowledge; includes alternative theoretical knowledge and practices; involves investigation and analysis of data by teachers in their own settings; involves critical reflection; inclusion of diversity; challenges beliefs and practices; and enhances insight into teachers' own thinking and actions. These principles are implicit to both studies discussed in this chapter, but there were variances in implementation. The studies explored the outcomes of different approaches to professional learning on literacy acquisition. The next section provides a brief overview of methodologies employed in each study and key findings in relation to promoting relationships between teachers and researchers to aid children's learning.

Methodology: Study One

Study One involved Claire McLachlan and Alison Arrow and was funded by Massey University Research Fund (MURF). Although we accepted some of the limitations of short-term professional learning to create changes in teachers' beliefs and practices, we trialed an intervention within four early childhood settings, using a fifth center as a control. Our aim was to see if we could promote change in teachers' understandings of alphabetic and phonological awareness and their literacy practices with children, using short-term professional learning. By deepening teachers' understandings of literacy acquisition, we hoped to promote change in children's knowledge and skills. Our research question was

> Does professional development for early childhood educators on facilitating alphabetic and phonological awareness, contribute to growth in alphabetic and phonological awareness in 3–5 year olds in full-time center-based care?

Our objectives were twofold:

1. To examine if professional development can improve teachers' knowledge regarding facilitating alphabetic and phonological awareness in 3- to 5-year-old children.
2. To examine if children's alphabetic and phonological awareness can be enhanced within a holistic, child-centered curriculum context within an eight week period.

A quasi-experimental design was used in which teachers' and children's knowledge was tested at the beginning and end of a data collection in five early childhood centers. We planned to conduct the intervention over a period of several weeks, beginning with pretesting of teachers and children's knowledge of phonological and alphabetic awareness. One center was used as a control, whereby teachers did not receive professional development until after the intervention period. The New Zealand Ministry of Education national database of early childhood centers and the College of Education coordinator of practicum placement's knowledge of centers were used to identify centers. Centers that had children who were primarily in full-time childcare and were located in the lower socioeconomic areas because this is one of the predictors of reading failure in young children in New Zealand (Tunmer, Chapman, & Prochnow, 2006).

We eliminated one center from the dataset because there were so many staff changes and only five children had completed surveys. The composition of the remaining sample in each setting is described in Table 5.1. Not all children were post-tested as some did not want to participate and some had gone to primary school. The number of teachers from each center who completed surveys is also indicated in Table 1.

Table 5.1 Composition of participants from four early childhood centers

Center*	Ownership model	Type	Number of teachers	Number of teachers with all data	Number of children (Pretest)	Number of children (Posttest)	Children with all data
CenterOne	"not for profit"	Full day care	6	4	22	18	16
CenterTwo	"not for profit"	sessional, parent educators	8	3	33	23	19
CenterThree	Private	Full day care	4	4	12	9	8
CenterFour	Private	Full day care	8	5	12	12	12

Note: *Centers 1–3 are intervention centers and Center 4 is the control group center.

Teachers

Across the five centers, 32 teachers completed pretests or posttests and a total of 16 teachers completed both pre-testing and post-testing data collections. The sample was all female and five (31.3 percent) had Bachelor's degrees, three (18.8 percent) held a Diploma in Teaching, two (12.5 percent) held Graduate Diplomas in early childhood education, three (18.8 percent) were currently training to become qualified, and a further three (18.8 percent) held no qualifications. There were no differences between the intervention and control centers in the distribution of qualifications (Mann–Whitney $U = 30$, $Z = 0.28$, $p = 0.77$). The number of years spent teaching varied from half a year to 24 years ($M = 8.84$ years, $SD = 8.79$), with no differences in distribution across intervention and control centers (Mann–Whitney $U = 31$, $Z = 0.41$, $p = 0.68$).

Children

Of the children who participated, 55 (27 boys, 28 girls) completed the data collection at both pretest and posttest. Children's ages ranged from 36 to 58 months ($M = 49.25$ months, $SD = 5.65$). There were no significant differences in children's age between intervention and control centers (Mann–Whitney $U = 232.5$, $Z = -0.521$, $p = 0.60$).

Measures

Teachers

Teachers were asked to complete a *questionnaire on current practices* concerning alphabetic and phonological awareness, which was based on surveys previously used for assessing teachers' knowledge and beliefs about literacy acquisition (McLachlan-Smith, 1996; McLachlan et al., 2006; Taylor, Blum, & Logdon, 1986). The questionnaire had three components. First, it identified teachers' perceptions of opportunities they give children within the center to develop literacy skills. Thirteen questions were scored to provide a measure of literacy opportunities, with a higher score indicating a high level of opportunity for literacy activities. The second component examined teachers' recognition of children's emergent literacy abilities, such as writing, reading signs, and alphabet recognition. This component has a maximum score of seven, indicating recognition of a wide range of children's abilities. Finally, teachers' knowledge of literacy development and their role in this development was examined. Teacher responses to this were analyzed qualitatively, using content and thematic analysis. Teachers were also asked to complete a *phonological awareness assessment* requiring phoneme segmentation (adapted from Moats, 2000). The maximum score for this assessment was 30.

Children

Children's data were collected with children in a quiet corner of each center. The first set of tasks for children were phonological awareness measures designed by the researchers. These tasks measured children's awareness of rhyme and onset sound using a picture of a cue word and three possible matches.

Children's emergent literacy skills were also assessed. The first tasks assessed children's *letter knowledge* in which children were presented with the 26 alphabet letters in a set random order in lower case and asked to name all the letters they knew. As the letter-sound knowledge of New Zealand young children lags behind their letter-name knowledge (Arrow, 2010) a letter-sound task was given to children who had scored 12 or more on the letter-name task. *Own-name knowledge*—children were given an A4 sheet with their name on it and asked to identify what the word said and they were also asked to write their name on a blank sheet of paper. Finally, children's *receptive vocabulary* was assessed at pretest only, using the British Picture Vocabulary Scale, 2nd edition, (Dunn, Dunn, Whetton, & Burley, 1997).

Procedures

The child pretest data were collected first, and once all the pretests on children had been completed in each center, a time was scheduled to meet with the teaching team in each of the intervention centers to provide a one-off professional development event. This event took approximately two hours for each center and included completion of the teacher phonological awareness assessment and survey. The professional development session focused on the predictors of literacy acquisition (NELP, 2009) and explained how to support literacy development through different pedagogies for story reading, language and rhyming games, and learning alphabet and vocabulary (e.g., Justice & Pullen, 2003; Justice et al., 2009; Phillips et al., 2008; Piasta & Wagner, 2010). After the professional development, teachers were asked to implement what they gained from the professional development for a period of approximately eight weeks and to keep brief records of the ways in which they had implemented their understandings.

Most groups of teachers queried how much detail was required and the log turned out to be a list of new activities from most centers with little to no detail of the effectiveness of the activities. In hindsight, requesting greater detail would have been useful but would have demanded more teacher time and reflection. For this study, we were asking teachers to participate on top of any self-review processes they had in place at the time.

At the end of the intervention period, the activities and teachers' surveys were repeated. Once the data were analyzed, the researchers returned to centers to talk about what the teachers had done during the intervention period and to discuss the data. At the control center the professional development program was offered after all data were collected.

Results

The initial analyses of children's data compared the pretest data across the intervention and control early childhood centers. There were no significant differences across the intervention and control groups, except for own name reading. More of the intervention group knew their own name to read, as a proportion, than the control group. However, the effect size for this difference was very low at $r^2 = 0.09$.

The posttest analyses of the 51 intervention children and the 12 control group children who completed all the analyses are reported in Table 5.2. There were no significant differences that favored the intervention group, but one significant difference that favored the control group was improvement in own name reading compared to the intervention group. However, the effect size for this was very low at $r^2 = 0.08$. What these results suggest is that children in the intervention groups had progressed in terms of literacy knowledge, as more children achieved higher scores on the simpler literacy tasks than the control group.

The teacher results were analyzed in terms of teachers' perceptions of the provision of literacy opportunities for children, the recognition of

Table 5.2 Mean Change from pretest to posttest for intervention and control groups

	Intervention N = 48	Control N = 12	t (58)	p	MSE
Rhyme identity	0.50 (1.83)	−0.17 (1.64)	1.15	ns	0.58
Onset identity	0.63 (1.55)	−0.33 (2.06)	1.79	ns	0.54
Own name reading	0.00 (0.46)	0.33 (.49)	2.21	<0.05	0.15
Own name spelling	0.19 (0.49)	0.00 (.00)	−		
Alphabet names	1.52 (2.93)	0.17 (1.95)	1.51	ns	0.89

literacy abilities within centers, and teachers' understanding of literacy and their role in facilitating literacy development. Both intervention and control centers considered they provided language and literacy-rich environments for children through the provision of song, nametags, books, posters, games, music, and puzzles. Our results indicated that teachers did not change their literacy opportunities for children in any significant way as a result of the intervention.

In recognition of literacy in young children measure, teachers at all centers indicated that they recognized all of the literacy abilities that the questionnaire asked about. However, understanding how children developed literacy was not well understood by teachers, as they did not mention specific forms of knowledge nor developmental progressions of literacy. The majority of responses to the question of how children develop literacy referred to the importance of literacy-rich environments and children being immersed in literacy. Teachers indicated that their roles were to encourage language development and provide literacy resources. The control center differed slightly in that the teachers considered that their role was to provide literacy experiences rather just resources. There was little change in the postintervention surveys, although in the intervention centers the preintervention role was identified as facilitating language development for literacy compared with the postintervention role, which had more emphasis on facilitating literacy itself. Also of interest is that teachers made little use of the early childhood curriculum *Te Whāriki* in their planning for literacy.

Teachers at all centers, including the control, commented that they were more conscious of supporting literacy during the intervention period. In the questionnaire one of the control center teachers commented, "Since viewing the questions your researchers were asking our children...I have instigated and supervised a specific letter recognition and sounds program." This response indicated that the control center initiated more formal literacy skills experiences for children than had been done for the intervention centers.

Methodology: Study Two

Study Two was designed to extend Study One, because we recognized that greater involvement with teachers might lead to greater change in pedagogies and stronger outcomes for children. It was also funded by MURF and this time involved Claire and Alison and Judy Watson, a Massey colleague. Our aim for Study Two was to examine if collaboratively planned reviews with teachers in low socioeconomic status (SES) kindergartens would enhance literacy learning for children of 3–5 years. Our research questions included

- Can collaborative planned reviews with kindergarten teachers in low-SES settings increase knowledge of literacy?
- Can collaborative planned reviews with kindergarten teachers change pedagogical practices related to literacy?
- Do changes in knowledge and pedagogies in teachers relate to changes in children's literacy knowledge, skills, abilities, and self-perceptions?

We used many of the instruments used for Study One, but made some different design decisions, based on our experiences of Study One. We hypothesized that greater time and greater involvement with teachers might be required. First, we recruited four low-decile kindergartens to participate with the assistance of our local kindergarten association, all of whom had decided to pursue a planned review of either literacy or numeracy in 2012. Two of the kindergartens planned to review literacy and two planned to review numeracy. The data reported here relate to only one of the kindergartens that reviewed literacy, as full analysis of all data is not yet complete. Linking the research to the planned review of literacy teaching and learning was important as it meant that we could develop working relationships with the kindergartens, rather than having research data being collected in isolation from their self-review practices, which happened in Study One.

The kindergarten had three trained teachers, who had been teaching together for nearly two years. The Head Teacher had 20 years of teaching experience and had a New Zealand Diploma of Teaching (ECE) and New Zealand Bachelor of Education (BEd). The other two teachers were new graduates and provisionally registered: one with BEd (Tchg) 0–8 and just over two years' experience; the other with a Graduate Diploma of Teaching and 18 months' experience. Parental consent was gained for 30 children, although we only collected data with 26 because of illness and absences.

For this study, we used a semistructured interview protocol at the beginning and end of the study. This provided more in-depth information from teachers. The research team regularly met with teachers and with a member of our University's Center for Educational Development, who was part of a Ministry of Education funded professional learning contract. The meetings were collegial and friendly and each meeting was documented by one of the teachers with agreement about what we would do before our next meeting. Over time, strong collaborative relationships were formed, which were attributable to each member. There were no difficult interactions to be resolved and we typically drank tea and talked for about two hours.

Table 5.3 Pre, mid, and post scores of literacy abilities in kindergarten children ($n = 26$)

Literacy measures	Pre	Range	Mid	Range	Post	Range
Alphabet names	8	0–24	7.8	0–26	9.2	0–26
Alphabet sounds	8.6	2–13	16.7	1–21	11.4	1–21
Name reading	8 yes		10 yes		12 yes	
Name writing	4 yes		4 yes		7 yes	
Rhyme identity (max 8)	3.3	0–8	3.8	1–8	4.1	2–8
Onset identity (max 8)	3.0	1–6	3.4	1–8	3.0	1–8
Vocabulary	93.4	55–112	97.3	76–117	99.4	76–117

We developed a questionnaire that was sent home to children's parents to assess home literacy activities to aid discussions with the teachers. The measures used with children were the same as in Study One, except that we gathered data at three intervals throughout the year (pre, mid, and post). We used the British Picture Vocabulary (BPV) scale at each interval, so that we tracked vocabulary development as a stable measure of language acquisition.

Results from children in this study show that children developed greater literacy skills than in Study One, although of course these are case study data and we are reporting preliminary data rather than full analyses. Of particular interest is the fact that children gained on average six vocabulary-standardized score points on the BPV scale, where typical development would suggest a stable score across the time period. Table 5.3 shows an overall positive pattern to literacy achievement for these children in all areas of literacy, not just for vocabulary development.

The teaching team had expressed confidence in their literacy teaching at the outset of the study and reviewed their current literacy practices, which looked at literacy environment, interactions, and routines. Teachers all agreed that their understandings of literacy and their practices had changed in specific ways. Some of the changes included the following:

- Increased use of alphabet by making alphabet resources using stones and sandpaper;
- Using alphabet resources inside and outside;
- Purchased an I-pad;
- Put writing materials inside and outside;
- Increased literacy resources in the kindergarten;
- Increased use of playdough and gloop for letter recognition;
- Increased focus on high-frequency words;

- Increased focus on reading stories, singing nursery rhymes and waiata and songs from other languages;
- Increased use of mats and cushions outside for reading; and
- Increased focus on selecting stories and resources to support learning of alphabet, sounds, new words.

As these findings suggest, teachers had mainly enriched the literacy environment but they had also reflected on their literacy practices within this environment and their pedagogical decision-making. All teachers said they were more confident about promoting literacy and had thought deeply about how to support and extend children's literacy especially using literacy resources more purposefully. All of them considered they supported foundational skills like fine motor skills for writing, knowledge of alphabet, and awareness of sounds. They discussed using resources to promote specific skills, such as puppets for phonological awareness and letter name resources for alphabet and writing. All commented that they were looking more explicitly at the link between teaching and children's outcomes and discussed issues related to assessment. Of significance in Study Two was that teachers were in accord about their role in collecting data that were revisited at each meeting and there was consequently no discernible debate or dissension within the team. This was in contrast to other centers, which were part of the larger study. In this center, the harmonious teaching team was a key factor in the changes to teachers' awareness and practices.

Discussion

What Were the Enablers for Effective Relationships across the Projects?

In Study One, both Claire and Alison spent time at each center prior to the start of this project to establish the parameters of the study, including the professional development component. The only exception to this was in the fifth center (the control), at which we offered the professional development on literacy after the data collection. The data collection took up to two weeks at each center which provided multiple opportunities to talk with staff about children, their learning, and teachers' approaches to supporting literacy learning. A further enabler was that all centers were interested in promoting literacy and were committed as teams to participate. With all groups, we met with either supervisors or groups of teachers at the center before the professional development session and explained the research and answered any questions. These meetings took more than an hour in all cases and meant that the subsequent professional development sessions were friendly and collegial and participants said they felt well informed of the purposes of the study.

In Study Two, the method involved greater involvement with the kindergarten teachers and over a longer period of time, enabling opportunities for stronger relationships to be formed. The study commenced by identifying teachers' beliefs about literacy and their thoughts about how they might enhance children's literacy. Researchers collected and collated data from children and then met with teachers to review the children's results at each stage of data collection and discussed possible implications for curriculum, pedagogy, assessment, and evaluation, as well as specific strategies for supporting individual children's learning. Teachers collected evidence of their approaches to literacy teaching and used these for their planned review of teaching literacy. Unlike Study One, the longer professional development relationship of nearly three school terms enabled greater relationship building and increased sharing between teachers and researchers. The sharing of child assessment data with staff for the purposes of reflecting on professional practice was a particularly strong enabler.

What Were the Barriers for Effective Relationships across the Projects?

Although we generally met with support and enthusiasm in Study One, at the intervention centers it was difficult to maintain the teacher sample, as although all teachers participated in the pretest survey of teachers' beliefs and attended the professional development sessions, we found in most centers that only qualified teachers turned up for the post test debriefing and explanation of the results, which impacted on the data collection and analysis. Possibly this was because the professional development session was seen as a one-off *class-type* session and thus the debrief session was not necessary. Additionally, the data collection may have been viewed as researcher-driven and not part of a relationship that may improve literacy for children. As in all centers there was a relatively high level of unqualified staff, this meant that the sample of teachers dropped from 30 to 16. As a consequence, for Study Two, we planned to collect the data in low-decile kindergartens instead of childcare centers, so that we would work with a smaller group of teachers, who were all qualified, in the hope of maintaining the sample throughout the study.

In addition, at the center that we used as a control in Study One, although we had asked the manager and supervisor to do "business as usual," the supervisor decided to use our intervention period to promote her own particular view of literacy, which differed from that provided in our professional development. It is clear in the data that all staff at the center did not share this view of literacy, but it did mean that we were very aware of a particular approach to literacy being adopted and were not surprised when this focus was reflected in the final results. Achieving an effective control group in an educational setting was a challenge that we hoped to overcome in Study Two by collecting literacy data in another kindergarten that had focused its planned review on numeracy but we did not provide professional development for these staff.

What Were the Perceptions of the Roles and Relationships within the Complexities of Teaching and Research? Were There Developmental Aspects to This throughout the Project?

Within Study One, roles and relationships were relatively straightforward, in that the study was carried out as an intervention study, designed to test the effectiveness of professional learning for promoting change in teachers' beliefs and children's knowledge, skills, and abilities. Researchers collected data and teachers taught, although they also kept brief records of any changes they had made to the literacy curriculum over the intervention period. In Study Two, teachers drove the frequency of meetings and researchers' involvement, over three kindergarten terms. This enabled our relationships to be more reciprocal and a greater sense of partnership and ownership of the research was established. This has extended to a recent opportunity to jointly present results of the review at a local early childhood symposium.

In the kindergarten the review involved semiregular meetings with the teaching team and the College of Education (CED) consultant. Both researchers and the consultant discussed children's results and shared suggestions for how to support the development of children's literacy knowledge and skills. The consultant and one of the researchers also generated two presentations for parents and the community where they showed a range of new resources for children and made suggestions to parents on how to support literacy at home.

What Was Seen as Knowledge, What Was Seen as Practice, and What Did Generating Knowledge Mean for the Projects?

In Study One, these concepts are reasonably clearly differentiated. Teachers' knowledge of literacy and linguistic knowledge and its relationship to practice was something that was assessed only by pre- and posttests and our only insights into practice were teachers' self-reports of how they had changed their practices during the intervention period. Data analysis suggests that only very minor shifts in teachers' beliefs and practices occurred as a result of professional development, although there are small but significant differences in children's literacy outcomes in the intervention centers. The nature of the research design meant that what counted as literacy knowledge was defined from the researchers' perspective, and not as something co-constructed between researchers and teachers.

In Study Two, we did not use a set format for professional learning. We asked teachers to tell us what would be helpful in terms of increasing their knowledge about literacy. At the meetings we talked in detail about the children who participated and about learning opportunities and evidence-based effective pedagogies. Giving teachers specific information about children's developing literacy knowledge and skills provided them with greater insights into how to change practice than the approach used in Study One had afforded. In particular, the nature of this professional learning relationship meant that children's knowledge was at the core of practice. There was a change in emphasis from generalized literacy practice and engagement, to teachers finding out more specific information about children's developing vocabulary, alphabet knowledge, and phonological awareness. This shifted teaching practices to focus on these specific outcomes.

Although teachers could not use the measures that we used to assess children's literacy (because they require time and specialist skill), teachers might want to record how children perform on different activities as part of their assessment of literacy to provide similar insights into how children are progressing. Teachers can also use some resources diagnostically to identify which children are having difficulties with key predictors of literacy, such as alphabet knowledge, phonological awareness, and vocabulary, as this would specifically target teaching those children who are *at risk* and need greater support. Children can, and do, develop specific forms of knowledge or ability, such as alphabet knowledge, and phonological awareness during early childhood education (Arrow, 2010), and children who have higher levels of knowledge or ability tend to do better once in primary school (Tunmer et al., 2006). Study Two also illustrated that once teachers have the knowledge of where children are in terms of this knowledge, they can facilitate further learning by providing experiences aimed at developing them.

Contextual Influences: How Did the Social, Political, and Temporal Position of Education Shape the Projects, Relationships, and Their Outcomes?

Although the focus on literacy is a passion of all authors of this chapter, literacy is also high on the New Zealand Government's agenda for education (Ministry of Education, 2010). For social and political reasons, we chose to conduct these studies in low-decile settings, because the Government is most concerned about achievement of children from low-decile settings. Arguably, if we want to make the most difference to outcomes for children, the research should be conducted in the settings where there are children who have the greatest need for effective teaching and learning opportunities. There is, to a certain extent, a social justice perspective underpinning our choices of research sites, as well as being responsive to the interests of government.

Both studies show that children in these lower-decile settings do have lower "literate cultural capital" (Tunmer, Chapman & Prochnow, 2006) than children from higher-decile settings. Although there is little available data on children's literacy abilities in early childhood, Arrow's (2007) doctoral research showed higher average scores for alphabet knowledge, phonological awareness, and vocabulary than children at these centers and kindergartens. Results from the Progress in Reading Literacy Study (PIRLS) (Ministry of Education, 2013) shows that children from lower-decile homes are more likely to be in New Zealand's significant tail of reading failure than children from higher-decile homes. Results from these two studies show that children are already showing lower levels of alphabet knowledge, phonological awareness, and vocabulary between three and five years, potentially predicting future difficulties in literacy acquisition. However, these difficulties may be preventable through stronger assessment of children's literacy knowledge and skills and targeted, specific teaching to support their development of requisite knowledge and skills.

Transformative Thinking and Practice—Possible or Not? Why or Why Not?

Study One showed that although there were small but significant differences in outcomes for children in intervention centers, there were less discernible changes in teachers' beliefs. Current research suggests that a coaching and guiding strategy, which more directly challenges teachers' thinking, is more likely to be effective in transforming thinking and practice (Cunningham Zibulsky, & Callahan, 2009). Study Two showed that spending greater time with teachers and using specific children's results as prompts for discussion resulted in greater transformation of thinking. The teachers in Study Two also felt more part of the developmental process.

Having examined both event and process approaches to professional learning, we consider that transformation of thinking is easier when teachers and researchers have more time together and have opportunities to discuss specific children and their literacy learning, but this is an expensive (time demanding) model. We undertook Study Two without much research funding, which meant that as researchers, our participation was limited to the time that we could fit in around our university workload and other commitments. Ideally, it would be good to have greater time for observations of teachers to include in the data collection or to videotape teachers' practice as prompts for discussion, but this is a costly model of professional learning, which few centers or governments could afford on a regular basis. The reality is that although our process approach is a more powerful model of professional learning, it is likely that most teachers are more likely to access event-based approaches because of affordability. Study One does suggest that professional learning events do have beneficial outcomes such as helping teachers to reflect on how they promote literacy, but Study Two shows that greater change may occur with a coaching and guiding strategy to professional learning.

Summary and Conclusions

Joce Nuttall (2010) provided the following challenges for early childhood researchers to consider:

a. The ... challenge of knowledge, practice, and research—separated but deeply connected;
b. Collaborations "demanding a level of relational expertise that must in itself be developed and enacted within the complex, social, political, cultural, environmental and economic agendas facing the education sector" (p. 3).
c. Collaborations that must "result in a higher level of research consciousness *amongst those practitioners* adding yet another level of complexity." (p. 3).

We consider that our studies of how to promote literacy in the early childhood setting have achieved all three goals above. We have addressed the complex nature of knowledge and practice in both studies, with a focus on planned review in Study Two focusing more deeply on how teachers can research their own practice. Study Two, in particular, involved collaboration with teachers and, for the one kindergarten site described here, also involved a Ministry of Education funded consultant. Working in collaboration with teachers over several months required a mutual commitment between researchers and teachers to share their knowledge and skills in order to achieve Nuttall's third challenge of reaching higher levels of consciousness. There is little doubt that partnerships between teachers and researchers are possible and mutually rewarding, but are premised upon the same principles that underpin any successful relationship: trust, empathy, and great communication. The implications of both studies are that professional learning can support both growth in teacher knowledge and enhance children's literacy learning.

References

Arrow, A. (2010). Emergent literacy skills in New Zealand kindergarten children: Implications for teaching and learning in ECE settings. *He Kupu, 2*(3), 57–69.

Arrow, A. W. (2007). *Potential precursors to the development of phonological awareness in preschool children.* Unpublished Doctoral thesis, University of Auckland, New Zealand.

Cullen, J. (2006, September). *Literacy education in the early years: Policies, polemics and practices.* Keynote speech to the Politics of Early Childhood Education Symposium. Auckland, New Zealand.

Cunningham, A. E., Perry, K. E., Stanovich, K. E., & Stanovich, P. J. (2004). Disciplinary knowledge of K-3 teachers and their knowledge calibration in the domain of early literacy. *Annals of Dyslexia, 54*(1), 139–166.

Cunningham, A. E., Zibulsky, J. & Callahan, M. D. (2009). Starting small: Building preschool teacher knowledge that supports early literacy development. *Reading and Writing, 22,* 487–510.

Doubek, M. B., & Cooper, E. J. (2007). Closing the gap through professional development: Implications for reading research. *Reading Research Quarterly, 42*(3), 411–415.

Dunn, L. M., Dunn, L. M., Whetton, C., & Burley, J. (1997). *The British picture vocabulary scale* (2nd ed.). Berkshire, UK: National Foundation for Educational Research.

Education Review Office. (2011). *Literacy teaching and learning in early childhood.* Wellington, NZ: Education Review Office.

Foote, L., Smith, J., & Ellis, F. (2004). The impact of teachers' beliefs on the literacy experiences of young children: A New Zealand perspective. *Early Years: Journal of International Research and Development, 24*(2), 135–148.

Hedges, H. (2003). A response to criticism and challenge: Early literacy and numeracy in Aotearoa/New Zealand. *New Zealand Research in Early Childhood Education, 6,* 13–22.

Justice, L. M., & Pullen, P. C. (2003). Promising interventions for promoting emergent literacy skills: Three evidence based approaches. *Topics in Early Childhood Special Education, 23*(3), 99–113.

Justice, L. M., Kaderavek, J. N., Fan, X., Sofka, A., & Hunt, A. (2009). Accelerating preschoolers' early literacy development through classroom-based teacher-child storybook reading and explicit print referencing. *Language, Speech and Hearing Services in Schools, 40,* 67–85.

McGill-Franzen, A. (2010). Guest editor's introduction. *Educational Researcher, 39,* 275–278.

McLachlan, C., & Arrow, A. (2011). Literacy in the early years in New Zealand: Policies, politics and pressing reasons for change. *Literacy, 45*(3), 126–133.
McLachlan, C., Carvalho, L., de Lautour, N., & Kumar, K. (2006). Literacy in early childhood settings in New Zealand: An examination of teachers' beliefs and practices. *Australian Journal of Early Childhood, 31*(2), 31–41.
McLachlan-Smith, C. J. (1996). *Emergent literacy in New Zealand kindergartens: An examination of policy and practices.* Unpublished doctoral thesis, Massey University, Palmerston North.
Ministry of Education. (1996). *Te Whāriki: He whāriki matauranga mō ngā mokopuna o Aotearoa: Early childhood curriculum.* Wellington, NZ: Learning Media.
Ministry of Education. (2005). *Kei tua o te pae. Assesment for learning: Early childhood exemplars.* Wellington, NZ: Learning Media.
Ministry of Education. (2007a). *Literacy learning progressions: Meeting the reading and writing demands of the curriculum.* Wellington, NZ: Learning Media.
Ministry of Education. (2007b). *The New Zealand curriculum.* Wellington, NZ: Learning Media.
Ministry of Education. (2010). *Literacy learning progressions: Report on feedback on the draft document.* Available at: http://www.educationcounts.govt.nz/publications/literacy/43632.
Ministry of Education. (2013). *PIRLS 2010/2011.* Retrieved from http://www.educationcounts.govt.nz/topics/research/pirls/pirls_201011
Mitchell, L. & Cubey, P. (2003). *Professional learning in early childhood settings: Best evidence synthesis.* Wellington, NZ: Ministry of Education.
Moats, L. C. (2000). *Speech to print: Language essentials for teachers.* Baltimore, MD: Paul H Brookes.
National Early Literacy Panel. (2009). *Developing early literacy: Report of the national early literacy panel.* Washington, DC: National Institute for Literacy.
Nicholson, T. (2005). *At the cutting edge: The importance of phonemic awareness in learning to read and spell.* Wellington, NZ: NZCER Press.
Nuttall, J. (2005). Looking back, looking forward: Three decades of early childhood curriculum development in New Zealand. *Curriculum Matters, 1,* 12–28.
Nuttall, J. (2010, November). The contribution of the Teaching and Learning Research Initiative to building knowledge about teaching and learning: A review of early years projects, 2004–2010. Paper presented to *TLRI Early Years Symposium*, Wellington, NZ: Teaching and Learning Research Initiative.
O'Connor, R. E., Notari-Syverson, A., & Vadasy, P. F. (1996). Ladders to literacy: The effects of teacher-led phonological activities for kindergarten children with and without disabilities. *Exceptional Children, 63,* 117–130.
Phillips, B. M., Clancy-Menchetti, J., & Lonigan, C. (2008). Successful phonological awareness instruction with preschool children. *Topics in Early Childhood Special Education, 28*(1), 3–17.
Phillips, G., McNaughton, S., & MacDonald, S. (2002). *Picking up the pace. Effective literacy interventions for accelerated progress over the transition into decile 1 schools.* Wellington, NZ: Ministry of Education.

Piasta, S. B., & Wagner, R. K. (2010). Developing early literacy skills: A meta-analysis of alphabet learning and instruction. *Reading Research Quarterly, 45*(1), 8–38.

Stanovich, K. (2000). *Progress in understanding reading: Scientific foundations and new frontiers.* New York, NY: Guilford Press.

Tagoilelagi-Leota, F., McNaughton, S., MacDonald, S., & Ferry, S. (2005). Bilingual and biliteracy development over the transition to school. *International Journal of Bilingual Education and Bilingualism, 8*(5), 455–479.

Taylor, N. E., Blum, I. H., & Logsdon, D. M. (1986). The development of written language awareness: Environmental aspects and program characteristics. *Reading Research Quarterly, Spring,* 132–149.

Tunmer, W. E., Chapman, J. W., & Prochnow, J. E. (2004). Why the reading achievement gap in New Zealand won't go away: Evidence from the PIRLS 2001 international study of reading achievement. *New Zealand Journal of Educational Studies, 39*(1), 127–145.

Tunmer, W. E., Chapman, J. W., & Prochnow, J. E. (2006). Literate cultural capital at school entry predicts later reading achievement: A seven year longitudinal study. *New Zealand Journal of Educational Studies, 41,* 183–204.

Whitehurst, G. J., & Lonigan, C. J. (1998). Child development and emergent literacy. *Child Development, 69,* 848–872.

Wong Fillmore, L., & Snow, C. E. (2000). *What teachers need to know about language. Special report.* Washington, DC: Eric Clearinghouse on Language and Linguistics.

6

Ko koe ki tēna, ko ahau ki tēnei kīwai o te kete: Exploring Collaboration across a Range of Recent Early Childhood Studies

Jenny Ritchie, Janita Craw, Cheryl Rau, and Iris Duhn

Introduction

The concept of relationality inherent in researching teaching and learning in early education is complex and multifaceted. It is well noted that relationships that make any kind of researching, teaching, and learning possible, let alone effective, are reliant on building collaborative partnerships between teachers, academic researchers, and others with an invested interest in the educational project (e.g., *tamariki* [children] and *whānau* [parents])—as well as striving to make (deep and meaningful) connections between knowledge, practice, and research (Nuttall, 2010). Developing possibilities for these relationships to be transformative (i.e., for teachers and researchers to view themselves/each other and the relationships developed as having agency to bring about social, cultural, educational change) relies on an understanding of the complexities and multifaceted nature of these relationships—in relation to experiences encountered in the wider (local/global) world we live in; an approach Taylor (2008) refers to as "a planetary view" (p. 9). From this perspective, transformation demands that those involved develop a critical and reflexive understanding of teaching, learning, early childhood care, and education, and of research. This chapter explores the complexities and possibilities of these intersecting relationships in response to our engagement in a number of Teaching and Learning Research Initiative (TLRI)[1] research projects (Dalli, Rockel, Duhn, Craw, & Doyle, 2011; Haynes, Cardno, & Craw, 2007; Ritchie, Duhn, Rau, & Craw, 2010; Ritchie & Rau, 2006, 2008).

With reference to these studies we discuss how the research methodologies themselves provided opportunities for the participant collaborators, both practitioners and researchers, to learn and to contribute not only to the research via a methodological approach of co-theorizing as knowledge generation but also to the ongoing development of practice. As part of these projects, challenges and possibilities emerged both in relation to giving voice to *tamariki* and *whānau* and to what extent the processes and relationships led to transformation. We consider ways in which the interdependence and intersubjectivities of the research directors and educator co-researchers enabled and constrained knowledge generation and social transformation.

First, Janita Craw offers a (re)-consideration of the research interview, using her recent research experiences to problematize traditional research interviewing from a range of poststructural lenses. In the following section, Iris Duhn reflects on the fluctuating collaborative choreography between researcher and teachers taking place within the context of the wider web of relationships in a busy early childhood care and education setting. Next, Cheryl Rau outlines the Indigenous conceptualizations underpinning research projects in 'mainstream' early childhood care and education settings. In the final section, Jenny Ritchie reflects on how researchers can unlock the doors to the circles of wisdom that surround *tamariki*, by adopting *precocious* methodologies (Malewski, 2005), ending with some provocations arising from the chapter.

Methodological Issues in (Re)conceptualizing the *Interview* (as Something Else?) in Early Childhood Education Research: Janita Craw

I have been involved in three different TLRI projects with three different research teams (Dalli et al., 2011; Haynes et al., 2007; Ritchie et al., 2010). Each project offered me a different teaching team to work with. In two cases, this involved working with kindergarten teaching teams of two or three teachers who worked with 40 or 45 children aged 3–5 years in, what were then, sessional (half-day) early childhood settings. In the third study, I worked with two teachers (from a team of up to four) who provided education and care for infants and toddlers in a fulltime education and care setting for children aged 2–5 years. Each project articulated a different qualitative methodology and methodological influences. These included (sometimes in combination): action research, phenomenology, sociocultural, ethnography, and poststructural thinking.

All three projects shared some similarities in the data gathering methods, including encouraging teachers to collect learning and teaching stories, and involved one (or two) researchers who spent time with the teacher-research participants, usually in their place of work. This was a way of enabling opportunities for teachers (and in one instance, the parents) to talk about their experience of teaching practices, children's learning, and the thinking that most influenced their knowledge and understandings of these in relation to the focus of the project (which included mathematics; sustainability; practices based in *Te Tiriti o Waitangi*[2]; infants and toddlers; pedagogy and curriculum). These talk sessions were most often audio-recorded and transcribed later. They were similar to what is identified in much of the qualitative research literature as semi-structured or informal interviews. These sessions were intended as opportunities for the researcher(s) to draw out from the educator-research partners, their ideas about the phenomenon central to the project. The informal nature of the format was an opportunity to give voice to those who might otherwise remain invisible—the teachers, children, their parents, and *whānau*.

In each instance, at the time of research design, the use of talk sessions was identified as a method for providing teachers with an opportunity to put forth their theoretical and philosophical knowledge and understandings, together with examples of practices in their particular settings. In each project the research design was constructed to integrate the diverse research and practice interests of the researchers and educator co-researchers involved. For example, one project aimed to integrate both phenomenological and poststructural research approaches. Exactly what this might mean in terms of how the complex relationship between diverse theoretical approaches to research practices might be managed, or even whether it needed to be managed, remained an open exercise. Hence, data analysis processes often involved identifying any themes evident in the (documented) talk sessions (and/or in the learning/teaching stories). Occasionally, but to a lesser extent, these processes involved an uncovering of the different discourses evident.

Although it is generally expected that the researcher be prepared with open-ended questions to guide the discussion, there is often an expectation that the researcher refrain from contributing. Active listening is to be exercised as the means of eliciting insights from teachers, children, parents, and *whānau*, reflections that reveal *truths*—or what Mazzei and Jackson (2009, p. 4) refer to as "voice as evidence" in relation to the focus of the study. However, my experiences on these projects left me with a desire to work differently, to ponder how (re)considering these talk sessions might enable the kind of critical discussion that problematizes "how voice is mediated, constrained, determined, and even commodified" (Mazzei & Jackson, 2009, p. 5). How does thinking about these talk sessions as conversations (or as *kōrero*—talking, or in this instance, storying) promote an examination of how voice is being—or might be—understood in early childhood education research? How can working with voice (or multiple voices) reveal the trickier moments, the voices that otherwise might escape, offering more dynamic ways of working in early childhood education and in research in early childhood education?

Although research interviewing may superficially appear to be a straightforward data collection method, it can also be recognized as an extremely complex process, which requires skill and craft, and involves a range of epistemological issues that make the very nature of the interviewing process problematic. Kvale and Brinkman (2009) offer two contrasting metaphors of the interviewer, which they believe "illustrate the different epistemological conceptions of interviewing as a process of knowledge collection or as a process of knowledge construction, respectively" (p. 48). These are the interviewer as *miner*, seeking predetermined nuggets of knowledge; and the interviewer as *traveler*, who meanders open-mindedly into the landscape of the interview process. Each metaphor determines how the interviewer or interviewers will approach and carry out the interviewing processes as well as how the data are gathered or produced, subsequently processed, and presented to an audience. Although theoretical discussions that include issues of representation, ethics, and power are essential for any approach to interviewing (Kvale & Brinkman, 2009; van Enk, 2009), other issues such as desire (Tuck, 2010) are also important because they offer alternative conceptualizations of the research process. Creating opportunities, for example, for teachers to interview the researchers may produce some interesting data.

From the first (positivistic and empirical) perspective, the 'miner' metaphor, the interview is understood as a site of data collection that enables the researcher to seek and extract knowledge waiting to be uncovered in the subject's interior. From this perspective, the knowledge and understandings offered by the teachers are understood as something that are fixed and will be expected to remain relatively constant throughout the research. From the second (postmodern) perspective, the *traveller* metaphor, the interview is understood as a special form of conversational practice that contributes to the socially constructed nature of knowledge and social reality. The knowledge and understandings offered by the teachers will be understood to exist in the "fabric of relations" between the persons (that include, e.g., the teachers, researchers) and the world

(Kvale & Brinkman, 2009, p. 48). The researcher/s roams freely through the research setting landscape, enter into conversations, and seek the potentialities of meaning in the stories that unfold. These narratives are then differentiated and interpreted by the researcher/s for a wider audience.

Kvale and Brinkman's (2009) metaphors may well, in the end, be only a partial contribution toward addressing the complexities identified in much of the literature and those that arose for me in my role as researcher-partner. For example, in one of the studies, the talk sessions were carried out with two teachers. I noticed that on several occasions, one teacher's voice was more prominent than another. I discussed this observation with the teachers on several occasions and the teachers insisted that, given the reflective and collaborative nature of their teaching team, that *one voice* be used to represent a combined and shared teacher voice throughout the research project.

It is evident that throughout the research activity—and over time—the teachers offer a range of different, and sometimes contradictory, discourses that may even change over time as the research activity progresses and through the conversations that take place. The challenge for researchers and teacher research partners is to consider how these complexities might be reflected upon, responded to, and recorded as the research unfolds.

Although the notion of an interview is rooted in the word *conversation*, it is interesting to recognize the very nature of research interviewing as a mechanism that has evolved in the social sciences over time. It has been heavily influenced by a *scientific* regime (or genre) that demands particular dynamics between the interviewer and the interviewee. All of the participants have expectations about how these dynamics are carried out. For example, the interviewer asks questions, rather than offering perspectives, opinions, and so on. In turn, the interviewee gives answers but does not ask questions of the interviewer. What might happen to the conversations if there was interviewer–interviewee reciprocity?

On one occasion, during a momentary pause that occurred while a teacher was actively engaged in response to a research question, I offered an idea that the teacher then ran with as if it was exactly what was on her mind. How can this be revealed in the final analysis in ways that contribute to revealing the complexity of researching (partnership-) voice in early childhood education research?

Rhedding-Jones (2008) has highlighted how clashes of opinion and epistemological dissonances, a critical issue in early childhood education research, occur when an adherence to positivism and the security of fixedness collides with the practices of those who seek to reconceptualize the field of early childhood care and education. Dockett and Sumsion (2004) consider, however, that such clashes and the dissonance they produce create a range of tensions and challenges that have the "potential to enliven debate and to be constructive for early childhood education research" (p. 7). The *mosaic* approach of Sumsion et al. (2011) provides a methodological pathway, which acknowledges these tensions. Encouraging a broad diversity of theoretical eclecticism by opening up shared dialogical spaces enables those involved to transcend paradigmatic boundaries, potentially making the knowledge thus generated accessible to a broader audience.

Van Enk (2009) identified a number of challenges that belie "the harmonious connotations conversation often carries" (p. 1270). There are some interesting parallels here with scenarios from my own research experiences. These include, for example,

- The inevitable tensions that resulted from the clashing agendas and different research interests (and epistemologies) of the partner researchers.
- The silencing or restraining of (researcher) voice is somewhat inevitable between interviewee and the interviewers when the potential for clashing agendas and different research interests (and epistemologies) arise.
- The *Othering* that happened when interviewees or interviewers were positioned in ways that fitted with former notions of *presumed truths* of what should (or should not) be said in early childhood education.
- Power being variously and subtly distributed in interviews. As is often the case, the researchers all worked in teacher education, and consequently several of the participants were ex-students of the researcher.

"To speak is to fight" (Lyotard, as cited in van Enk, 2009, p. 1270), hence a productive approach to determining meaning can involve making space for interactive interviewing styles that range from cooperative to the conflictual. Respecting this productive capacity and thereby making deliberate space for conflict in the interviewing processes is something that many researchers shy away from. Understanding what motivates people to participate in research, and making sure these motivations are supported and represented in the research, is essential (van Enk, 2009). From my experience, it has been interesting to note that over time many teachers are becoming motivated to participate in research projects because of the opportunities it might offer them to engage in more challenging ways (to think about and work with ideas as well as their practices) than a professional development model might once have offered.

Many of the issues discussed here are reflected in the growing interest in the notion of *dialogue* and in an understanding of research interviewing processes as a *dialogic encounter*. Kvale and Brinkman (2009) attribute this interest being responsive (at least in part) to an uptake of Russian literary critic and philosopher Michael Bahktin's dialogic theory—a theory that is influenced by a Marxist dialectical materialism. Bahktin's dialogic theory emphasizes the tensions that exist in the deep structures of all human experiences and that these tensions operate as a catalyst for continual change (as cited in Kvale & Brinkman, 2009, p. 226). A *dialogical intersubjectivity* operates through "interview (as) a conversation and a negotiation of meaning" between research participants (Kvale & Brinkman, 2009, p. 243). Although this approach to research method values the ability to accommodate tension, co-construct, and collaboratively produce (new) knowledge, elements that might be highly valued within early childhood education research, creating a research culture whereby these tensions can be enacted is somewhat more challenging. Tanggaard's (2009) overview of Bahktin's two key concepts provides an understanding of the mechanisms inherent in this approach; these are

1. Understanding the research interview as a social setting for the proliferation of *polyphonic* dialogues—that is, dialogues (or conversations) are understood as personal narratives that incorporate, many voices, words, and multiple discourses; and,
2. Understanding the interview dialogues as *heteroglot*—that is, language and society are inherently impregnated with diverse (hetereo) speeches (glossia) that need to be synthesized, unified in a somewhat cohesive manner.

The mosaic methodological approach of Sumsion et al. (2011) is an example of this in practice.

From a *polyphonic* perspective, teachers' personal meanings are understood as dialogical and performed in a borderline area between (one-) self and others. For example, one teacher's stories are closely (socially, culturally, historically) intertwined with others—including that of the researchers (Tanggaard, 2009). Understanding the interview dialogue as *heteroglot* involves an understanding of language as *heteroglossic*. That is, language is composed of a combination of social languages, some of which are engaged in opposition and struggle. Language gives voice to the coexistence of socio-ideological contradictions; conflicting discourses that may stand in opposition to official or dominant (political) discourses. From this perspective, it is important the interviewing processes be seen as a "coming to know more about the social life within particular communities" (Tanggaard, 2009, p. 1507). Hence, though somewhat challenging, perhaps it becomes important in any partnership to make visible the oppositional and struggling epistemological, ontological, educational aspirations, et cetera, evident in the narratives of both the teacher-participants as well as those of the researcher-participants.

Working with oppositional and struggling narratives in research in early childhood education is a challenge, one that opens up spaces for experimentation that might demand new research tools. Olsson (2009) draws on the works of Deleuze and Guattari to describe research as "a practice engaging in collective, intense and unpredictable experimentation" (p. 46). Interviewing processes, she suggests, can be understood as an assemblage, "a collective process of the simultaneous creation of lines of flights" (Olsson, 2009, p. 47). However, the use of discourse analyses and deconstructive techniques that are often already used to challenge dominant discourses or reveal the different discourses within early childhood care and education have yet to become common tools used in collaboration with teachers as partners in TLRI projects. Yet these theoretical domains open up further spaces for other researchers to pick up, and to play with these threads in productive and meaningful ways, that may benefit very young children, teachers, parents, *whānau* in early childhood education.

Collaborative Research as an Opportunity to Learn to Choreograph a Dance Together: Iris Duhn

This section of the chapter explores possibilities for research subjectivities that enable collaboration, trust, and high-level analysis. The focus is on the research relationship that developed between one researcher (Iris) and two teachers (Marina and Kate) of a small privately owned suburban childcare center in Auckland during a recent TLRI study (Ritchie et al., 2010). Specifically, this section reflects critically on the emerging *learning self* as a professional subjectivity in collaborative research. The collaborative ethos that guided this project was based explicitly on notions of care, including care for the self and for the other. I consider that the way the notion of how care for self and other has been thought and practiced in the project remains an area for critical analysis after the project has been completed. However, as a guiding principle it served as a constant reminder of the intentions of the research.

Finding Rhythms, Searching for the Tune

From the beginning, it was understood by the teachers and I that a strong commitment to ethics would keep us on track, almost as a honing device. Nevertheless our relationships were, at least initially, governed by caution and reserve. What exactly does it mean to work collaboratively and with care for self and other in an overarching global research context where institutionalized hierarchies continue to rule (Cannella & Lincoln, 2004)? Is it not naïve to expect that people who barely know each other will learn to trust and work collaboratively just because the title of the research project says so? There is no getting around the fact that even in the most *collaborative* project teachers are the ones under the researcher's gaze, at least at some point if not all the time. This governs the relationship by making one side seemingly more vulnerable, especially in a new research relationship (Langan & Morton, 2009). Without giving it specific attention as a focus in our project, Marina, Kate[3], and I were aware of the power relations throughout our work. At times, we would talk about how understandings of *the self* as, for example, teacher, as researcher, as mother, or as a member of the local community, worked their way into relationships with others. At one point, Marina, who is the owner and one of the lead teachers in the center, and I came close to a direct discussion on how *the self* is thought and embodied in her professional practice (Duhn, 2010). However, with a busy research project that demanded to stay *on task*, we did not have the time and energy to venture into a closer examination of how power governs the self in our collaborative research.

Rather than seeing power as a barrier or an enabler for effective relationships, we saw ourselves, perhaps, as novice dancers in a complex choreography of our own making. The tune was set but we explored variations. The length of the piece was set but we created intensities that lingered (Duhn, Bachmann, & Harris, 2010). As rhythms and repetitions developed through particular research practices and ways of doing things, confidence in our ability to work collaboratively flourished. We were keen for other teachers to become as involved, but it proved to be a huge challenge to keep the momentum strong enough for other teachers to be swept along by the rhythm.

For instance, while Marina and Kate were particularly keen to research their own and the center's practice and policies over the duration of the project, their colleagues dipped in and out at various times. The reasons for this are complex and have to do with time, both in terms of investing precious time in someone else's research and also in terms of length of employment. Kate and Marina have worked together for many years. Their relationship is based on care for the other, which has its foundation in knowing the other, trusting the other, and feeling safe in the environment that has been created together. For others who had been members of this center community for a shorter period of time, the web of relationships that hold the community together seems, perhaps, less connected than it appears to someone who intimately knows, and consequently moves around, the web with confidence. Care for the self and for each other takes time and place to manifest and flourish (Cuomo, 1998).

Thinking about the center community itself as a web, makes it possible to consider the research relationships as embedded within this existing network. As a researcher, I entered into the network on a new tangent. My presence created a new node, with new possibilities, which in this case were intensified by Kate and Marina's collaboration. All this newness could lead to isolation of the research node within the network. Success depended on the integration of the new node into the existing structures. We challenged each other. Did I spend enough time with the children, the families, and the teachers? I remained an outsider to the network within. I heavily depended on my guides, Marina, Kate, and the other teachers who found parents for me to talk to, and documented what children thought and did. I led the dance when it came to narrating the story of the center, and *going public* with the narratives. In between, we talked and got to know one another and we shared moments of vulnerability and strength, for instance when we presented at an overseas conference together. How long would it take for me to become *an insider*? Does the idea of collaborative, reciprocal research relationships assume that everyone is equal but different—what exactly does that mean in a research context? Is it achievable, and is it desirable? Perhaps we made each other feel *other* in the process of working together. I became aware of the limitations to becoming even a temporary member of this community. My collaborative teacher-research partners may have become aware of the challenges in relation to *telling the research story* to a wider audience.

Complicated Research Conversations

Over the course of the two-year project, we came to know each other as research participants and collaborators, critical thinkers and writers, and as people and friends. In many ways, the project led us toward *complicated conversations* (Gough, 2009), which were only a starting point for an opening toward "encounters with *remarkable difference* (difference that puzzles, provokes, surprises or shocks us)" (Gough, 2009, p. 74, emphasis in original). Did we go far enough in our enquiries? Do we ever have the opportunity to encounter remarkable difference in our research projects? Or, and this is a question that makes me sit up and pay attention, am I blind and deaf to such encounters because I am governed by a focus on results, findings, conclusions? Where is my learning?

Ellsworth (2005) proposes to think of learning as an encounter with sensation and movement, as deeply experiential and sensory. The learning self emerges in that moment of recognition, or in a bodily felt shift, when the self knows herself differently. In this sense, the collaborative research relationship we entered into, asked of us to *know ourselves differently* if we intended to learn from our research partnership. I cannot speak for my research partners, but for me our collaboration has generated moments of knowing myself anew. Even if those moments were fleeting, in hindsight they may well have been the most significant ones for me.

Te Ao Māori Epistemology: Re-Lensing the Research Paradigm: Cheryl Rau

A critical *Māori* research approach prioritizes *tikanga* (ways of doing) alongside that which is *tika* (right), ancient indigenous rituals guided by "ethical codes of conduct" (Smith, 1999, p. 120). A *Māori* worldview also highlights responsibility and respectfulness to the collective, to our "interconnected relationships with each other and the universe" (Smith, 1999, p. 120). This section considers how these ways of knowing, doing, and being shape, influence, and determine the methodology and findings of our TLRI research (Ritchie et al., 2010; Ritchie & Rau, 2006, 2008).

Our methodology positions *kaumātua* (elders) as integral to the collaborative co-researcher collective. They are the sages who bring a breadth of knowledge, understanding, and experiences, as the *pou* (foundations) of strength for the research *rōpu* (collective). Our *kuia* (female elder), Rahera Barrett-Douglas, a member of the *Ngāti Maniapoto* tribe, is connected closely to both Jenny and I through Rahera's previous roles as a lecturer at the University of Waikato and as a director for *Ngāhihi*, a *Māori* organization providing professional learning for the early childhood care and education sector. Rahera's educational contributions include a long-term history within early childhood care and education beginning with involvement in Playcentre[4]; becoming a qualified kindergarten teacher; working for the government as a *Māori* advisor in the Department of Education and then in the Early Childhood Development support service for the early childhood care and education sector; and being a lecturer at the University of Waikato and a director of *Ngāhihi*. A writer of published works, a committed *Māori* Welfare Women's League member, and a contributor to the strategic educational initiatives of her *Maniapoto* tribe, Rahera has been a *taonga* (treasure) to our three TLRI projects, offering her wisdom with generosity, *aroha* (love), and *ngākau māhaki* (gentle heart), and providing a third space lens beyond the dual scholarship of *te ao Māori* and *te ao Pākehā (Māori* world and the Western world).

Our *kaumātua* across our three TLRI projects has been Huata Holmes, a navigator, aviator, and educator from *Ta Va'i Poenemu* (The South Island of New Zealand), a *kaumātua* recognized by the *Kai Tahu, Kāti Mamoe*, and *Waitaha* tribes, and *Pou Here Tangata* (the person who binds people together) of the Education Department of the University of Otago (Bishop, 1996). Huata offers his wisdom through story, song, and "by applying the traditional Southern *Māori* learning method, *tū taha kē ai*: 'to stand at the side of or be an adjunct to.' This metaphoric journey represents the pursuit of knowledge across both intercultural and transcultural paradigms" (Halba, McCallum, & Holmes, 2011, p. 69).

The prioritization of *kaumātua* within our projects recognizes the invaluable role they have in serving as *kaitiaki* (stewards, guardians) of both spiritual well-being and knowledge. Rahera Barrett-Douglas and Huata Holmes represent different *hapū* and *iwi* (sub-tribes and tribes) and their respectful modeling of awareness of differences lifted our research *rōpu* awareness and understanding of tribal specificities, which inadvertently alert us to the dangers of homogenizing and essentializing Indigenous constructs.

Commitment to *Te Tiriti o Waitangi*, the 1840 Treaty that allowed for British settlers to reside alongside the *tangata whenua* (Indigenous people) in Aotearoa New Zealand, formulated a model of relationality in which two peoples were to live, respectfully, side-by-side in our country. This treaty-based relationship underpins the partnership between Jenny and I, and is a critical element in evolving research collaborations and co-researcher collectives who will work alongside *Māori tamariki* (children) and *whānau* (parents). The relationships have developed through our ongoing partnership while facilitating *kanohi ki te kanohi* (face-to-face) professional learning programs. This platform enabled teachers, lecturers, *whānau Māori* (Māori families), and early childhood sector management to engage with us, allowing us all to build a working knowledge of each other's values, beliefs, ethics, and processes, which we were then able to carry forward into the TLRI projects. These shared professional learning experiences highlighted commitment to *Te Tiriti o Waitangi* partnership and established relationships anchored in trust, transparency, openness, and respect.

Wairuatanga (spiritual interconnectedness) recognizes *Māori* spiritual systems encoded within *Māori* literacies. The process of *whakatau* (greeting ceremony) is concerned with establishing a space of spiritual protection, of ensuring that *kanohi ki te kanohi* (face to face, in person) encounters are enhanced through interconnected spirituality. Indigenous articulation asserts that *karakia* (spiritual invocation) has the potential to shift one's state from *ordinary*, to one of raised spiritual awareness, which connects people with the heavens, the winds, the stars, those long since departed deities, and the forces of nature. The effect is to elevate everyday mental preoccupations to a higher state of awareness, thereby promoting improved understanding based on higher levels of contextualization. By connecting planes of thinking and symbolism there is a psychological energy flow away from the centre, outwards to broader conceptual domains, a centrifugal force away from micro dimensions (an individual, a single issue) to macro levels (groups, broad encounters, spiritual influences).

(Durie, 2002, p. 22)

Wairuatanga is significant to the collective well-being of our research cohort and co-researcher collective and therefore includes rituals that nurture the *rōpu* and the environment.

A *Māori* worldview prioritizes *manaakitanga* (caring, generosity, hospitality), with a reciprocal responsibility to uphold the *mana* (prestige, integrity) of people, to ensure that their prestige remains intact or is enhanced through shared interactions. This concept sets a premise and provides a blueprint of how we might behave ethically in conducting and representing ourselves within a research paradigm. Upholding prestige and demonstrating responsibility to the wider co-researcher collective offers an alternative way of being. Integral to this is respecting the ideas and contributions of others, of in fact encouraging co-researchers to draw from their expertise, creativity, and life experiences. It was not surprising to us that some of the educator co-researchers, having attended an initial one-day workshop at the start of each project, then proceeded to instigate and design their own particular research questions, generating their own research frameworks, thus providing leadership in *te ao Māori*. One co-researcher group articulated strongly an approach of contribution to *Māori* rather than of asking what *whānau Māori* might give to the center. This active belief upholds the idea of reciprocal responsibility, *whānau Māori* in turn responding to the *manaaki* (support) of the teachers. One of our roles was to *manaaki* co-researchers in their role in engaging and inviting *tamariki* and *whānau Māori* articulation, visibility, and validation of *te ao Māori*. We were privileged to be both collaborators and to be led within the research collaboratives.

Whakapapa (origins, genealogy) is a conceptual belief that has influenced all of our research projects. Our collective co-researcher *whakapapa* begins in the north of the North Island, in Auckland, moves to the Waikato region, across to Tauranga, through to Hawera and then on to the south of the South Island, to Dunedin. A *Māori* worldview prioritizes *kaitiakitanga* (exercising stewardship) of the land and applies a *te ao Māori* lens toward knowing, doing and being alongside the environment. Regional specificities pertaining to each area are evident, with co-researchers sharing local ecological engagement highlighting *tamariki* and *whānau* praxis of *Māori* knowledge and belief systems. As a *Te Tiriti* based partnership, Jenny and I honor the specificities of *hapū* and *iwi*, acknowledging the *mana* and prestige, the *mana whenua* (tribal precedence) of each area. Reflexive openness and responsiveness from the research cohort to *te ao Māori* resulted in narratives generated from *tamariki* and *whānau Māori* along with *Pākehā* voice resonating respect for *whakapapa*. The enactment of *whanaungatanga* (relationships) implies a principle of collectivism— individual contribution benefitting the collective and the collective benefitting all. It is an imperative part of our research methodology, a central foci being the organizing, at the beginning of each project of a collective research cohort *hui* (gathering). This *kanohi ki te kanohi* (sharing experience) allows faces to be seen and to be known. It opens spaces for dialogue, for questions, for discussion, through which is generated a sense of cohesion. Throughout the research projects, liaisons between the co-researchers in early childhood care and education centers are developed with *kanohi ki te kanohi* facilitation occurring throughout the year. We believe this to be critical in developing connected collaborative relationships.

Te ao Māori celebrates empowerment, with our co-researcher *ropū* applying self-empowering praxis through applying their own insights to their research design, evolving processes connected to *iwi* boundaries, taking opportunities to lead, and contributing to the collective in order to benefit all. Our co-researcher collaborative model supported transformative thinking and practice through the capacity of the educator co-researchers to shift from a dominant gaze and apply instead a *Te Tiriti o Waitangi* framed lens; to re-lens from the eye of an individual to that of the collective; recognizing and being responsive to *tamariki* and *whānau Māori* ways of knowing, doing, and being. That is revolutionary.

Ehara taku toa i te toa taki tahi, engari he toa taki tini
(My valor is not that of the individual, but that of the collective).

"Committed Sapiential Circles": Jenny Ritchie

In her 1978 foreword to a book written by my parents, Margaret Mead recognized the importance of a small nation such as New Zealand in offering examples of hope for the future, derived from such illuminations as

> long lineages and committed sapiential circles; for new ways in which the peoples of this planet, lost in an unrealised over-mechanical immensity, can again feel their feet firmly planted on some piece of loved earth, washed

by the seven seas and under an over-arching atmosphere which they share with all the peoples of the world. One of the great contributions which New Zealand can make is people, who after a healthy, happy childhood, relate to the natural world they love, are able to go anywhere—or stay at home—and make important contributions to an emerging world community.

(Mead, 1978, pp. xi–xii)

In our three TLRI studies (Ritchie et al., 2010; Ritchie & Rau, 2006, 2008), Cheryl and I, along with co-directors and educator co-researchers, have endeavored to facilitate, through long-standing, connected relationships, the illumination of the potentialities for *Tiriti based* pedagogies as signaled in *Te Whāriki. He whāriki mātauranga mō ngā mokopuna o Aotearoa: Early childhood curriculum* (Ministry of Education, 1996). These are pedagogies that validate a dual epistemological approach, honoring the promise of *Te Tiriti o Waitangi* to protect *Māori* resources and aspirations, by enacting *Māori* language, values, and cultural practices in an integrated, holistic way throughout the early childhood care and education program.

Both children and Indigenous peoples have a long history of having been treated as the objects of research studies, that is, having been *colonized* by researchers for many years (Harwood, 2010; Smith, 1999). Central to our methodological approach has been a commitment to a counter-colonial approach, deeply committed to including the voices of children generally as well as those of Indigenous scholars, educators, families, and children within the *sapiential circles* of relationality within our projects. In our first TLRI study (Ritchie & Rau, 2006), we had sought from educator co-researchers stories of children's experiences in early childhood care and education settings with a strong commitment to *Tiriti*-based practice, yet this had not been a particular focus in the data. So in our second and third projects (Ritchie et al., 2010; Ritchie & Rau, 2008), we asked our co-researchers to "foreground the voices of children" (Stephenson, 2009, p. 132) within their range of narrative data collection methodologies, relying on the depth of their relationships with *tamariki* and *whānau* to elicit material, rather than imposing ourselves into the settings to obtain data directly from children.

We followed our educator co-researchers' strategies with interest, as some of them experimented with various ways of *capturing* children's often elusive wisdom. Some of the methods that co-researchers employed were formal interviews with individual children; with the child and parent together; recording mat-time discussions; videoing children's activities; and gathering examples of children's art and accompanying narratives. We also learned from our co-researchers that we need not take our pursuit of *child voice* to be a search for an adult-determined mode of literacy. When the teachers and *whānau* of Belmont—*Te Kupenga* Kindergarten were invited by Tainui *kuia* (elders of the Tainui tribe) to the commemorations on the anniversary of the death of the *Māori* Queen *Te Arikinui*, Dame *Te Atairangikaahu*, the two teachers *Pera Paekau* and Pat Leyland spent hours preparing the children (and parents) from this multicultural urban kindergarten for the experience of attending the formal *pōwhiri* (greeting ceremony). Photos they shared with us afterwards showed the children playing absorbedly with river-stones on the bank of the Waikato River. Here was a narrative that while not portraying *literal child voice*, was imbued with deep layers of sentience and meaning.

Possibilities for Post/Counter-Colonial Research with Children

Early childhood care and education settings are sites of potentiality, of "immense possibility and power" (Batycky, 2008, p. 176), yet situated in contexts imbued with the historicity and legacy of colonization, racism, and cultural and economic inequities. Cannella and Viruru (2004) have alerted us to the pervasive nature of colonialist thinking, and how constructions of *child* and *education* are implicated within this. They challenge us to construct a *postcolonial disposition*, which problematizes the *will to power*, *othering*, and simplistic interpretations constructed by adults in the name of children (p. 155). This confronts us in regard to our commitment to perform post/counter-colonial research with children, and how we might conceive this research as praxis, that is "reflection and action upon the world in order to transform it" (Freire, 1972, p. 28). In a counter-colonialist praxis-oriented research mode, "children would be encouraged to engage in continual critique of the situations within which we have placed them" (Cannella & Viruru, 2004, p. 155). Further, this ongoing praxis needs to engage with both "local and global community actions" as determined by the children themselves (p. 155).

When we view and relate to children as agentic and powerful, we recognize their *mana* and *tino rangatiratanga* (self-determination). Our most recent project, *Titiro Whakamuri, Hoki Whakamua. We are the future, the present and the past: caring for self, others and the environment in early years' teaching and learning* (Ritchie et al., 2010), demonstrated children's agency, supported through the *kaupapa* (philosophy) of the research project as enacted and facilitated by committed educator co-researchers. Children demonstrated their empathy and compassion for *Papatūanuku* (Mother Earth) and *Ranginui* (Sky Father), and were actively and consciously pursuing practices that would protect *Papatūanuku* and *Ranginui*, such as recycling, beach, and park clean-ups, tree-planting, gardening, and so forth. Parents and communities were also drawn into these activities, demonstrating the catalytic potential of young children, supported by responsive, engaged adults, of revolutionary transformative praxis who were in service of our planet.

Eric Malewski (2005), in his epilogue to Soto and Swadener's edited collection *Power and Voice in Research with Young Children* (Soto & Swadener, 2005), has called for "precocious methodologies" that resist and transcend traditional, formal modes of researching with children whereby "the authority invested in the investigator is one of omnipotence, of orchestrating research protocols and delicately pulling already formulated thought from [children's] minds" (Malewski, 2005, p. 219). For Malewski:

> Precociousness indicates an enacted nature, a symbiotic view of research as a foundation for participatory democratic education that integrates the belief that all people deserve high-quality, rigorous schooling with research and assessment that is culturally relevant ... and methodologies that emerge from various subcultures, informed by the dispossessed and made relevant through nuanced understandings of voice.
>
> (Malewski, 2005, pp. 220–221)

He pātai anō (Some Questions for Further Reflection)

This section of our chapter ends, in the spirit of *Te Whāriki* (Ministry of Education, 1996), with a series of *questions for reflection*. We are always asking ourselves, and each other, questions, especially those that focus on how we might conduct ourselves alongside our research cohort of educator co-researchers, *tamariki* and *whānau*. One of the frameworks that we have found useful is that offered by Bishop (2005). A particular question arising from his work is: "How will those who contribute to this research project benefit from their participation?"

Further questions that we might consider in future research endeavors are: How will the *kaupapa* of this study contribute to social, cultural and environmental justice? How *precocious* are we in our research design? How attentive are we in establishing our research foci, processes, and collectives, of embedding *Tiriti o Waitangi* based/decolonizing commitments? How do we, in our research design and processes simultaneously maintain responsiveness to the *taonga* (treasures) of the local Indigenous people, along with the richness of cultural diversity present in many early childhood care and education contexts? How can we ensure that we, and our educator co-researchers, maintain a strong ethical reflexivity (Phelan &

Kinsella, 2013) throughout the research process? Finally, in what ways can we allow children to determine the research focus, in order that it follow a praxis orientation responsive to children's priorities, one that operates from a democratic, participatory paradigm (Pascal & Bertram, 2009), while retaining our role as facilitators of research and education committed to social, cultural, and environmental justice?

Notes

1. The New Zealand Teaching and Learning Initiative (TLRI) is a government funding body for the education sector, which aims to support research collaborations between practitioners and researchers. We would like to acknowledge the TLRI for their funding of our various projects. For further information about the TLRI, see their website http://www.tlri.org.nz/.
2. *Te Tiriti o Waitangi* (The Treaty of Waitangi) is the 1840 agreement between the British Crown and *Māori* chiefs, which preceded the settlement of *Aotearoa* New Zealand by the British. In exchange for ceding to Britain the role of governance, *Māori* were promised their ongoing chieftainship and self-determination over their resources and everything of value to them as well as equal citizenship rights with the British.
3. Educator co-researchers and *kuia/kaumātua* (elders) who are named in this chapter were also identified in the original research reports and have consented to having their real names used in subsequent publications.
4. Playcentre is a national New Zealand parent cooperative early childhood and family education organization that offers early learning sessions and parent education programs.

References

Batycky, J. (2008). Early childhood voices: Who is really talking? *Contemporary Issues in Early Childhood, 9*(2), 173–177.

Bishop, R. (1996). *Collaborative research stories: Whakawhanaungatanga.* Palmerston North, NZ: Dunmore Press.

Bishop, R. (2005). Freeing ourselves from neocolonial domination in research: A kaupapa Māori approach to creating knowledge. In N. K. Denzin & Y. S. Lincoln (Eds.), *The sage handbook of qualitative research* (3rd ed., pp. 109–164). Thousand Oaks, CA: Sage.

Cannella, G., & Viruru, R. (2004). *Childhood and (post) colonization: Power, education and contemporary practice.* London, UK: Routledge.

Cannella, G. S., & Lincoln, Y. S. (2004). Epilogue: Claiming a critical public social science: Reconceptualizing and redeploying research. *Qualitative Inquiry, 10*(2), 298–309.

Cuomo, C. (1998). *Feminism and ecological communities: An ethic of flourishing.* London, UK: Routledge.

Dalli, C., Rockel, J., Duhn, I., Craw, J., & Doyle, K. (2011). *What's special about teaching and learning in the first years? Investigating the "what, hows and whys" of relational pedagogy with infants and toddlers*. Wellington, NZ: Teaching and Learning Research Initiative. Retrieved from http://www.tlri.org.nz/sites/default/files/projects/9267_summaryreport.pdf.

Dockett, S., & Sumsion, J. (2004). Australian research in early childhood education: Contexts, tensions, challenges and future directions. *The Australian Educational Researcher, 31*(3), 3–18.

Duhn, I. (2010). Professionalism/s. In J. L. Miller & C. Cable (Eds.), *Professionalization, leadership and management in the early years* (pp. 133–146). London, UK: Sage.

Duhn, I., Bachmann, M., & Harris, K. (2010). Becoming ecologically sustainable in early childhood education. *Early Childhood Folio, 14*(1), 2–7.

Durie, M. (2002, November). Is there a distinctive Māori psychology? Paper presented at the *National Māori Graduates of Psychology Symposium: Making a difference*. University of Waikato, Hamilton, New Zealand.

Ellsworth, A. (2005). *Places of learning: Media, architecture, pedagogy*. New York, NY: RoutledgeFalmer.

Freire, P. (1972). *Pedagogy of the Oppressed*. London, UK: Penguin.

Gough, N. (2009). Becoming transnational: Rhizosemiosis, complicated conversation and curriculum inquiry. In M. McKenzie, P. Hart, B. Heeson, & B. Jickling (Eds.), *Fields of green: Restorying culture, environment, and education* (pp. 67–84). Cresskill, NJ: Hampton Press.

Halba, H., McCallum, R., & Holmes, H. (2011). Tū Taha, Tū Kaha: Transcultural dialogues. Hilary Halba and Rua McCallum with Huata Holmes. *Australasian Drama Studies, 59*, 69–87.

Harwood, D. (2010). Finding a voice for child participants within doctoral research: Experiences from the field. *Australasian Journal of Early Childhood, 35*(4), 4–13.

Haynes, M., Cardno, C., & Craw, J. (2007). *Enhancing mathematics teaching and learning in early childhood settings. Final report to the Teaching & Learning Research Initiative Project*. Wellington, NZ: Teaching and Learning Research Initiative. Retrieved from http://www.tlri.org.nz/tlri-research/research-completed/ece-sector/enhancing-mathematics-teaching-and-learning-early

Kvale, S., & Brinkman, S. (2009). *Interviews: Learning the craft of qualitative research interviewing*. Los Angeles, CA: Sage.

Langan, D., & Morton, M. (2009). Reflecting on community/academic 'collaboration': The challenge of 'doing' feminist participatory action research. *Action Research, 7*(2), 165–184.

Malewski, E. (2005). Epilogue: When children and youth talk back. Precocious research practices and the cleverest voices. In L. D. Soto & B. B. Swadener (Eds.), *Power and voice in research with children* (pp. 215–222). New York, NY: Peter Lang.

Mazzei, L. A., & Jackson, A. Y. (2009). Introduction: The limit of voice. In L. A. Mazzei & A. Y. Jackson (Eds.), *Voice in qualitative inquiry: Challenging conventional, interpretive, and critical conceptions in qualitative research* (pp. 1–14). New York, NY: Routledge.

Mead, M. (1978). Foreword. In J. Ritchie & J. Ritchie (Eds.), *Growing up in New Zealand* (pp. ix–xii). Sydney, Australia: George Allen & Unwin.

Ministry of Education. (1996). *Te Whāriki. He whāriki mātauranga mō ngā mokopuna o Aotearoa: Early childhood curriculum.* Wellington, NZ: Learning Media. Retrieved from http://www.educate.ece.govt.nz/~/media/Educate/Files/Reference%20Downloads/whariki.pdf.

Nuttall, J. (2010, November). *The contribution of the Teaching and Learning Research Initiative to building knowledge about teaching and learning: A review of early years projects, 2004–2010.* Paper presented to TLRI Early Years Symposium, Wellington, New Zealand.

Olsson, L. (2009). *Movement and experimentation in young children's learning: Deleuze and Guattari in early childhood education.* London, UK/New York, NY: Routledge.

Pascal, C., & Bertram, T. (2009). Listening to young citizens: The struggle to make real a participatory paradigm in research with young children. *European Early Childhood Education Research Journal, 17*(2), 249–262.

Phelan, S. K., & Kinsella, E. A. (2013). Picture this...safety, dignity, and voice—ethical research with children: Practical considerations for the reflexive researcher. *Qualitative Inquiry, 19*(2), 81–90.

Rhedding-Jones, J. (2008). The OECD and the notion of expert in early childhood education and care: A play. *International Critical Childhood Policy Studies, 1*(1), 28–41.

Ritchie, J., Duhn, I., Rau, C., & Craw, J. (2010). *Titiro Whakamuri, Hoki Whakamua. We are the future, the present and the past: Caring for self, others and the environment in early years' teaching and learning. Final report for the Teaching and Learning Research Initiative.* Wellington, NZ: Teaching and Learning Research Initiative. Retrieved from http://www.tlri.org.nz/sites/default/files/projects/9260-finalreport.pdf.

Ritchie, J., & Rau, C. (2006). *Whakawhanaungatanga. Partnerships in bicultural development in early childhood education. Final report to the Teaching & Learning Research Initiative Project.* Wellington, NZ: Teaching Learning Research Institute. Retrieved from http://www.tlri.org.nz/pdfs/9207_finalreport.pdf.

Ritchie, J., & Rau, C. (2008). *Te Puawaitanga—partnerships with tamariki and whānau in bicultural early childhood care and education. Final report to the Teaching Learning Research Initiative.* Wellington, NZ: Teaching Learning Research Institute. Retrieved from http://www.tlri.org.nz/pdfs/9238_finalreport.pdf.

Smith, L. T. (1999). *Decolonizing methodologies. Research and indigenous peoples.* London, UK: Zed Books Ltd.

Soto, L. D., & Swadener, B. B. (Eds.). (2005). *Power and voice in research with children.* New York, NY: Peter Lang.

Stephenson, A. (2009). Horses in the sandpit: Photography, prolonged involvement and 'stepping back' as strategies for listening to children's voices. *Early Child Development and Care, 179*(2), 131–141.

Sumsion, J., Harrison, L., Press, F., McLeod, S., Goodfellow, J., & Bradley, B. (2011). Researching infants' experiences of early childhood education and care. In

D. Harcourt, B. Perry, & T. Waller (Eds.), *Researching young children's perspectives: Debating the ethics and dilemmas of educational research with children* (pp. 113–127). London, UK: Routledge.

Tanggaard, L. (2009). The research interview as a dialogical context for the production of social life and personal narratives. *Qualitative Inquiry, 15*(9), 1498–1515.

Taylor, E. W. (2008). Transformative learning theory. *New Directions for Adult and Continuing Education, 2008*(119), 5–15.

Tuck, E. (2010). Breaking up with Deleuze: Desire and valuing the irreconcilable. *International Journal of Qualitative Studies in Education, 23*(5), 635–650.

van Enk, A. A. J. (2009). The shaping effects of the conversational interview. An examination using Bakhtin's theory of genre. *Qualitative Inquiry, 15*(7), 1265–1286.

7

An Ongoing Exploration of Uncertainty: Ethical Identities—Ours and Children's

Kim Atkinson and Enid Elliot, with input from the Victoria IQ group

Introduction

Kim and I have been thinking together about issues in early childhood practice since 2007. I have been involved in a research project, *Investigating Quality* (IQ), (Pacini-Ketchabaw, Nxumalo, Kocher, Elliot, & Sanchez, 2013) that had begun in 2006 under the auspices of the University of Victoria, British Columbia (BC), Canada. This project invited early childhood educators to gather together to think critically, question assumptions, and look more deeply into their practice. Kim had joined the monthly meetings in the second year as a preschool teacher from a local cooperative preschool where she was the teacher of a group of 18 children with parents helping her; she was an articulate and reflective member of our group.

The IQ project was a five-year project and involved several groups of educators in different locations: Vancouver, Victoria; online; and for a year in Nelson, BC. The groups had 10–15 participants who volunteered to spend an afternoon a month looking closely at their practice by sharing ideas, reading current papers, and questioning long-held assumptions. Centers were given money to hire substitutes in order that staff could attend what we called *Learning Circles*. As a facilitator with the initial groups, I (Enid Elliot) listened and reflected with the educators as we explored some of our beliefs and questioned some of our common understandings of our practice. As topics arose, I shared resources and ideas to challenge and provide inspiration for thinking.

Each year the Learning Circles met together in a *Sharing Circle*. These Sharing Circles had speakers from other contexts who shared their practice and ideas in order to expand our local thinking and learning. During each Sharing Circle, each group would share some of the work with which they had been engaged.

In the last Sharing Circle before the project ended, our group created a collage of narratives to reflect some of our struggles. For several years we had been thinking of some of the difficult places that are found in practice. Early on in our group two years before Kim's investigation with the *Bad Guy Beavers*, which she recounts below, an educator from North Vancouver Island had shared an emotional reaction to gunplay at her center. This particular topic triggered deeply felt reactions in our group and was revisited several times and in different forms. Our discussions over the next two years formed a background to Kim's subsequent decision to listen carefully to the children's deep interest in bad guy play and to wonder what an ethical response would be.

The Victoria group asked Kim to present her narrative, which is recounted below, as it reflected our explorations of early childhood practice as a *pedagogy of uncertainty* (Britzman, 2009) and our questions about children's and educators' ethical responsibilities. As Kim said, "we wanted to highlight the silences, the places where we are frozen" (personal communication, Kim Atkinson, 2011). Too often we are faced with small injustices, unkind comments, or even larger issues to which we do not know how to respond or even think. Within our own particular group, we had created for ourselves a space that felt safe for that thinking; we worked to reserve judgment about others' difficult choices. After being part of our discussions, Kim had taken a careful decision to explore the idea of listening deeply to children and she found herself in a place of discomfort over the year that this narrative unfolded. Sharing this narrative (below) with the other Provincial groups, who had engaged in their own process, Kim felt vulnerable, aware that this piece might be controversial. While we presented other stories alongside this one to illustrate some of the issues we had struggled with as a group, this one created emotional reactions from the Sharing Circle.

The following narrative raises issues that many educators do not usually want to explore. The traditional stance among early childhood programs is to ban guns and bad guy play. Many educators believe that gunplay and bad guy play leads to increased violence. This story might lend credence to that belief, but perhaps the time the children spent in exploring these issues allowed them to develop a deeper understanding of *badness*. In the year leading up to this narration, we had looked at Edmiston's (2008) work on children developing ethical identities where he argues, "in pretend play people create space-times where through evaluation of the deeds of possible selves they form and shape their ethical identities" (p. 23).

This narrative is an example of children's play that often goes untold. Our group realized over our time together that there are other stories that challenged our emotions and thinking. Within a caring and supportive group these stories can be shared, new perspectives gained, and new narratives created.

Kim's Story

Four boys have stacked large blocks to create a wall and they now crouch behind it, peering over the top now and again. A group of girls walk by and the boys spring into action. They point long narrow blocks at the passing girls and shout: "Shoot the girls! Only the girls!" They make shooting noises as they train their *guns* on the girls. The girls quickly leave the area and the boys continue the conversation:

> "This is my gun"
> "But they can also be skis right?"
> "No we can hide here"
> "This is a gun. You guys sit here"
> "Shoot the girls, only the girls. Shoot the teacher!"
> "Put them here. Hide them quick you guys."
> "My bullet can shoot through a window."
> "If someone's talking you say 'Yes Sir' (saluting) and you walk 'Huh Huh Huh!' " (marching)
> "What power does your gun shoot?"
> "One hundred and sixty-eight meters"
> "Mine shoots fire"
> "My gun shoots pistols"

As the boys prepare to go outside, they discuss what they are going to play. They decide to play the game they have invented, called "Surrender Die," and as soon as they are outside they begin running and shouting, "Kill the girls!"

Later that week I receive an email from a parent:

> I am writing to you for some advice on how to respond to (my daughter) Maria. She is still worrying about coming to school because of relationships

with some of the *bad guy* boys. Yesterday she told me that she needed to have her hair straightened before she went back to school "so Tori won't know it's me." "Or else they will kill me," she added.

The boys called themselves *Bad Guy Beavers* and spying, shooting girls, stockpiling weapons, fighting and being *bad guys* made up their constant occupation for the year we (at the preschool) spent together. The *Bad Guy Beavers* led me, along with the other children and the parents, into places of tension and discomfort, of stormy confrontations and of great silences. We were all caught up in the tales they told, some of us were frightened, some angry or appalled, some were judgmental, and others felt judged.

As the sole educator in the preschool, I struggled to listen to all the voices, and to find my own voice. Uncertainty became my constant companion as I peered into *the cracks* of my practice. One question kept surfacing for me: what is my ethical responsibility?

In the years prior to encountering the *Bad Guy Beavers*, I, like so many early childhood educators, adhered to a strict *No Guns* policy in my work with children. I routinely used phrases such as "We don't use guns. Can you make that into something else?" Often the response was a pleading "But we're just pretending!" to which I replied, "But we don't want to even pretend to hurt people, do we?" I neither expected nor waited for a reply.

At meetings with parents, I informed them of this policy and it was never challenged. Either the idea was consistent with their personal philosophies, or my perceived authority as an early childhood expert deterred dissention.

But where did such unquestioning acceptance of this rule originate? In 25 years of working in various childcare settings, I had never seen a written policy instructing educators to adhere to this approach, nor were there any directives from governing bodies such as licensing regulations. As Penny Holland (2003) observed:

> [Z]ero tolerance practices are not explicitly based on any hard evidence of a causal connection between early toy gun, weapon and super hero play and the development of aggressive behavior, but rather on a common sense, nurture-based belief that there might well be, and that no harm could be done by acting on that assumption. While few practitioners make specific reference to theory or research supporting this assumption, many believe that such research exists and supports a zero tolerance approach. (p. 10)

The *No Guns* rule fitted with my feminist perspective. By disrupting gendered stereotyped violent play with proactive interventions, I could do my part to create a new generation of non-violent boys. It was best practice.

Or was it? When I joined with the early childhood practitioners in the IQ Project and we began a dialogue about our practice, we, tentatively at first, talked of our shared experiences and, over time as trust was built within the group, engaged more deeply and more reflectively, allowing more of ourselves to be revealed. Slowly, we began to touch on issues we had never previously discussed, issues we thought were outside the realm of early childhood care. We opened dialogues on power, violence, gender, racialization, sexuality, and politics, and reflected on our image of the child. We examined our assumptions about the ability to *know* a child through the developmental theories that dominated our field. Within a relationship of trust, we negotiated new understandings and opened ourselves to a *pedagogy of uncertainty* (Britzman, 2009).

Central to these dialogues was critical reflection. I began to ask questions of myself, examining my routines, my rules, my *daily-ness* that had become the truths of my practice. I asked myself: why and how had these truths become so embedded, so certain? How was it that I had the power to decide that these truths were privileged? And whose voices were silenced by my rules and my assumptions of what was right? My certainties were beginning to crumble.

What was it about *gun play* that I was afraid of? What would happen if I no longer enforced the *No Gun* rule? These were new questions, uncomfortable questions, but once they were raised I could not ignore them. I began to consider my role as an educator, the choices I made and the effects those choices had on children and myself. As MacNaughton (2005) notes,

> Education is about choices—for example, choices to 'do' curriculum in particular ways, choices to prioritize one set of goals over another and choices to address an issue or not. Each of these choices is linked to a set of meanings about who a child is, what education is for and who should take decisions about what the child needs. (p. 105)

By critically reflecting on my practice I was becoming aware of "taken-for-granted ways of knowing and acting that remain unquestioned precisely because they seem natural to us" (MacNaughton, 2005, p. 10).

The conversations in our IQ group became more intense as we stripped away layers of meanings around gun play, violence, aggression, and power, both real and pretend. We examined how the image of the *innocent child* played into our discomfort. We wondered for whom we imposed the rules—the children or the parents? We wondered why gun play continued despite our collective efforts to make it *go away*. These dialogues took us to places of vulnerability, pushed us to reconsider core values, and allowed us to expose moments in our practice of which we were not proud and in which we responded to a child in anger or frustration or with silence.

As we shared of ourselves, we built a community of collegiality where determining answers was not the goal. Instead we found satisfaction and reassurance in the collaboration, the multiple perspectives enriching our understandings. Within the uncertainty, I had support, which in turn gave me the courage to experiment with change. And so I took a tentative step: a few boys made guns from a construction toy and I simply observed, saying nothing. I was beginning a process that Davies (2011) terms "open listening": "Such listening is not a simple extension of usual practices of listening. It involves working, to some extent, against oneself, and against those habitual practices through which one establishes 'this is who I am'" (p. 4).

I had just begun to dip my toes into *working against myself*, and wondering *who I am* when the *Bad Guy Beavers* entered my preschool. As Carlina Rinaldi puts it, "I had to decide what kind of teacher I wanted to be, what kind of human I wanted to be" (presentation at University of Victoria, July 2012).

The preschool in which I worked was a cooperative where parents participated as teacher assistants on a rotating schedule, and attended regular parent meetings. As the only educator, I built close relationships with families. Parents felt connected to the preschool, knew all the children, and were keen observers of all that happened in the classroom.

The class of 18 children had been with me the previous year as three-year-olds, and now they were four. The *Bad Guy Beavers* were composed of a group of eight boys; some were bad guys every day, others moved in and out of the play. A few boys in the preschool group never joined in, and none of the girls participated. The eight *Bad Guy Beavers* established themselves a couple of months into the school year with this story:

> We go Cha! And then we eat some wood. This time we eat wood. We are beaver spies. When we see writing cha cha cha we want to write too. Cha cha cha. We go and fight people and then we go and get girls and then we turn them into wood and we eat them. Cha cha cha. We eat wood all the time, every night too. Cha cha cha. Birds come and eat the worms and they bring them to us and we eat them. And then they turn into wood. Then we pooed them out. And we go cheer cheer cha cha cha.

Every day the *Bad Guy Beavers* would find their fort, create their arsenal, then begin spying and shooting at girls. There was constant conflict and hurt feelings among themselves; they hit, pinched, and called each another names. Angry and tearful, they accused one another of being mean. The girls were afraid to be in the same area as the boys, and parents were nervous as well, alarmed and unsure how to respond. I spent all my time monitoring and watching the boys, feeling that I was abandoning the rest of the class.

I used strategies that many would. I negotiated conflict by having the boys talk with one another. I encouraged empathy, reminded about kindness, asked how everyone felt. But where previously I would have simply shut down the play, I now felt an ethical responsibility to listen. Davies (2011) suggests:

> Open listening makes the listener vulnerable to the not-yet-known.... On the part of the teacher, it involves the courage to let go of oneself as a figure of certainty and authority. It involves opening oneself to an ongoing process of what Deleuze (1994) named differentiation, that is, to becoming other to oneself, and to a process of evolution that takes the self beyond what it already knows. (p. 4)

These boys were giving voice to ideas, thoughts, and images that were powerful and scary: what would the consequences be if I refused to listen? I needed to go *beyond what I knew*.

I wanted to extend my understanding about children's conceptualization of good guys and bad guys, so I asked some questions:

> Kim: "What is a bad guy?"
> "Robbers and be rude and steal stuff."
> "Be really bad. They kiss girls!"
> "Good guys kill bad guys in a movie."
> Kim: "Are bad guys bad all the time?"
> "Yes, bad guys are bad all the time."
> "Can be both. Bad guys can be good."
> Kim: "Do your families like this game?" Twelve children say, "No."
> One child says, "Yes."
> Mary: "Sometimes I like to play Batman, I like to play bad guys in Batman. I only play bad guys with a friend or by myself. I could be a mermaid bad guy."
> Nina: "I like to play good guy as long there's no bad guy."
> Thomas: "A bad guy you chase around and you go to jail.
> *Bad Guy Beavers* just fight and eat girls."
> Kim: "Why do they fight?"
> Thomas: "'cause they eat girl food."
> Nina: "I don't really like that part of the story. Everything Thomas says is about dying."
> Freddie: "They kind of do bad stuff like hurt people. They really hurt people. Really hurt. I know, I play it."

Kim: "Is it pretend or real?"
Everyone agrees: Pretend game.

This conversation revealed some nuances in the children's thinking that was not apparent in their play, such as the idea that bad guys could sometimes be good, and that some girls were not entirely opposed to bad guys and would, in fact, play it under certain circumstances, such as when they were with a friend, though Nina was clear that she did not like bad guys and did not want to play death. Freddie's statement that bad guys really hurt people and he knew because he played it, suggests that he recognized that hurting in play and hurting in real life were quite separate. The children were unanimous that the play was a pretend game, which makes me wonder if we, as adults, are the ones who are confused about pretend and real.

Despite my best efforts to engage the girls in talking about the bad guys, this was the first time they had spoken of their concerns. I felt I needed to give them greater voice, a way into the dialogue, so I wrote a story that incorporated elements of stories they had previously dictated to me, as O'Loughlin (2009) says, "to return to the [girls] what is already theirs, but now in a manner that increases their capacity to own their own histories" (p. 19), and to negotiate their understanding.

> Once upon a time there was a curious girl named Goldilocks who was walking in the jungle with her jungle cats and jungle dogs. As they walked they touched the shiny leaves and vines that hung from the trees. They listened to the thud thud thud of the buffalo running. It sounded like this:
>
> Thud Thud Cha cha cha
>
> Thud thud cha cha cha
>
> The jungle cats and the jungle dogs did a jungle dance.
>
> Goldilocks and the jungle cats and the jungle dogs kept walking. They heard some jungle birds. They looked up where the birds were flying and there was a princess sitting in a tree eating pineapple. Goldilocks said 'Come on down' so the princess jumped but she didn't fall because she had wings and she could fly. They kept walking together in the jungle and suddenly they heard a terrible sound, terrible hissing, terrible gnashing of teeth. It was snakes having a wild rumpus. 'Let's get out of here' said Goldilocks. So the princess and Goldilocks and the jungle cats and the jungle dogs ran and ran. Then they saw a puff of smoke. It was a little dragon. 'Hello, my name is Puff' said the dragon. 'Do you want to go to a land named Honah Lee?' 'Yes' said Goldilocks and the princess. The jungle cats and the jungle dogs did another jungle dance.

Thud thud cha cha cha

Thud thud cha cha cha

That meant yes.

So they all got on a boat and they crossed the ocean that was full of sharks. They came to a land called Honah Lee and they went to a house and had some tea and went to sleep.

Everyone sings Puff the Magic Dragon

The girls enthusiastically embraced the story and acted it out, with the boys taking on the roles of the snakes and the sharks. But the girls remained in control of the narrative and kept the sharks and snakes at a distance. As Rinaldi (2006) notes: "metaphorical language, precisely because it is more undefined, allusive and sometimes ambiguous, but at the same time open to new concepts, becomes the only tool available to the new understanding that is seeking to emerge" (p. 76). Edmiston (2008) agrees, asserting that children interpret play events metaphorically, as a means of inquiry into "possible ways that people can relate to each other" (p. 68). He proposes that within this play children are involved in complex ethical situations, taking on the perspective of other identities, evaluating them, and by doing so begin *authoring* their own identities. He says:

> By projecting into the viewpoints and actions of the heroes, monsters, and people in whatever narratives engage them, children inquire about those aspects of life that are difficult to examine in the everyday world. How do you experience and contemplate the power to kill, the power to heal, or the power to love? How do you discover what might happen if you really hurt someone without actually hurting? How do you know how to respond to violence without being in danger?
>
> (Edmiston, 2008, p. 75)

Re-conceptualizing bad guy play as a metaphor, as a tool to explore themes of power, courage, fear, and compassion allowed me to reimagine my role. These children needed to investigate difficult, frightening narratives and they needed to be heard. They trusted me to listen, felt safe enough within our preschool community, within our relationship, that I would serve as the "receiver of (their) unconscious knowledge" (O'Loughlin, 2009, p. 30). Just as within our IQ group, we created a place of trust in which we could reveal our difficult stories; the children trusted me and revealed their difficult stories. Having someone listen to us gives us meaning, identity, value. Rinaldi (2006) tells us

> Listening legitimizes the other person, because communication is one of the fundamental means of giving form to thought. The communicative act that takes place through listening produces meanings and reciprocal modifications that enrich all the participants in this type of exchange. (p. 126)

But it is not enough to simply listen passively, I needed to be prepared to move into what Davies (2011) calls "ethical teaching" which involves relinquishing the status quo and opening up "to a more multiple and fluid reality." She calls on us to

> listen without judgment, and with an openness of mind that does not rest on the fixing of one's own, or the other's identity. It involves abandoning the demands of ego and resisting the allure of seemingly neutral and reasonable normalizing discourses.
>
> (Davies, 2011, p. 15)

The *normalizing discourse* here may be that these are *challenging behaviors* that need to be *fixed*. This discourse assumes that children who behave in *socially unacceptable ways* are too immature to find solutions and should be *taught how to behave*. My role as teacher would be to decide on some guiding rules, explain to children why these rules are important, and enforce them (MacNaughton, Hughes, & Smith, 2007).

But I could not ignore the refrain of *ethical teaching* that had lodged itself in my mind. I knew that creating and enforcing my rules would be disrespectful, a misuse of power, would diminish the agency of children, and likely wouldn't work anyway. The simplistic act of creating a rule would deny the complexity of life in our preschool. Davies (2011) tells us that "ethical teaching" involves "living in the complexity of one's life and adhering to the truth of that complexity, a truth that involves assuming responsibility for the way one's desires and psychic investments conjure and inform that irreducible complexity" (p. 15).

I had a close and very affectionate relationship with each of the *Bad Guy Beavers*, and I could catch glimpses of what might lie behind the play. They each had their own uncertainties: about who they were in the preschool, about who they might become. I sensed that some boys carried the persona of the *Bad Guy Beaver* as a shield, to guard against vulnerability, others found in it a way to experiment with power and courage, others wanted the camaraderie, the mutual narrative. These were my musings, my hunches, certainly incomplete for we will never truly know another's full story. But I was aware that each *Bad Guy Beaver* had a story; I was not willing to make rule that told them their story was wrong.

As the school year went on, the play continued unchanged as the boys yelled, "Get the girls!" and argued and fought among themselves. I continued to ask questions, to talk to the boys about respect, empathy, kindness, to listen to one another, to think of how the girls might feel. Parents took me aside to express their concerns with the bad guy play, told me their children were afraid, that they themselves were afraid to be in the area where the boys played. Another parent approached me upset and frustrated at being judged as the parent of a *bad guy*.

As with the boys, I had close relationships with the parents, so as they shared their concerns, I could also share my thinking. I talked about how I saw the *Bad Guy Beavers* as exploring themes of good and evil, power and courage, and how I could not ethically ask them to stop. We talked of the fears of the other children, and what we could do to create spaces for their voices to be heard alongside the *Bad Guy Beavers*. We all felt uncomfortable with the gendered aspect of the play but had no clear solution. Within our relationships of trust these dialogues between the parents and I were emotional, but respectful. No one hinted they might withdraw their child from the program, and if they disagreed with my approach, they did not say so.

The girls acted out their story but couldn't find their voice to directly address the boys. It was clear they did not like the play but they seemed unable to articulate it to me or to the boys. Our daily group time had become a time for the boys to discuss the *Bad Guy Beaver* play, to talk about the arguments and hurt feelings. The girls would listen attentively, and though I invited them to speak, they remained silent. Months went by until finally Maria spoke out during one of these discussions.

> *Maria*: "I don't think you can trap us, not kill us or anything. I want them to have happy things and have a nice time. I want the bad guy to not put us in jail. I want to get them to be kind. I want to get them to be nice."
> *Mary*: "I don't want them to fight us and chase us."
> *Cara*: "They can't run and catch me and put you in jail."
> *Freddie*: "They don't like us chopping them up for eating."
> *Marc*: "And definitely not with real knives."
> *Neil*: "They probably don't like playing that game."

The boys listen, but as soon as they go outside Thomas and Casey shout, "Let's get the girls!" I remind them of what the girls have said and ask them what we should do. They decide to stop playing this game until they go to kindergarten. They tell me they need a note that they will keep in their pockets as a reminder:

> I want to remember that we can play the star wars game and Surrender Die game when we are in kindergarten.
> And the Surrender Die game we have to remember.

A few days later Thomas told me that they would only kill pretend bad guys. This came at the beginning of the play without any previous conversation from me. Later, Jona pointed to Thomas and said, "He's using a gun." I asked, "Did you decide not to use guns today?" Jona replied, "Yes."

These boys were wrestling with ethical issues, about what it is to be right or good. They were choosing their own responses, not adhering to an imposed response. As Edmiston (2008) says, "We want children, as ethical beings, both to take responsibility for their actions and to be ready to question other people's actions, in particular events and specific relationships" (p. 177). He also says that, "when children have the opportunity to experiment with multiple identities in their play (not just identities adults approve of) they can test actions, evaluate characters and begin authoring their own ethical identities" (p. 19).

As I struggled with my uncertainty and the *Bad Guy Beavers*, I knew that within the IQ group I would be listened to, heard, and not judged. Our conversations went to difficult places, and focused on topics that we had never previously discussed in our practice. But all of us in our IQ group felt safe going to these difficult places together, discussing these difficult topics. Together we recognized and acknowledged the emotion, the tension, our fears and our vulnerability in opening ourselves to these dialogues. Answers or agreement on the *right way* to respond to guns, violence, power and fear never emerged, and we came to see it was opening the dialogue that mattered. We saw that uncertainty had become our constant companion, and as time went by it became a companion we could feel comfortable with.

The ongoing dialogue reframed our image of ourselves from *educator as expert* to *educator as co-learner*, and gave us a voice to begin to talk with children and parents about the difficult issues, the places of silence. From the safety of IQ we could begin to see beyond the bounds of *the good teacher* who has all the answers and controls the program, including what is talked about and what is not. We were liberated to explore possibilities (MacNaughton, 2005, p. 59) of becoming a different kind of teacher who is open to uncertainty, who questions, listens, and who explores the uncomfortable.

With that liberation to explore possibilities came the courage to take risks, to try new approaches, to "provide space to move through different terrains" (MacNaughton, 2005, p. 59). I felt safe to approach issues, terrains, and topics I would have left unexplored before IQ. By not silencing the issues the children brought to me, but instead listening, being open to dialogue about guns, violence, fear, and hurt, I could create a space of safety for children to move through their difficult issues and terrains. The *Bad Guy Beavers* needed the preschool as a place of safety and trust where they could explore their story, just as I needed IQ as a place of safety and trust to explore mine.

Enid's Reflection

For the Sharing Circles, each Learning Circle would chose narratives to share with the other groups that reflected some aspects of our journey that year. Our group had asked Kim to share a PowerPoint of this story, which she had shared with the group. We presented it along with an introduction, which I wrote, and two other stories from other participants. Working on this chapter we met to discuss this narrative again with members of our IQ group, as well as we discussed our reflections on the process of presenting the narrative to the larger audience.

Kim's story revealed some of the struggles facing many educators in our group. Early childhood educators, like many adults, are tempted to offer to children a simple view of life: safe, trustworthy, and reasonable. Violence and gender issues are hard topics to discuss. Children know these issues are complex; they want to think about them deeply as they understand at some level that *Bad Guy Beavers* can be both bad and good. While the play was *pretend*, it was also real and while the boys were going to eat the girls, they didn't and some of the girls also wanted to play. Through the game the children created dialogues with their teacher, with their parents and among each other.

In our IQ group we often found ourselves wondering about issues that seemed to have no easy answers and we began to realize how often we might choose to close places of ambiguity by creating a rule, such as, *no guns*. The *Bad Guy Beavers* challenge our belief about children as *innocent* and in need of protection. These children sense the ambiguity in the world and the difficult issues; they see or sense that life is more complicated. Children actively explore the darker side of life, which can create tensions for educators. Children struggle with issues of power, control, and relationship and their ethical responses, so do educators. These are legitimate struggles and we have a responsibility to think about them with children and with each other. It can be difficult because some of the ambiguities can mirror our own tensions.

In their daily work situations, early childhood practitioners can find themselves in places of ambivalence and experience longings, desires, and conflicts (Elliot, 2013); at times they can be overwhelmed by the tensions they find in their work. Hoffman (2004) writes, "It is ambiguity, not certainty that poses a threat to our convictions and forces us into harder positions. But it is ambiguity that can—or should be—a provocation to thought" (p. 143). A chance to name and think about the ambiguities and difficulties that face us as educators can provide us with a path to deeper understanding and perhaps more authentic action.

Educators need time, space, and others with whom to share their doubts, their discomfort, and their fears. But often there is no space for sharing, for listening, and for thinking through the complexities of practice. In education to become an early childhood educator, students are encouraged to see children's strengths, to leave their issues outside the door and to empathize with parents (Langford, 2008). Seeing children as capable, reflecting on the educative value of their practice and understanding parents' positions are certainly important, is only part of the work of an early childhood educator. Focusing solely on children and families leaves little room for educators to focus on their own questions, growth, and learning when there are moments of insecurity, of anger, and of sadness. These moments are often repressed or ignored as not *appropriate* for the practice of being an early childhood educator.

The pressure to be *so* sympathetic and empathetic comes at a psychic price (Lear, 1990). Acknowledging that as educators we can be uncertain and fearful, takes courage and trust, in ourselves as well as in our listeners. Writing about the image of the early childhood educator as reflected in students' perceptions and textbook portrayals, Langford (2008) notes "the discourses of the good ECE focus primarily on the personal qualities of passion, happiness, inner strength, caring, and alertness to an individual child's needs and interests" (p. 82). There is little room for uncertainty, indecisiveness, or discomfort. Focusing on happiness, caring for the other, and calling on one's inner strength can mute the voices of doubt, fear, and insecurity—and yet those voices are still there.

Children do not have such restrictions on their play and their questioning. Edmiston (2008) talks about what he calls mythic play, where children can "not only speak what adults often leave 'unspoken' they can also act out and reflect on what is often regarded as 'unactable'—death, birth, hatred, injury and violence" (p. 112). Their play and conversations can range widely and touch upon issues that have no comfortable answers. Often our response is to repress this play.

Educators are also faced with questions and situations that are ambiguous, fraught with layers of emotions, and difficult to resolve. Often there is no place in practice for reflecting on feelings, fears, and concerns and they remain unacknowledged. We can, and should, be able to explore these emotions, yet not wallowing in them and not allowing them to imprison us. Sharing our narratives and our questions can open up a valuable dialogue with children, parents, and colleagues that can uncover emotional layers. As Bakhtin suggested, we learn of ourselves through engagement with the other: "the two languages frankly and intensely peered into each other's faces, and each became more aware of itself, of its potentialities and limitations, in the light of the other" (Bakhtin, 1994, p. 465). To invite someone to join you in a dialogue and to listen and to be heard, is to be vulnerable within that encounter. As the dialogue deepens and each starts to learn the other's language, it is possible to face some of the uncertainty of practice and perhaps engage with children's deep and searching questions.

In our IQ group in Victoria, we shared stories like Kim's narrative, allowing our group to explore the *cracks* in our practice and ourselves—places of discomfort and uncertainty. Becoming vulnerable, we open to our own possibilities and growth; we also must come face to face with our own ghosts and fears. If we are going to listen fully to children's struggles with unspoken issues then we must have space to listen to our own. We too have ghosts in our background narratives (Fraiberg, Adelson, & Shapiro, 1975; O'Loughlin, 2009) which can influence our responses and feelings. We can share stories and find new perspectives, and in the sharing become more comfortable with the uncertainty we face as we engage with children and families. Becoming aware of our darker emotions and how they might structure our responses to children and families can deepen our practice and help us listen more carefully to the feelings with which children struggle.

Within our IQ group we tried to listen to each other closely and to think beyond the story we were hearing. These difficult places became our curriculum and focus as we made deeper meaning of the work in which we were all engaged. As Pinar, Reynolds, Slattery, and Taubman (1995) suggest,

> curriculum is an extraordinarily complicated conversation. Curriculum as institutionalized text is a formalized and abstract version of conversation, a term we usually use to refer to those open-ended, highly personal, and interest-driven events in which persons encounter each other. (p. 848)

MacNaughton (2005) suggests that educators need the time and space to grow into an understanding of the "messiness, uncertainties and ethical dilemmas of relationships in teaching" (p. 193).

Tensions existed in our discussions. Educators brought their beliefs and understandings to the group; through sharing narratives and questioning those narratives, they came to question previously held values or beliefs. Creating dynamics that challenge assumptions and encourage reflection calls for trust and openness within the group. Aldo Fortunati (2006) argues that the educators' role is to be more attentive to creating possibilities than pursuing predefined goals... [to be] removed from the fallacy of certainties, [assuming instead] responsibility to choose, experiment, discuss, reflect and change, focusing on the organisation of opportunities rather than the anxiety of pursuing outcomes, and maintaining in her work the pleasure of amazement and wonder. (p. 37)

Our mutual agreement to look at the tensions and to challenge our beliefs helped create feelings of trust.

As the facilitator of our group I was committed to following the interests and concerns of the educators, believing that within the group process, pedagogical issues would surface. Trying to listen closely, I was not always sure as to how we would proceed. We usually started with narratives of practice, some of which were simple while others uncovered tensions in someone's practice, which often could be understood to reflect wider tensions within the early childhood field or the dominant discourses around us. Once we found the place where uncertainty and discomfort resided, we struggled with naming the issues that were provoked. Like the *Bad Guy Beavers*, we found ourselves returning to the topic from different angles and perspectives.

Sharing stories and selves is challenging; putting words to emotions is uncomfortable. As we grew to trust and respect each other, we shared more difficult narratives. It took some courage for a participant to share the first gunplay narrative and her anger at having a pretend gun pointed at her as she made room for the exploration of gun-play. Telling the story, she re-lived the anger and shared her discomfort at realizing how intensely she reacted. Holding her narrative gently, other educators began to share moments of confusion and intense emotion. Finding theoretical structures, which could support these narratives, helped contain the emotional responses and began to give us language to discuss them.

I suggested the group read parts of Edmiston's work (2008) as one explanation of children's play as explorations of how to be in relationships in meaningful and ethical ways. Edmiston argues that children create "space-times where through evaluation of the deeds of possible selves they form and shape their ethical identities" (p. 23). Children explore different issues and ideas in their intense play; they bring up topics with which we are uncomfortable. We had to recognize that children want to explore areas that are disquieting and part of our discomfort comes from a dissonance that arises from the widespread discourse of children's innocence and ignorance.

Children's moments of fear and anger, their uncertainties, and their intense desires are not so different from our own. How we manage our own longings and terrors that lurk beneath the surface depends on our own histories, our own values and beliefs, our own ethical responses. Finding a path through the powerful emotions elicited by children and their families by sharing narratives in order to make sense of those emotions can be comforting and allow caregivers to continue to be present for the children in their care. This path is not easy or untangled: "the intention to understand is already an emotionally wrought experience, for it returns us to times when we cannot understand and when we ourselves feel misunderstood " (Britzman, 2009, p. 95).

There is a need to widen the discourses of the *good early childhood educator* and how our ethical selves respond. Paying attention to the places of discomfort led us to reading other theorists who made us question, modify, or move to deeper thinking. Britzman (2009) says,

> development is uneven because we are born too soon and become responsible for a world we have not made. If we have the strange work of trying to understand the minds of others and still keep our own mind, if we have the work of welcoming what cannot be understood and the responsibility for a hospitality without reserve, if we confront a world that is wearing out, and if we must work from all this ignorance, teacher education may begin. (p. 44)

Once a year during this project, in the Sharing Circle all the groups met to discuss their work and listen to a guest speaker who shared their own work. Presenting her narrative within this Sharing Circle, Kim was unsettled by the reactions that it provoked. During the previous Sharing Circle we had done a presentation on the complexity of story and the responsibility involved in telling a story, which had been well received. Having been with the project for three years, Kim was comfortable sharing a narrative that was personal and revealing. Having been with the project for three years, Kim was comfortable sharing a narrative that was personal and revealing. She knew that the group supported her and that she represented a genuine expression of our group's dialogues.

Afterwards, she reflected on the tension she felt in the room and how uncomfortable it had made her. While some educators from the other groups had understood the value of opening up a crack in their practice, others judged her as irresponsible for not stopping this play and there was a lively discussion. One participant extended our narrative by sharing a story of having had a child whose father was in jail for murder and her center had chosen to be open about this child's reality and encouraged the child along with the other children to draw pictures to send to her father, thus giving the children a greater understanding of the world and a way to engage with that understanding.

Kim's story provides an example of how educators can take up a dialogue about children's play, children's philosophizing, and how we can respond in a way that leads to much greater learning for all. It is through discussing narratives such as these that we can provoke thinking about our own beliefs and understandings about these issues. Where are we, as educators, in response to children's play about violence, gender, and power? Thinking together with children about these questions would connect us to the human quest to understand life and its meaning more deeply. Sharing our own personal stories with one another and considering others' responses will inform our own responses; our image of ourselves as educators will influence our replies.

Acknowledging and articulating the darker aspects of our work can provoke others to explore uneasy or uncomfortable situations related to their roles. If we listen deeply to children to hear their underlying questions and fears, we may find some of our own reflected. How can we pay proper attention to these places of unease? It is through welcoming dialogue with colleagues and listening closely that we begin to disclose the complexity of children's play, how it reflects real-life concerns, and how to be more mindful of our own responses. Farquhar (2010) reminds us that by "using a narrative, dialogical approach to recover memory, to understand systems of reasoning and categories of inclusion, is a challenge for all involved in early childhood education" (p. 8).

Having found the process valuable, the group in Victoria, BC, continues to meet. We have discussed Kim's narrative, the ideas within this chapter, and the impacts of the Sharing Circle. Many in our group wondered if they would have been able to stand up and share a narrative like Kim's in the more public venue of the Sharing Circle. Fearing judgment tends to silence many of us. Feeling that Kim's story was powerful, the group agreed that it had an impact on their practice and encouraged them to be more open to children's play and to think of it differently. One person said she had thought about the narrative "a lot" and without this particular story she might "have shut it [the play] down without thinking." Like the girls who eventually found their voice to tell the boys they didn't like the play, the group had created a space for uncomfortable stories to be shared. If Kim had not allowed the play and the *Bad Guy Beavers* to explore their *badness*, the girls might not have had the opportunity to go through a process of finding their voice. During our learning circles we were learning to find our voices and think about practice more deeply.

References

Bakhtin, M. M. (1994). The dialogic imagination (M. Holquist & C. Emerson, Trans.). In P. Morris (Ed.), *The Bakhtin reader; selected writings of Bakhtin, Medvedev, Voloshinov* (pp. 74–80). London, UK: Arnold.

Britzman, D. P. (2009). *The very thought of education: Psychoanalysis and the impossible professions.* Albany, NY: State University of New York Press.

Davies, B. (2011). Open listening: Creative evolution in early childhood settings. *International Journal of Early Childhood, 43*(2), 119–132. doi: 10.1007/s13158-011-0030-1.

Edmiston, B. (2008). *Forming ethical identities in early childhood play.* New York, NY: Routledge.

Deleuze, G. (1994). *Difference and repitition.* London, UK: Continuum.

Elliot, E. (2013). Listening with two ears: Caregivers listening deeply to babies and to self. In M. O'Loughlin (Ed.), *The uses of psychoanalysis in working with children's emotional lives* (pp. 47–67). Plymouth, UK: Jason Aronson.

Farquhar, S. (2010). Narrative identity and early childhood education. *Educational Philosophy and Theory, 44*(3), 1–13.

Fortunati, A. (2006). *The education of young children as a community project: Children, teachers and parents in the infant-toddler centers and the new early childhood services, the experience of San Miniato.* San Paolo, Italy: Edizioni Junior.

Fraiberg, S., Adelson, E., & Shapiro, V. (1975). Ghosts in the nursery: A psychoanalytic approach to the problems of impaired infant-mother relationships. *Journal of the American Academy of Child Pyschiatry, 14,* 387–421.

Hoffman, E. (2004). *After such knowledge: Memory, history, and the legacy of the Holocaust.* New York, NY: Public Affairs.

Holland, P. (2003). *We don't play with guns here: War, weapon and superhero play in the early years.* Philidelphia, PA: Open University Press.

Langford, R. (2008). Making a difference in the lives of young children: A critical analysis of a pedagogical discourse for motivating young women to become early childhood educators. *Canadian Journal of Education/Revue canadienne de l'éducation, 31*(1), 78–101.

Lear, J. (1990). *Love and its place in nature: A philosophical interpretation of Freudian psychoanalysis.* New York, NY: Farrar, Straus & Giroux.

MacNaughton, G. (2005). *Doing Foucault in early childhood studies: Applying poststructural ideas.* Oxford, UK: Routledge.

MacNaughton, G., Hughes, P., & Smith, K. (2007). Rethinking approaches to working with children who challenge: Action learning for emancipatory practice. *International Journal of Early Childhood, 39*(1), 39–57.

O'Loughlin, M. (2009). *The subject of childhood.* New York, NY: Peter Lang.

Pacini-Ketchabaw, V., Nxumalo, F., Kocher, L., Elliot, E., & Sanchez, A. (2013). *Journeys: Complexifying early childhood practices through pedagogical narration.* Victoria, BC: University of Victoria.

Pinar, W., Reynolds, W., Slattery, P., & Taubman, P. (1995). *Understanding curriculum: An introduction to the study of historical and contemporary curriculum discourses.* New York, NY: Peter Lang.

Rinaldi, C. (2006). *In dialogue with Reggio Emilia: Listening, researching and learning.* New York, NY: Routledge.

8

Teacher Reflection in Early Years Partnership Research Projects: But It's No Use Going Back to Yesterday, because I Was a Different Person Then (Says Alice from *Alice's Adventures in Wonderland*)

Judith Duncan

Introduction

This chapter discusses two Aotearoa New Zealand early childhood research projects, based on partnerships between university academics (myself and others) and teachers, where reflection and reflective records formed the data gathering methodology, as well as generating our new understandings. The teachers, discussed in this chapter, describe their experiences with reflective writing in the two projects. Drawing on the theoretical concepts of Foucault, and Deleuze and Guattari, the use of reflective writing within partnership projects is reexamined.

When Alice was asked to repeat and explain some of her adventures in Wonderland to the Gryphon and the Mock Turtle, her reply was " 'I could tell you my adventures—beginning from this morning,' said Alice a little timidly: 'but it's no use going back to yesterday, because I was a different person then'" (Carroll, 1980, p. 156). Often in our educational research this is what we ask teachers to do—begin when the research project needs to begin and end when the funding, or the project, has finished. Where we begin and end is often dictated by the parameters of the research, rather than the lived realities of the teacher and the educational setting. Where to start—to begin—is the first question in undertaking research investigations: where along the *reflective* journey does one begin? Which line of *reflection* do you follow? Stephenson (2011) suggests in her understanding of Deleuze and Guattari's approach to beginning: "the beginning is never really the beginning but the middle.... Recognizing the impossibility of this position, we must choose a starting point if we are to start" (p. xi).

Where is the starting the place for reflection? The *now*? The *then*? The *before*? The *after*? How do the processes of being asked to reflect and record for a research study influence the decision of what, when, and how to record thoughts? Yet, do we attempt to answer these questions when we ask teachers to reflect on their teaching lives? We present reflective practice and reflective recording as a problem-free way of supporting teachers to understand their pedagogical practices, their teaching lives, and the learning experiences of their students/children. The place of reflection and reflective writing in a research partnership can demonstrate unequal expectations, uneven risks, and contrasting investments in the project. Cochran-Smith and Lytle (2009) highlight how in university–teacher partnerships what is shared and omitted, what is disclosed, and by whom, demonstrates the differences in partnerships, in what counts as knowledge and what can or cannot become possible in a research endeavor. They highlight how academic researchers and teachers have different perspectives and different positions in this regard:

> Even deciding what to disclose and what to obscure or omit entails very different risks and consequences for the differently positioned writers in the group. What is troubling is that as university researchers, we tend to argue for pushing boundaries and writing about unsettling subjects. But we are also much more likely to get credit for doing this and much less likely than some of our school-based colleagues to have to deal directly with the fallout of our choices. (p. 104)

Reflective journals, which are closely tied with what becomes possible to disclose, what is safe to share, what counts as knowledge, have become a leading research method for teachers. Teachers are familiar with journaling for reflective practice within their everyday professional experiences (O'Connor & Diggins, 2002) and appear to use these without question, particularly when they are required to do so, for example, in renewal of teacher registration (see New Zealand Teachers Council: http://

www.teacherscouncil.govt.nz). In Aotearoa New Zealand, action research methodologies have become commonly accepted as a leading paradigm of teacher research, both within teacher-led projects, and partnership projects with professionals from outside of the immediate setting, where reflection has been integrated into each cycle or phase of the investigation (Citizens Preschool and Nursery Centre of Innovation, 2008).

Kiri Gould wrote in 1997 that reflection had become the buzzword for teachers in the late 1990s. As Gould indicated, reflective practice had become "hailed in the literature as a powerful means by which teachers can change their practice" (Gould, 1997, p. 12). The concept of reflection was developed by Schön (1983, 1987, 1996), for whom reflective practice was not only a *conscious* mental activity but also an *unconscious* one. He distinguished between two forms of reflection, reflection-in-action and reflection-on-action, defining the former as "tacit and spontaneous and often delivered without taking thought" (Schön, 1987, p. 3, cited Chiu, 2006, p. 186) and the latter as retrospective, "an intellectual [activity which] requires verbalisation and symbolisation" (Schön, 1987, cited Chiu, 2006, p. 186). Cherrington (2012) discusses how reflective practice is considered an essential aspect of teaching and professionalism in Aotearoa New Zealand. In her doctoral study she builds on the notions of Schön's *reflection-in-action, reflection-on-action* (1983, 1987). She defines them as

> Reflection-in-action occurs within the moment of the activity, often in response to the unexpected, and results in an immediate change in practice. In contrast, reflection-on-action generally takes place after the event and does not influence or impact on the original episode. (p. 14)

Grey (2012) argues that reflection and reflective practice provides a new way of conceptualizing the teaching professional and professionalism. The benefit, she asserts, is in "the 'inside-out' professional tak[ing] a questioning approach to teaching that emphasizes critical reflection and dialogue based on authentic situations pertaining to each teacher's immediate teaching context" (Grey, 2012, p. 11). The teacher, then, is able to combine expert knowledge with sound judgment and thoughtful action.

Mayo (2006) has identified how reflection and reflective practice have become "glorified in recent decades as an important element in teachers' professional work" (p. 130). She quotes John Smyth (1992) who has raised concerns for some time over the use of reflective practice when it:

> becomes a means of focusing upon ends that are determined by others, not as an active process of contesting, debating and determining the nature of those ends.
> (Smyth, 1992, p. 280 cited in Mayo, 2006, p. 130)

Mayo's (2006) concern is that reflection and reflective practices can become tools for "recycling assumptions (or myths) rather than identifying and addressing issues within a professional community" (p. 130). Other scholars, who have similar concerns that reflection can merely reproduce existing practices, have attempted to address this reification of practice by making the reflection more collaborative or public. Perhaps one of the most significant and prolific scholars of reflective practice and self-study is John Loughran. Loughran suggests that

> Teacher educators engaging in self-study commonly share a broad motivation to improve the experience of teacher education through improving their teaching practice... it is this overarching desire to better align theory and practice, to be more fully informed about the nature of a knowledge of practice, and to explore and build on these 'learnings' in public ways that appears to be an underlying common purpose in self-study—a tacit catalyst for self-study.
>
> (Loughran, 2007, pp. 14–15)

Combining self-reflection with shared dialogue with others, exploring ideas with others, debating and sharing professional reflections, have become known as "self-study" (Loughran & Russell, 2002). Self-study approaches are regularly used in educational research projects, particularly ones including action research methods (see, e.g., Meade, 2005, 2006, 2007, 2009, 2010; Sandretto et al., 2006; Sandretto & Critical Literacy Research Team, 2008). Thus, the methods of eliciting and using reflection have come to be unproblematized within research projects involving partnerships with teachers, for example, Teaching and Learning Research Initiative (TLRI) projects and Centre of Innovation projects (COI)[1].

Teacher-Partnership Research and Reflection

Making sense of the *here-and-now* through reflection (looking back) and critical reflection (looking back and forwards) were key methods in the two early childhood education research projects discussed in this chapter. Two teacher-partnership research projects[2], where I was the principal researcher, relied heavily on reflection and reflective recording to gather data (or evidence from the investigations) and to involve the teachers in changes in pedagogy—meaningful changes that originated from the teachers' own understandings and willing engagement with difference from their everyday pedagogical practices. At the time of establishing both of the projects, the use of reflective practice and reflective writing was a professional expectation of all the teams, so this mode, or tool for the research, appeared to be a suitable and appropriate tool for our teacher-partnership research. The two projects described below demonstrated that the use of reflective writing was problematic for the teachers within the understanding of the teacher-partnership relationships within the projects. Revisiting Alice's confusion at how to describe herself when each day she is different—her *becoming* (Deleuze & Guattari, 1987)—combined with Foucault's thinking about the *confessional self* as a surveillance and governing device, provide concepts that demonstrate the complexity of thinking expected of teachers and the risks to the nature of the partnership between the teachers and the researcher-academic (for full details of the research studies included in this chapter, see Duncan et al., 2006; Duncan et al., 2011)[3].

Project One was a partnership between university researchers with kindergarten teachers in three case-study kindergartens, who were working for the first time with large numbers of under-three-year-olds in their program. Kindergartens, in New Zealand, had historically been for three to five-year-olds, but a fall in demographics and a change in social trends early this century (2000–2002) created a situation where younger children began to attend in large numbers and where teachers had been underprepared for their inclusion. The research was carried out over a two-year period. Teachers completed research diaries reflecting on their interactions with children, and engaged in reflective conversations with myself, one of two university researchers, and three university research assistants (see Duncan, 2005, 2009; Duncan et al., 2006).

Project Two was a partnership between Visiting Teachers, in a home-based organization, and myself (as the university researcher)[4] (see Duncan et al., 2011). The Visiting Teachers were qualified early childhood teachers who regularly visited educators (who provided early childhood education in their homes, known internationally as family daycare providers). The visits involved support and guidance for the educator, as well as the mandatory functions of ensuring that all the educators were working to national regulations (educational as well as health and safety). This was also a two-year project and involved Visiting Teachers undertaking self-study tasks, including writing regular reflective journal entries, and a *buddy visit* where the teachers videoed each other during regular visits with educators.

In each case, the projects were negotiated between the managers or senior management of each of the organizations in which the research was undertaken. For both projects I (Judith) had established relationships with either the organization itself (the kindergarten associations) or with individual managers in the organization (home-based organization). In both projects the ideas were developed with the managers and then individual teachers were approached to partner with the university researchers in the research. Teachers within the project were the main players and the key partners in the research, while the managers were the advisors and supporters of the projects in their organizations. It quickly became apparent that this way of establishing partnerships within the body of teachers caused tensions, particularly with the educators within both projects. The teachers became cautious about what this project would mean for their day-to-day experiences, as well as concerned that this was actually a hidden attempt by managers to improve *deficits* or problems within the teaching teams. For example:

> It was an interesting beginning. We first received a fax from the senior teacher at the kindergarten association asking us how many children under-three we had in our programme. Little did we know when we replied that Judith had a cunning plan and we very honestly replied and soon Judith arrived armed with many consent forms for us to sign.
> (Teacher cited in Duncan et al., 2006, pp. 38–39)

> When the subject of research was first mooted we, [Visiting Teachers] as a group, thought we would be looking at educators' practice. However, this was quickly challenged by Judith and [Manager] who felt that there would be instability among educators through their leaving the service and pregnancy. They felt we should be looking at the Visiting Teachers' role. We definitely felt this had been preplanned with an agenda to *fix us*, which [Manager] had alluded to on various occasions.
> (Unpublished Visiting Teacher reflection)

With the increased accountability in early childhood education in Aotearoa New Zealand, which has seen more internal and external surveillance and auditing of services and teachers (Duncan, 2007, 2008), it is not surprising that teachers were wary of research that was instigated by their managers with an *outsider* from a university. No matter how well known or liked I was (having worked alongside several of the teachers in my own early childhood teaching career prior to moving into the academic world), the concern that the projects were the *cover* for other agendas by their employers continued to sit closely to the surface of the projects for the first few months for each study. Asking the teachers to reflect on their teaching and share these reflections increased the feelings of vulnerability by the teachers, the surveillance, and the exposure not only to their *doing* but also to their *being* and *becoming*.

However, over time, each of the teachers began to see that as the *outsider* I brought support and useful provocations for them—support to grow as a *researching-teacher*, as a critical thinker, and as an investigator of best possible pedagogical practices. This shift was based around the relational work that occurred between each of the teachers and myself, as lead investigator in the project, as the "constructive disruption" (Cochran-Smith & Lytle, 2009, p. 86) of working together shifted the expected teacher-researcher roles. For example, in Project One I scrubbed the tables and did dishes to free the teachers to write in their reflective journals.

In both projects we spent equal times discussing readings, insights, and *learnings* with the teachers taking the role of teaching me the knowledges that only they had access to. Examples:

> So after a while we even started looking forward to Judith coming and she then started to bring her own lunch and we would have wonderful conversations and discussions over lunch, which was really great so we looked forward to that too.
>
> (Teacher cited in Duncan et al., 2006, pp. 38–39)

> Our research journey started with readings. As action research was a new concept for our Visiting Teacher team it was really important for us all to have a good understanding of what action research meant. Judith very happily supplied us with as many readings as were required. This really helped us to get our heads around the idea and set us all in the right direction. During the course of the research Judith would provide us with readings relating to the certain area that we were focusing on at that particular time. The readings were shared amongst the Visiting Teacher team sharing and photocopying the ones that were practically beneficial to read. There was always lots of professional discussion about the readings. It was then decided that we put research on the agenda to be discussed at our weekly staff meetings, readings were shared at these meetings.
>
> (Visiting Teacher notes; Duncan et al., 2008)

Early in both projects reflective writing was introduced. In Project One the teachers kept daily diaries to record their interactions with each case study child in their center, and engaged in reflective conversations each week with the university researcher. Project Two was based on an action method which required the teachers to engage in regular reflection at each stage of the planning, data gathering, assessing, and evaluating and planning the next phase. In this second project we also introduced the *buddy visit*, which entailed each Visiting Teacher to accompany their colleague to the home visit of an educator, video the interactions, and then sit together to reflect on the visit (with key reflective questions to guide the watching and discussion). In both of these projects the use of *reflection* was expected by all the teachers (and also by the university researchers) but was presented as an unproblematic tool that teachers, already familiar with in their professional lives, would find as (a) an easy tool to use; and (b) an effective tool for sustainable pedagogical change. The teachers themselves through the projects often expressed discomfort in using these tools—citing time constraints, workload issues, and concerns as to the use of the written records as the reasons for struggling with them. The ill-ease that the teachers experienced may have been indicative of the concerns raised around the use of reflection more generally—the reification of existing practice, the increased evaluation of their work being made public, the limitations of critical thought within an existing community of practice. Building on the ideas of Deleuze and Guattari (1987), Olsson (2009) cautions on the use of reflection, and challenges the critical thinking that is often promoted as an aspect of the reflection. Olsson encourages researchers and teachers to open up new ways of thinking through *experimentation* to enable knowledge to be experienced and created in new ways. She warns that critical thinking (as part of reflection) does not open up new possibilities. Rather

> research efforts must find other means to engage with practice than through conscious critique.... Critical thinking seems to lock up movement and experimentation in subjectivity and learning through a transcendent principle, where critique is undertaken from above or beyond the empirical features. Empirical features are consequently always immobilized by abstract logical thinking. Critical thinking, even though twisted and turned in different methodological approaches, is always in trouble by the end. (p. 50)

These problems identified by Olsson—the worries of relational research—critical thinking and reflection shape the rest of this chapter. The challenge she poses is to understand that teaching (and educational research) is always in the process of happening, changing, moving, and *becoming*. To try to critique an event that happened in the past, removing the relational and *becoming* aspects of the event locks up thought, restricts possibilities, and limits new ways of knowing. Seeing reflective writing as a limiting tool for *thinking* for building relational work, also ignores the constructive role that the act of the writing plays in the creation of the *self*, and the knowledge that then becomes generated.

Disciplinary Technologies and Becomings

Michel Foucault's (1961, 1977, 1980a, 1980b, 1980c) tools provide us with useful lenses to examine pedagogical reflective writing. In his study of the evolution of the modern prison, hospital, and asylum, Foucault demonstrated a shift from overt brutal physical punishment as a form of power to ensure population control and compliance, to that of a more insidious form of power—that of self-control. He argued that this self-control became the most effective form of control over populations as it is gained, not through repression, but by eliciting consent from individuals through coercive procedures. Through procedures such as the religious confession, medical examination, and military exercise, modern society has more effective and subtle forms of social control that move away from direct punishments. These procedures coerce individuals into behaving in a way that has been classified by any given society at that time as *normal* (Roth, 1992). This is achieved, according to Foucault, through three new forms of, what he calls, disciplinary technology—surveillance, written examination, and the normalizing judgment (Duncan, 2008).

Surveillance

The concept of surveillance (the "all-seeing gaze") as a form of normalizing power (Foucault, 1961, 1977, 1980b, 1980c) presents a provocation when thinking about reflection in teaching—reflective journals, reflection activities, and reflective conversations. In his discussion of surveillance, Foucault used the example of the Panopticon, Bentham's nineteenth-century prison model; a design for the constant visual monitoring of prisoners. How it works is as follows: the significance of *the gaze* generates morally self-monitoring subjects (Foucault, 1977, p. 202) who are controlled inwardly by their own constraints and actions. Reflecting on one's own teaching, one's own thinking about one's teaching can be seen as *the gaze* that constructs an obedient and compliant teacher. Being watched and observed in a research project is a natural part of most research endeavors; however, adding in the reflection task had been an attempt to increase the understanding of the teachers' thinking around their pedagogy—to examine their construction of selves as teachers, teachers of two-year-olds, and teachers with educators. Michelle, from Project One, describes it in this way:

> I also had, what Judith calls the 'researcher effect' on relationships, while the children were being observed. In the second phase of the research I began to examine my motives for interacting with children and I would ask myself: Am I going to interact with this child now because Judith's here and I haven't had an interaction with this child yet today? Or am I going to interact with this child because I see the need for it, at this point in time, with what they're doing? I'd also examine how many interactions perhaps I'd had with the children of the group, as such, because we had a larger number of children in our afternoon session at that time and I really wanted to have some equity for the children that she was observing at the time. So that became quite

difficult for me to determine. When I should and shouldn't interact with the children? Whether I was doing it purely because Judith was there, or whether it was authentic? And the more I queried it, the harder it became for me to determine whether it was authentic or not. [emphasis in original]

(Duncan et al., 2006, p. 40)

The usefulness of Foucault's ideas in this context then is in the production of reflective teachers who are *producing themselves* and each other through the *written word*. Michelle's written reflections presented above were shared in a public presentation and in our final report. For her, the more she reflected on her reflections the more she came to doubt and wonder about her own teaching and her construction of herself as a *successful teacher*—what should her interactions 'look like to others'? In her exit interview Michelle expressed her frustrations that being involved in a research project had a significant impact on how and who she felt she was as a teacher:

I saw what—the way that I was really stilted and nervous and self-conscious of every word I was saying and I just couldn't relax with the children. I couldn't even do what I'd normally do with them. . . . And it was that—and it was that whole thing that fed into it, do I chat with this child now? . . . . But I did just feel incredibly self-conscious and hated it. And I think that came down to the fact that I knew that I wasn't doing a good job.

For Michelle the double surveillance of being physically observed and having to reflect on those observations and share them with her research partners reinforced her self-doubt in herself as a *good teacher* and what *good teaching* would *look like*.

The Examination (Written Reflections)

Foucault (1977) argues that the examination or written record functions to discipline individuals in modern society. Not only does it expose the individual to the world but also it turns real lives into writing (Foucault, 1977, pp. 189–190). This documentation functions to produce objectification and subjection where "the individual becomes a 'case' whose individuality is observed, documented and thereby emphasized" (Hall & Millard, 1994, p. 158). Written records represent the *teacher* and allow others to judge, evaluate, and categorize *the teacher:* a docile (normalized) teacher begins to take shape. Reflective writing in a research project can be seen to do just this—the private becomes public, the thoughts and wondering become documented and frozen in time. Where Alice may have been a different person yesterday, journaling of her adventures would set her as a *case* open to scrutiny, surveillance, and judgment, set in time, and open to critique, hence Alice's resistance to revisit her *yesterday*. Through the written reflection the teachers begin to not only reflect on their work but also they begin to judge what is good, bad, could be better, et cetera. For example, in an exit interview in Project One, a teacher described how the intersection of writing a reflective journal (Year One) and then *not* writing a journal (Year Two) were equally problematic for her:

> The journal almost gave you the right to be more involved [with the children], whereas not having it; it was like where do I sit with this now? Whereas the journal was, kind of, like I am going to make more connections and I am going to write it down, so I am going to feed that back, so I have to know it. Whereas when the journal wasn't there it was like, it was like what I was saying at conference the other day, it's that whole equity thing. How many other children have I spent time with today out of all these children? Am I doing it for you [researcher] because you are recording at this time, or am I doing it because I would have interacted with that child at that moment? Don't know.
>
> (Exit interview with Teacher Project One)

This teacher demonstrated the tensions that arose for her in the written tasks. The requirement within the project, to record reflective diaries, was uncomfortable for her in Year One, yet when we made a decision to remove them in Year Two, the teacher no longer had a public record to demonstrate how well she knew the children—public evidence of a *good teacher* and a *good research participant*.

Normalizing Judgment

Combining surveillance and the written examination (written reflection or reflective journal) provides for, what Foucault calls, the normalizing judgment—the *good* teacher. This normalizing judgment has become a powerful tool in the functioning of modern disciplinary power (Foucault, 1977; Gore, 1995; Roth, 1992) and is aided by the notion of a *confessional*, or confessing, society, which plays a large part in the construction of this manageable, self-regulating populace. The notion of *confession* makes previously inconspicuous individuals audible as well as visible. This behavior has become an everyday event where we *confess*:

> in justice, medicine, education, family relationships, and love relations, in the most ordinary affairs of everyday life, and in the most solemn rites; one

> confesses one's crimes, one's sins, one's thoughts and desires, one's illnesses and troubles; one goes about telling, with the greatest precision, whatever is most difficult to tell.
>
> (Foucault, 1980c, p. 59)

Increased accountability in education has seen a rise of *confessing*: self-reviews and professional assessment procedures, staff meetings to report to, parents to explain and justify actions and practices, et cetera. Deacon and Parker (1995) chose to identify the disciplinary mechanisms of the examination and the confession as keys to the power relations that constitute teachers. They see the ritual of "to tell what one is" as a discernible effect of power, that once the telling has been done, it "produces intrinsic modifications in the person who articulates it" (Foucault, 1981 cited in Deacon & Parker, 1995, p. 115). Seen through this lens, the use of reflective journaling and reflections through educational research, the teacher can become motivated, engaged, and stimulated within their educational work. However, they can also be judged for not only what is *seen* by others, but what the teacher thinks, how the teacher thinks, what the teacher's thought processes/considerations are at the moment and over time. Across the two projects, there was evidence that the reflective tasks increased the articulation of normalization and awareness of surveillance of thought as well as deed, and rather than to problematize this way of gathering data, or celebrate the different ways that the teachers approached their work with teaching, the teachers problematized their own teaching and their relationships with each other, including the university researcher.

If we reframe the examples shared in this chapter and use the ideas of Deleuze and Guattari (1987) to think about reflection within teaching and research, another possibility emerges—one that encourages change, difference, movement, and experimentation. Their concepts of *becoming* provide another provocation to the notion of reflection. They argue that understanding *knowledge* and *thinking* are not about recognizing facts, or solutions, to problems, but rather *making connections,* of *fundamental encounters,* of teachers in the "here-and-now" (Dahlberg & Bloch, 2006, p. 114). They argue that we are always in the process of *becoming*; therefore to reflect on a stable identity or a *fact*, or on something that occurred yesterday is problematic and unhelpful. Stagoll (2010) argues that "becoming is...a characteristic of the very production of events" (p. 26). In contrast to a fixed stable identity or self, where reflection can measure the essence of a person (conscious and unconscious) Deleuze's notions of *becoming* sees one's self as "a constantly changing assemblage of forces, an epiphenomenon arising from chance confluences of languages, organisms, societies, expectations, laws and so on" (p. 27). An example: a Visiting Teacher explored the notion of *who she was* in her wondering about her own language in describing her work with educators:

> I see in my journal that sometimes I was very clear about my role and then the entries would slide into talking about the educators' role, without any reflection or thought about what I was doing or thinking or trying. On reflection, thinking about my role is a lot more difficult for me than reflecting on others' role. This is interesting to me, as when I am teaching children I think I am quite skilled at observing children, supporting learning, adding complexity, trying lots of different strategies to encourage change and learning and most importantly thinking hard about how my teaching impacts on children. I find this hard when working with adults—notice I say 'working with adults' rather than 'teaching adults'. This, I think is an important use in words as it shows my values and feelings about being a Visiting Teacher and the difficulties I have with 'teaching' adults/educators. 'Working with' is embedded in the idea of partnership, a flat power structure and my liberal leanings—'that everyone is the same'. Whereas teaching is embedded in a discourse that is a lot more complex, for example, that power and agency is acknowledged and positions are negotiated. Somehow in my head I work with educators and I teach children and when working in a centre I am a head teacher so I see it as my role to be a teacher of teachers. Oh, I just thought of something. Even though my role is that of a Visiting Teacher I think or have thought that—'*I work alongside educators*' and that *I'm the children's Visiting Teacher*. These thoughts must guide the way I work. [emphasis in original]
> (Unpublished Visiting Teacher reflection)

This Visiting Teacher had used her reflections to trouble and unsettle her own thinking and discursive language, to rethink her encounters, and reframe her *becoming*. Like Alice, she is changing with each day, and in each encounter with educators, she encounters her thinking about the encounters, and her experimentation in what a Visiting Teacher could look like and be like.

Another example demonstrates the *becoming* that a Visiting Teacher engages in as she constructs herself into that role rather than a teacher with children. Her reflections provided her with the space to begin to wonder about who she is as a Visiting Teacher:

> Entering into the world of the Visiting Teacher would be an easy transition, I thought. I never expected to be taken on such a steep learning curve or find such reward. I recently confessed to my colleagues how on my very first visit I practically knocked the educator out of the way to get to the children and enthrall them with my talents—after my home-based version of mat

time, I left secure in the knowledge I had taught well! As I have been relieving in the Visiting Teacher role for a year or so, I picked up on some of the changes the research was bringing and as my understanding and thus my confidence grew, it has been my choice to buy into the research challenge of making a difference. Most of the time, I think I have been lucky to be in the right place at the right time, as I didn't really have many preconceived ideas about being a Visiting Teacher. I soon learned it wasn't a modified version of being a kindergarten teacher. What I have gained from being a part of the research is, through the conversations and discussions, with other Visiting Teachers and the readings, to be provoked to reflect and analyze my own beliefs and practices... What is happening for my practice is this feedback from the educators is stimulating me to strive to have a genuine understanding of how I can follow up to best match where the educator and children are at so that my work does have high value (or make a difference) for both their learning. This is often supported by further discussion with the other Visiting Teachers—a valuable tool for me to reflect and make decisions and share ideas.... I have adapted to not feeling sure, as every day is potentially filled with a new challenge, every visit is different, every educator is unique, every parent has a need, every child has a purpose—it no longer scares me to not know everything and I am excited to be a part of the sharing in these relationships as a Visiting Teacher.

(Visiting Teacher reflection on being in the research project, presentation notes, Duncan et al., 2008)

In this teacher's reflection, she expresses the *becoming* of a Visiting Teacher, through her encounters with others, through her experimentation with different ways of being, and through embracing the notions of difference and uncertainty. Her feelings of being a *good Visiting Teacher* were not about being normalized or *fitting* into any particular vision of a Visiting Teacher, but, for this teacher, her sense of pride in her work was making a difference with children and educators—through her own experimentation and encounters.

Both examples of *becoming* from these two teachers demonstrate different uses of reflection within research, and present a useful critique of the traditional *reflective writing* that teachers are more familiar with, and which more usually appears in research reports.

Conclusion

Using Foucault's and Deleuze and Guattari's theoretical tools, this chapter has explored two partnership projects and demonstrated how transformative thinking and practice had impact on both the nature of the partnerships (an outsider working with insider personnel) and the political nature of making the personal (reflection) open for scrutiny and judgment. Foucault's ideas of surveillance position the creation and recording of knowledge in reflection journals very differently from a technical recording of teachers' practices. The emphasis on recording *reflective journals* on the *before, the here and now,* the *after,* positions teachers in a static and unchanging position where they are allowed to neither be fluid nor *becoming* but rather have *come to be something* that can be measured, assessed, judged, and passed sentence on. Deleuze and Guattari discuss the idea of *becomings* and how through encounters we are always in the acts of *becomings* and have never *become,* yet this *becoming something* is often the focus of reflection—becoming a better teacher, a more reflective teacher, a teacher-who-fits-in (normalized teacher). To return to Alice, in her reply to the Gryphon and the Mock Turtle, she indicated her own understanding of *becoming* when she replied "But it's no use going back to yesterday, because I was a different person then." The teachers discussed in this chapter experienced reflective writing in the two projects as both a barrier and a support for the relationships that they shared across the projects, but more importantly, drawing on Foucault, they were examined, surveyed, and normalized by their partnership projects. What was usually silent became shared (research meetings) and public (presentations as part of the requirements of TLRI funding). While their stories tell of *becomings,* they were treated as *research data stories* to be examined and judged. Given the prevalence and promotion of reflection as both a teaching tool and a research method, this chapter argues that we should move from this method to one that encourages experimentation, difference, and becomings. By *reflecting* on these two projects using the *all-seeing gaze* and *becomings,* this chapter has opened up discussions on the use of reflection within university-teacher research partnerships.

Notes

1. TLRI projects, see above. Centre of Innovation projects were New Zealand collaborative projects between professional researchers and early childhood teachers. For more details, see http://www.educate.ece.govt.nz/Programmes/CentresofInnovation.aspx.
2. Both studies were funded by the New Zealand Teaching and Learning Research Initiative (TLRI). This fund supports research that "seeks to enhance the links between educational research and teaching practices to improve outcomes for learners" (see www.tlri.org.nz) and is based on a partnership between teachers and academic/professional researchers.
3. While the nature of the *partnership* is not spelt out by TLRI the intent is that together teachers and skilled researchers can create understandings, which,

individually, may not be possible. The projects are funded on the basis that there will be a strong partnership and that the research will meet all the other criteria for valid, reliable, and trustworthy research (see Garvey Berger & Baker, 2008).
4. Visiting Teachers is the New Zealand term for family daycare coordinators; Homebased ECE is the New Zealand term for family daycare.

References

Carroll, L. (1980). *Alice's adventures in wonderland.* London, UK: Octopus Books Ltd.
Cherrington, S. (2012). Professionalism in practice: Teachers thinking together about teaching. *Early Education, 52*(Spring/Summer), 13–17.
Chiu, L. F. (2006). Critical reflection: More than nuts and bolts. *Action Research, 4*(2), 183–203.
Citizens Preschool and Nursery Centre of Innovation. (2008). *Collaborations: Teachers and a Family Whānau Support Worker in an early childhood setting. Centre of innovation final report.* Wellington, NZ: Ministry of Education. Retrieved from http://www.educationcounts.govt.nz/publications/ECE/22551/26635/26636.
Corcoran, C. A., & Leahy, R. (2003). Growing professionally through reflective practice. *Kappa Delta Pi Record, 40*(1), 30–33.
Cochran-Smith, M., & Lytle, S. L. (Eds.). (2009). *Inquiry as stance: Practitioner research for the next generation.* New York, NY: Teachers College Press.
Dahlberg, G., & Bloch, M. N. (2006). Is the power to see and visualize always the power to control? In T. S. Popkewitz, K. Petersson, U. Olsson, & J. Kowalczyk (Eds.), *"The future is not what it appears to be." Pedagogy, genealogy and political epistemology. In honor and in memory of Kenneth Hultqvist* (pp. 105–123). Stockholm, Sweden: HLS Förlag.
Deacon, R., & Parker, B. (1995). Education as subjection and refusal: An elaboration on Foucault. *Curriculum Studies, 3*(2), 109–122.
Deleuze, G., & Guattari, F. (1987). *A thousand plateaus: Capitalism and schizophrenia* (B. Massumi, Trans.). Minneapolis, MN: University of Minnesota Press.
Duncan, J. (2005). Two year olds in kindergarten: What are they doing there?! *The First Years: New Zealand Journal of Infant and Toddler Education, 7*(2), 4–8.
Duncan, J. (2007). New Zealand Free Kindergartens: Free or freely forgotten? *Qualitative Studies in Education, 20*(3), 319–333.
Duncan, J. (2008). *Restructuring lives: Kindergarten teachers and education reforms, 1984–1996.* Köln, Germany: Lambert Academic Publishing.
Duncan, J. (2009). "If you think they can do it—then they can": Two-year-olds in Aotearoa New Zealand kindergartens and changing professional perspectives. In D. C. Berthelsen, J. Brownlee, & E. Johansson (Eds.), *Participatory learning in the early years: Research and pedagogy* (pp. 164–184). New York, NY: Routledge.
Duncan, J., Auld, S., Fagan, H., Irvine, P., Smith, C., & Weir, S. (2008, August). *Homebased early childhood education (family day care): The visiting teachers' role in improving educators' practices—What makes a difference? Keynote address at the*

University of Otago College of Education Early Childhood Research Hui, Dunedin, New Zealand.

Duncan, J., Dalli, C., Becker, R., Butcher, M., Foster, K., Hayes, K., Lake-Ryan, S., Mackie, B., Montgomery, H., McCormack, P., Muller, R., Sherburd, R., Taita, J., & Walker, W. (2006). *Under three-year-olds in kindergarten: Children's experiences and teacher's practices*. Report prepared for the Teaching And Learning Research Initiative, New Zealand Council For Educational Research. Retrieved from http://www.tlri.org.nz/under-three-year-olds-kindergarten-children%E2%80%99s-experiences-and-teachers%E2%80%99-practices/.

Duncan, J., Irvine, P., Auld, S., Cross, T., Fagan, H., Seiuli, T., Smith, C., Sutton, A., & Weir, S. (2011). *Homebased early childhood education (family day care)—The Visiting Teacher's role in improving educators' practices. A Summary.* Retrieved from http://www.tlri.org.nz/home-based-early-childhood-education-family-day-care-visiting-teachers%E2%80%99-role-improving-educators%E2%80%99-0/.

Foucault, M. (1961). *Madness and civilization: A history of insanity in the age of reason*. London, UK: Tavistock Publications.

Foucault, M. (1977). *Discipline and punish* (Alan Sheridan, Trans.). London, UK: Penguin Books.

Foucault, M. (1980a). The confession of the flesh. In C. Gordon (Ed.), *Power/knowledge: Selected interviews and other writings, 1972–1977: Michel Foucault* (pp. 194–228). Hemel Hempstead, UK: The Harvester Press.

Foucault, M. (1980b). The eye of power. In C. Gordon (Ed.), *Power/knowledge: Selected interviews and other writings, 1972–1977: Michel Foucault* (pp. 146–165). Hemel Hempstead, UK: The Harvester Press.

Foucault, M. (1980c). *The History of sexuality* (Robert Hurley, Trans.). New York, NY: Pantheon Books.

Garvey Berger, J. G., & Baker, R. (2008). *Developing new knowledge and practice through teacher—researcher partnerships? Discussion Paper*. Wellington, NZ: Teaching and Learning Initiative, New Zealand Council for Educational Research. Retrieved from http://www.tlri.org.nz/tlri-research/discussion-papers.

Gore, J. M. (1995). On the continuity of power relations in pedagogy. *International Studies in Sociology of Education*, 5(2), 165–188.

Gould, K. (1997). *Professional development: A literature review. Position Paper 4*. Hamilton: Department of Early Childhood Studies, University of Waikato, New Zealand.

Grey, A. (2012). The inside-out professional. *Early Education, 52*(Spring/Summer), 9–12.

Hall, C., & Millard, E. (1994). The means of correct training? Teachers, Foucault and disciplining. *Journal of Education for Teaching, 20*(2), 153–160.

Loughran, J. J. (2007). Researching teacher education practices: Responding to the challenges, demands and expectations of self-study. *Journal of Teacher Education, 58* (1), 12–20.

Loughran, J. J., & Russell, T. (Eds.). (2002). *Improving teacher education practices through self-study*. London, UK: Routledge/Falmer.

Mayo, E. (2006). Researching together: Praxis-based research among practitioners. In C. Mutch (Ed.), *Challenging the notion of "other". Reframing research in the Aotearoa New Zealand context* (pp. 119–140). Wellington, NZ: NZCER Press.

Meade, A. (Ed.). (2005). *Catching the waves: Innovation in early childhood education.* Wellington, NZ: NZCER Press.

Meade, A. (Ed.). (2006). *Riding the waves: Innovation in early childhood education.* Wellington, NZ: NZCER Press.

Meade, A. (Ed.). (2007). *Cresting the waves: Innovation in early childhood education.* Wellington, NZ: NZCER Press.

Meade, A. (Ed.). (2009). *Generating waves: Innovation in early childhood education.* Wellington, NZ: NZCER Press.

Meade, A. (Ed.). (2010). *Dispersing waves: Innovation in early childhood education.* Wellington, NZ: NZCER Press.

O'Connor, A., & Diggins, C. (2002). *On reflection: Reflective practice for early childhood educators.* Lower Hutt, NZ: Open Mind Publishing.

Olsson, L. M. (2009). *Movement and experimentation in young children's learning: Deleuze and Guattari in early childhood education.* London, UK: Routledge.

Roth, J. (1992). Of what help is he? A review of Foucault and education. *American Educational Research Journal, 29*(4), 683–694.

Sandretto, S., & Critical Literacy Research Team. (2008). *A collaborative self-study into the development and integration of critical literacy practices.* Wellington, NZ: Teaching and Learning Research Initiative, NZCER. Retrieved from http://www.tlri.org.nz/tlri-research/research-completed/school-sector/collaborative-self-study-development-and-integration.

Sandretto, S., Tilson, J., Hill, P., Upton, J., Howland, R., & Parker, R. (2006). *A collaborative self-study into the development of critical-literacy practices—A pilot study.* Wellington, NZ: Teaching and Learning Research Initiative. NZCER. Retrieved from http://www.tlri.org.nz/tlri-research/research-completed/school-sector/collaborative-self-study-development-critical.

Schön, D. A. (1983). *The reflective practitioner: How professionals think in action.* London, UK: Temple Smith.

Schön, D. A. (1987). *Educating the reflective practitioner: Toward a new design for teaching and learning in the professions.* San Francisco, California: Jossey-Bass Inc.

Schön, D. A. (1996). *Educating the reflective practitioner: Towards a new design for teaching and learning in the professions.* San Francisco, CA: Jossey-Bass.

Stagoll, C. (2010). Becoming. In A. Parr (Ed.), *The Deleuze dictionary. Revised Edition* (pp. 25–27). Edinburgh, UK: Edinburgh University Press.

Stephenson, A. M. (2011). Foreword. In R. Faber, & A. M. Stephenson (Eds.), *Secrets of becoming: Negotiating Whitehead, Deleuze and Butler* (pp. xi–xx). New York, NY: Fordham University Press.

9

Conclusion: Research Partnerships in Early Years Education

Judith Duncan and Lindsey Conner

> [T]eaching as profession in itself nowadays is seen as an area of knowledge, being a subject of inquiry and research. The dichotomy between head and hand is in this respect a thing of the past. Teachers should be good doers because they are qualified as good 'knowers'. Not all teachers are expected to be scholars but all teacher students urgently need to be trained in critical thought and theoretical reasoning. This is the major task and possibility of educational research today.
>
> (Franck, 2006, p. 9)

Introduction

Teachers are more than technicians, more than *doers*. The old saying that "those who can do, those who can't teach" can no longer be applied to teachers in the twenty-first century. Those who engage in teaching, whatever their title (educator, carer, teacher, pedagogista), are required to understand why they do what they do at both the theoretical and the technical levels. The authors in this collection have discussed how teachers engaged in research, at various levels of engagement, are supported in new ways to rethink their *taken-for-granted ways of working*, to be *troubled* within their pedagogical habits, to encounter tensions and uncertainties around and about *best practice* or *evidence-based practices*. Alongside the teachers, the partners in the research, whatever their title (university researcher, academic researcher, outsider, expert researcher, research associate), are challenged to rethink their areas of expertise, to reassess what counts as knowledge, to encounter uncertainty, diversity, innovation in ways and forms that challenge traditional research methods, traditional ways of writing in the academic world, and more familiar forms of knowledge, understanding, and learning. Across the chapters the authors have provided examples where the partnership of teachers and researchers has challenged predictable, linear, causal links among professional development, research, and teacher transformation. Each chapter has provided the context and examples that highlight the importance of teachers engaged in research—whatever method or form that this may have taken.

The Researching Teacher

Teaching and research, once seen as separate activities carried out by separate individuals, are now regular aspects of many teachers' lives. Oliver (2005) describes the traditional understanding of the teaching and learning process as the teachers having been "the consumers of knowledge and academic researchers as its producers" (p. 1). Gilmore (2007) traced the practitioner researcher in the following roles:

- research/passive participant—the subject of research;
- active participant—taking part in the research as an active participant by examining the outcomes of changes to their practices (sometimes they have been described as 'teacher-researchers'); and
- teacher-researcher—designing and carrying out an action research project within their classroom, supported by a researcher—this is the most typical role. (p. 27)

The shift from seeing teachers as consumers (and often passive consumers) to active generators and creators of knowledge through research and investigation has increased in all the education sectors over the last two decades. Beginning with involving teachers more actively in professional development models that included self-review, self-study, and action research models, teachers began to research their own practices (often using the softer term of investigation rather than research). Cochrane-Smith and Lytle (1999) identified the emergence of this change in thinking about teaching and suggested, "in its broadest sense, the emphasis of the movement is on teacher as knower and as agent for change" (Cochrane-Smith & Lytle, 1999, p. 22). These roles for teachers—as knowers and as agents of change—are the focus of a substantial body of scholarship published between 1995 and 2012; scholarship asking how teacher knowledge is constructed, how teachers can change their practice, and how teachers' practices change the world in which they teach.

Mayo (2006) describes the justifications for practitioners (teachers) becoming researchers, rather than researched-on or *othered*, as follows:

1. To recognise that the practitioner is at the forefront of knowledge construction because she or he works at the point where social issues emerge and are addressed.
2. To value these experiential insights of practitioners that cannot be captured by realist forms of normalising or interpretive research.
3. To provide the teacher practitioner access to voice and power so that she or he, and the profession, grow in statutre.
4. To redress the balance: the voice of the teacher as practitioner has been silenced in political debates in recent educational reforms. (Mayo, 2006, p. 129)

Cochrane-Smith and Lytle (1999) revealed that teacher research had become increasingly prominent in teacher education, professional development, and school reform, and that a number of conceptual frameworks for teacher research emerged or were further developed during the 1990s. These frameworks included teacher research as social inquiry, teacher research as ways of knowing within communities and teacher research as practical inquiry. While important critiques were made of teacher research on epistemological and methodological grounds, and on the basis of its purposes, teacher research has continued to grow as a movement and field of inquiry. Potter (2001) argues that teachers "can no longer be regarded as irrelevant to the discourse on curriculum and pedagogy. They must be given the opportunity within their workplaces to enter the conversations in knowledgeable and meaningful ways" (p. 12).

Teachers' theorization, critique, and construction of their own practice have become a major focus of previous and current publications. There is now a significant body of work examining action research and self-study of teaching, both in terms of how and why they should be done and in terms of their benefits for teaching and for society generally.

Researching Partnerships: Researchers and Researching Teachers

Research partnerships between academics and practicing teachers have gained tremendous interest internationally as a transformative way to advance knowledge about teaching and learning. This shift to emphasizing the importance of partnerships in educational research developed from a strand of literature that began to question the efficacy of teachers researching in their isolated context. The co-construction of knowledge between research partners—teachers and other professionals—has become central to the discussions and experiences of researching education, both for practicing teachers and for other professionals interested in educational settings, particularly ongoing professional learning. Educational research partnerships are now one of the most well supported forms of research in many countries, with funding made available by universities and governments to support such partnerships within educational investigations.

There are numerous ways in which a partnership can operate, but the underlying premise is that there is collaboration and sharing of tasks, in which each individual accepts some level of responsibility for the overall task and the team establishes processes that "promote learning, mutual accountability and shared power over relevant decisions" (Timperley & Robinson, 2002, cited in Oliver, 2005, p. 1). Potter (2001) discusses "the power of collaboration, professional dialogue, and social interaction in teacher-researchers' professional growth [and] calls for a departure from the traditional theory-into-practice model which has historically seen university-based researchers generating knowledge or research questions for teachers who, in turn, are expected to respond" (Potter, 2001, p. 8). Potter recognized the teacher as a knowledge generator and sees knowledge production as a shared responsibility of school-based and university-based researchers. Potter's own study, a qualitative research project conducted collaboratively by school-based and university-based researchers, aimed to explore the home literacies of children from socioculturally diverse contexts. The project assessed the role of collaboration in challenging and generating new professional understandings about the complexity of teachers' work. Potter suggests that relationships between university-based and school-based researchers vary from those in which the teacher is an *object* of study by the university-based researcher, to those in which the teacher is an active participant as a teacher-researcher. It is not often the case that the teacher-researcher is involved in the conceptualization of a research project, posing research questions, identifying methodology, engaging in collaborative analysis and interpretation, and giving voice to the findings.

In a review of Early Childhood Centres of Innovation (COI), a New Zealand initiative, which was funded nationally from 2003 to 2009 and developed around research partnerships between early years teachers and researchers (mostly from tertiary institutions), Meade (2010) identified that the success of these partnerships were dependent on the complementary skills that each partner brought to the project. She emphasizes the importance of the different roles that the partners play at different times that enabled research capabilities to emerge—for teachers building up research skills, and for *ivory tower academics* to be immersed in early years settings once again. This has been confirmed by the projects discussed in this volume. For example, Duncan, and Ritchie, Craw, Rau, and Duhn.

The values of research partnerships within research projects have been recorded as continuing past the life of the research itself. In a recent New Zealand study (Brennan, Everiss, & Mara, 2011) in which three academics joined together as teachers and researchers to investigate a field-based initial teacher education program with the tutors and students, the benefits were extended beyond the project by generating a longer-term interest and a willingness to work together. They described it as follows:

> An additional dimension has been the development of positive working relationships between three tertiary institutions and a community of practice, which extends beyond the research project itself to a more general scenario of support for, and interest in, each other's work. Significantly, the participants have expressed interest in following through on the findings of this study to research their own pedagogy. This ongoing desire to engage is indicative of the importance of the study for teacher educators' own professional practice and commitment to ongoing articulation and understanding of effective field-based pedagogies in ITE [Initial Teacher Education].
>
> (Brennan, Everiss, & Mara, 2011, p. 5)

In another New Zealand early years partnership project, the authors have identified successful outcomes for their research between two academics and a team of kindergarten teachers to be as follows:

> Through action research, the research team has addressed the teachers' questions associated with (a) the strengthening of relationships (how this has been done so far, and how might it be furthered); (b) changes in practice (what is possible, what appears to be effective); (c) diversity (how a range of "funds of knowledge" (González, Moll, & Amanti, 2005) can be shared and included in curriculum); and (d) documentation (how this can engage families and learners).
>
> (Clarkin-Phillips & Carr, n. d., p. 1)

Oliver (2005), in her study of partnerships across 16 Teaching and Learning Research Initiative (TLRI) projects in New Zealand, found that

> while in some project teams all the members may work in unison on the tasks, in others it may be more practical for partners with differing experience to divide the work into distinct tasks and assign them appropriately.

> In these situations members of the partnership may be working independently of each other, and there may be differing levels of interaction between various members of the project team.
>
> (Timperley & Robinson, 2002, cited in Oliver, 2005, p. 2)

Meade (2010), in a review of New Zealand's COI teaching and research partnerships, described the division of responsibilities for the early childhood teachers and the expert researchers (known as research associates in this program). In clearly differentiating these roles, there were different expectations of the expertise in terms of skills and knowledge that partners would bring, but that these could complement each other. Indeed, Meade pointed out that there was not always a clear distinction as to who was the expert in what: "Sometimes... different practitioners took up research roles in later cycles, and the research associates needed to increase their research capability" (Meade, 2010, p. 9). These forms of negotiation are clearly articulated in Atkinson and Elliot, Duncan, Fleer, and Ritchie et al. chapters in this volume.

Garvey Berger and Baker (2008) in reviewing the role of partnership in the New Zealand TLRI projects funded from 2002 till 2008, observed the models that were more commonly favored in the projects. These fell under two approaches: practitioner as research assistant, or researcher and practitioner as associates. They argue that the first approach is not as dissimilar to traditional research models as to not purport to be partnership projects. For example, the ideas, research questions, and decisions around methods come from the researcher and they do most of the data gathering. The role of the teacher in this approach is to be an informant, possibly coordinate the data gathering (giving out and collecting surveys, hosting focus groups), and support the researcher. The second approach, where the partners are *associates*, is based on the teachers and the researcher/s as collaborators.

> Researchers teach teachers about research, but teachers often decide on the questions that interest them (often under a particular umbrella) and investigate those questions inside their own classroom. Teachers and researchers collect data (sometimes with the teachers collecting data in their classroom and the researchers collecting data on the teacher/researcher partnership) and talk about what they're learning. The partners analyse the data together. Sometimes they even write up and present the findings together.
>
> (Garvey Berger & Baker, 2008, p. 4)

The benefits of this *associates* model are agreed upon across many writers' discussions of research/academic partnerships. Garvey Berger and

Baker (2008) claim that this form of partnership makes real changes to teaching, "ensuring the connection between [teachers] research and their practice" (p. 5). However, Pacini-Ketchabaw and Nxumalo's chapter opens with the statement, "we feel it is naïve to talk about research partnerships as opportunities that bring about change in educator's practices" (p. 28). Partnerships do not guarantee that there will be successful outcomes either for the research itself or for improving the education of children or educational environments. What might we learn from projects where there was a deliberate partnership approach to research in education?

While the outcomes of many of partnership research projects in educational settings have been reported elsewhere, the experiences of building workable, long-term relationships between academics and teachers/educators has received very little attention. Partnerships afford multiple perspectives within educational settings; however, in this book we were interested in how partners developed their relationships within the contexts of investigation, how these led to either expected or unanticipated outcomes, and the enablers or barriers to the research projects. The authors in this edited book have provided in-depth case studies of their collaborations across their own projects to discuss how they addressed the complexities of working in partnerships to meet the aims of each project and any longer-term outcomes. Indeed, while all the contributors to this book have been able to identify the benefits of partnership research in education, they also all provide caution in simplifying both the processes and the outcomes from such endeavors. Across and between the chapters, the following cautions and encouragers can be understood.

The Importance of Context—Place, Space, Time

Nuttall (2010), in her review of partnership-funded educational research, identified how COI teachers were expected to use "their skills with the complementary skills of researchers" (p. 3). She argued that both COI and TLRI projects demanded "a level of relational expertise that must in itself be developed and enacted within the complex social, political, cultural, environmental and economic agendas facing the education sector" (Nuttall, 2010, p. 3). While research may often *describe* the context of the project, educational research must look wider at the educational terrain that the research is occurring in. For education, this terrain includes, as Nuttall states, "the complex social, political, cultural, environmental and economic agendas facing the education sector" (p. 3). How more complex this becomes when partnerships and relationships are added into the research environment? Fleer, in this collection, identifies the complexity of working across agencies and providers, all the while working within the wider Australian Government agenda for implementing their first national early years curriculum. She discusses how each partner brought their own expertise in theoretical frameworks and in cultural and social conditions to each meeting. The focus for this partnership was shaped by the objective to provide an *end-product*—resources to support the curriculum document. She argues that this shared focus, or common research goal, played a key part in the projects' success, while the collaborative approach to working combined "and extended collective expertise, while simultaneously learning from each other" (p. 58). Fleer's discussion of the negotiations, the shifts, the compromises, the challenges, and the excitement that the processes involved demonstrates "relational agency" across time and place, within a political context. McLachlan, Arrow, and Watson discuss the political interest in literacy, which shaped the shared engagement of their research partners in the studies they describe in their contribution. Having a shared desire to increase the literacy of children and the complementary skills of the early childhood teachers/educators formed the focal point in both chapters 4 and 5. In both chapters, having the shared academic focus enabled the relationships and partnerships to focus on the tasks in hand, thus giving a *safe place* to begin, to debate, and to work together on professionally focused contexts.

Pacini-Ketchabaw and Nxumalo reflect on the potential of relationships that include place/land and with the colonial past and present. The importance of the colonialism is apparent in all the contributions to this book. Our authors, who are from New Zealand, Australia, and Canada, all Commonwealth countries, trace their European influences from a colonized history (Britain). In each of these countries, the position of the Indigenous/First Nations people present social, cultural, and political concerns. Ritchie, Craw, Rau, and Duhn discuss the Indigenous conceptual underpinnings to their partnership projects. They conclude their explorations of partnerships with the reminder that while early childhood education, and partnerships within these settings, are sites of potentiality, they are however imbued with "the historicity and legacy of colonization, racism, and cultural and economic inequities" (p. 159). Time, another condition, is shaped by these legacies and impacts our relationships, our processes, and our understandings. This has been described by Brown and Jones (2001) in the following way.

> [H]ow we might construe time as practitioner-researcher. It questions the limits of our capacity to enter into *projects of action* as intentional beings (Schutz, 1962), embedded as we are in socially derived constructions of the world we experience. It offers versions of how we map out time into the future and how we situate ourselves as being derived from our pasts. It hints

that construing practice as "aiming for an ideal" has a questionable track record, but also that we necessarily experience difficulty in making sense of the present since we understand our present through cultural filters to which we contribute. [emphasis in original]

(Brown & Jones, 2001, p. 57)

Mei Lai and McNaughton emphasized that time is not just bounded by the length of the project, but involves the ongoing relationships that the partners have—in the prior planning of the projects and in the life after the project. Time is discussed in regard to establishing and building the relationships to begin a project with partners; for example, Duncan stresses the importance of time—time to be known and become known so as to build relationships that can move past unfamiliarity and strangeness. Her work built on prior relationships that proved to be valuable in a research partnership context so that there was willingness by the teachers to invest time and effort for the longer-term benefit of the project. McLachlan et al. described shared time between researchers and teachers as pivotal to the transformation of thinking for both the researchers and the teachers. However, they also pointed out that in terms of resources and funding, it is this shared time that is the most expensive and is often the area where research partners cut back to *afford* the project (i.e., paid release time for teachers and researchers to meet together).

Complexity of Change and Transformation

Brown and Jones (2001) question the value of action research in education as challenging the traditional understanding of the reflective practitioner, education's answerable questions (or unanswerable questions), and whether teacher-research is actually about better teaching or better lives for children. They de-emphasize the research process itself and instead argue for the "centrality of the writing process" (p. 7) to bring about both an awareness of the self and a construction of the teacher/researcher:

> We thus understand the task of practitioner research as being targeted at producing a construction of self in relation to the professional/social context being faced. (p. 8)

They go on to argue that this writing process, undertaken by a teacher, changes both the teacher and the reality that the teacher is describing. Reminiscent of the theories of Deleuze and Guattari (1987), this sense of teachers *becoming* and constructing themselves and their research through engaging in research and writing runs through the chapters. In their chapter, Pacini-Ketchabaw and Nxumalo, draw on postfoundational theorizing to make sense of the relationality of partnerships. They, too, argue that traditional educational research has too often taken a linear progression of improvement trajectories as a sign of success. They argue for the complexity of change within teaching. Rather than seeing change as something that researchers can bring about in teachers, Pacini-Ketchabaw and Nxumalo argue that change is "a pervasive state of life," that is, a *becoming*. They summarize:

> If we accept that we are in a process of becoming, of constant change, then we must abandon our idea of a static change, knowable educator and move to a view of on educator in a state of constant becoming and change. (p. 27)

Several of the authors discuss the role and place of professional development as part of their research projects—thus blurring the boundaries for both data gathering and creating and constructing change. Presenting research as professional development enabled teachers to see the projects in a more familiar light, and enabled the university researchers to build on methods that teachers are already familiar with; for example, McLachlan et al., Mei Lai and McNaughton, and Pacini-Ketchabaw and Nxumalo explain how professional development blurs within their research as both forms of action with teachers are known to support change and difference.

Ritchie et al. reflect that teachers themselves see this blurring but are increasingly interested in the research side of the partnerships:

> From my experience, it has been interesting to note that over time many teachers are becoming motivated to participate in research projects because of the opportunities it might offer them to engage in more challenging ways (to think about and work ideas as well as their practices) than a 'professional development' model might once have offered. (p. 145)

Power: The Elephant in the Room in Teacher-Researcher Partnerships

Pacini-Ketchabaw and Nxumalo introduce their chapter with the argument on the complexities of relationality in research. They highlight the non-innocent relations in educational research and the potentials for conflict and dissension with research partners. Duncan and Ritchie et al. discuss the cautions and tensions at the beginning of their partnership projects: what are the *real* agendas going on here? Friend or foe? Despite already being known, the nature of being the *outsider,* or the one who is seen to be the *knower* or *expert*, poses tensions within all the chapters in this collection. Atkinson and Elliot highlight how stepping outside the usual roles when discussing pedagogical episodes was also *risky*, despite their *insider* relationships with the teachers. When Kim Atkinson discussed her teaching experiences, her confrontation with the tough issues that are often silenced, was an example of making the comfortable uncomfortable, of changing the power dynamics in the group, of contesting the *good-teacher-as-normalized* discourse. In their pedagogical example, Kim opened herself and her actions to scrutiny and judgment, depending on the relational expertise of the group to support her reconceptualization of her teaching responses, and those of the others in the group. While "pedagogy of uncertainty" had been the focus of their "Sharing Circle," they also positioned themselves as *becoming-vulnerable*:

> To invite someone to join you in a dialogue and to listen and to be heard is to be vulnerable within that encounter.... [E]xploring the cracks in our practice and ourselves—places of discomfort and uncertainty. (p. 190)

Ritchie et al. discuss the power of voice in research partnerships. Whose voice is being heard? What do we count as *voice*? Why do researchers interview teachers and not the other way around in a partnership? Remembering, as discussed above, that all relationships are positioned within social, cultural, and historical contexts adds another layer of complexity to capturing, hearing, listening, and recording voice. Relationality is a key to disempowering or reempowering the *voice* of partners within a project.

The authors use a range of terms to talk about research relations: relational agency, relationality, and relationships. McLachlan et al. summarize the possibilities and success of research partnerships as "premised upon the same principles that underpin any successful relationship: trust, empathy and great communication" (p. 131). Within these relationships all the authors discuss the theories that the partners bring to the research: the university partners often offer the *theories*: cultural-historical, poststructural, postfoundational, developmental, et cetera; the teachers offer theories in action, pedagogical theories, and theory-as-lived. Mei Lai and McNaughton emphasize the importance of taking into account all the partners' "theories of action." Across the chapters there are examples of how opportunities were used to explore and understand the theories of partners in the projects ranging from building learning communities, collaborative critically engaged communities, and professional learning communities, to types of communities of practice. Within such shared communities not only do the partners begin to understand and share their knowledge with others but also there can be significant changes in the perception of who-holds-the-power.

The chapters in this collection themselves demonstrate the shift in recognizing and acknowledging the expertise, knowledges, and understanding that the partners bring to the projects in their constructions. While several of the chapters have a more traditional approach to writing about the partnership (the researcher writes about the project and inserts quotes and evidence from the partners), several of the chapters have been written/constructed/created with the whole teams; for example, the chapter by Atkinson and Elliot. This shift in the writing process as well as the researching process represents a significant shift in reframing the partnership from beginning to end.

Ending on a Beginning

The chapters provide examples of teachers as researchers, researchers as teachers, teachers as learners, and researchers as learners. Each chapter poses many questions for thinking about and investigating the *unanswerable* questions within education. The examples have demonstrated uncertainty, entanglements, pleasures, regrets, successes, cautions, risks, adventures, and challenges. We have not tried to provide instructions or models of educational research partnerships to follow, nor have we tried to capture guidelines or exemplars. What we have hoped to do in this contribution to educational research is to begin a conversation. A conversation that encourages others to work alongside and with *others* to provoke "experimentation" within teaching, pedagogy, teaching lives, and children's learning (Olsson, 2009). To engage in the performance of partnership research as creating reality as much as recording reality (Brown & Jones, 2001); to recognize the fluidity of research within time, place, context, and relationality (Brown & Jones, 2001; Deleuze & Guattari, 1987; Olsson, 2009); to reshift *the gaze* from anticipated or predicted change, or a hoped-for outcome or objective, to one of viewing with excitement the *becomings* of teachers, and the innovation and experimentation of teaching and learning.

The contribution that this edited volume makes is that it simultaneously addresses how early years education makes a difference, what early years teachers do to make the difference, and the significance of researching early years education collaboratively. We hope that this collection will be the beginning of many more conversations.

References

Brennan, M., Everiss, L., & Mara, D. (2011). *Field-based early childhood teacher education: "But they are already teachers..." Summary report*. Wellington, NZ: Teaching Learning Research Initiative. Retrieved from http://www.tlri.org.nz/cross-sector-list.

Brown, T., & Jones, L. (2001). *Action research and postmodernism: Congruence and critique.* Buckingham, UK: Open University Press.

Clarkin-Phillips, J., & Carr, M. (n. d.). *Strengthening responsive and reciprocal relationships in a Whānau Tangata centre: An action research project. Summary report.* Wellington, NZ: Teaching Learning Research Initiative. Retrieved from http://www.tlri.org.nz/strengthening-responsive-and-reciprocal-relationships-wh%C3%A4nau-tangata-centre-action-research-project/.

Cochrane-Smith, M., & Lytle, S. L. (1999). The teacher research movement: A decade later. *Educational Researcher, 28*(7), 15–25.

Deleuze, G., & Guattari, F. (1987). *A thousand plateaus: Capitalism and schizophrenia* (B. Massumi, Trans.). Minneapolis, MN: University of Minnesota Press.

Franck, E. (2006). Foreword. In T. S. Popkewitz, K. Petersson, U. Olsson, & J. Kowalczyk (Eds.), *"The future is not what it appears to be." Pedagogy, genealogy and political epistemology. In honor and in memory of Kenneth Hultqvist* (p. 9). Stockholm, Sweden: HLS Förlag.

Garvey Berger, J., & Baker, R. (2008). *Developing new knowledge and practice through teacher—researcher partnerships? Discussion paper.* Wellington, NZ: Teaching and Learning Initiative, New Zealand Council for Educational Research. Retrieved from http://www.tlri.org.nz/tlri-research/discussion-papers.

Gilmore, A. (2007). *Review of the teaching and learning research initiative: Discussion paper* Wellington, NZ: Teaching and Learning Research Initiative. Retrieved from http://www.tlri.org.nz/tlri-research/discussion-papers.

Mayo, E. (2006). Researching together: Praxis-based research among practitioners. In C. Mutch (Ed.), *Challenging the notion of "other." Reframing research in the Aotearoa New Zealand context* (pp. 119–140). Wellington, NZ: NZCER Press.

Meade, A. (2010, November). *The contribution of ECE Centres of Innovation to building knowledge about teaching and learning 2003–2010.* Paper presented to TLRI Early Years Symposium. Wellington, NZ: Teaching and Learning Research Initiative.

Nuttall, J. (2010, November). *The contribution of The Teaching And Learning Research Initiative to building knowledge about teaching and learning: A review of early years projects, 2004–2010.* Paper presented to TLRI Early Years Symposium. Wellington, NZ: Teaching and Learning Research Initiative.

Oliver, A. (2005). *The TLRI: Teachers' perspectives on partnership and research. Final summary.* Wellington, NZ: Teaching and Learning Research Initiative. Retrieved from http://www.tlri.org.nz/tlri-research/discussion-papers.

Olsson, L. M. (2009). *Movement and experimentation in young children's learning: Deleuze and Guattari in early childhood education.* London, UK: Routledge.

Potter, G. (2001). The power of collaborative research in teacher's professional development. *Australian Journal of Early Childhood Education, 26*(2), 8–13.

Index

accountability, xiii, xv, xxi, 140, 146, 156
action research, 16, 17, 19, 54, 58, 66, 95, 137, 138, 141, 154, 155, 157, 161
agency
 child's, 37, 108, 124
 create change, 13, 93
 relational, 3, 5, 6, 27, 28, 29, 30, 32, 39, 41, 43, 47, 160, 163
 teachers, xv–xvi, 35, 147
alliances, 3, 8, 13, 29, 38, 40, 44, 47
approaches to teaching, xv, xix, 50, 55–8, 61–4, 71, 73, 81, 86, 90, 95, 137, 144, 154
assessment, xxvii, 51, 52, 60, 61, 68, 74, 78, 83, 84, 86, 87, 109, 146
assumptions, xiii, xxi, 3, 5, 8, 16, 17, 42, 55, 56, 59, 115, 118, 119, 129, 138
Australia, xiii, xv, xxii, xxvi, xxvii, 5, 6, 10, 28, 30, 34, 36, 41, 43, 47, 90, 111, 112, 160
authentic action, 128, 137, 144

Bahktin, 99
Bandura, 62, 67
barriers/boundaries
 paradigmatic, 28, 159
 relational, xvii, 9, 11, 40, 84, 85, 159
becoming (Deleuzian), xviii, xxi, 17, 18, 19, 21, 121, 126, 129, 139, 140, 142, 146, 147, 148, 149, 161, 162, 163, 164

Canada, xiii, xv, xxiii, xxv–xxviii, 14, 23, 68, 115, 160

caring, xxviii, 13, 17, 20, 105, 108, 112, 117, 128
case studies, xiv, 82, 139, 141, 159
Centres of Innovation (COI), 138, 156, 158, 159
challenges
 beliefs, xix, 5, 6, 30, 32, 33, 39, 42, 55, 59, 62, 72, 75, 85, 87, 89–90, 104, 116, 129–30, 132
 setting up partnerships, 5
 sustaining successful partnerships, 1, 3–6, 9, 28, 29, 43, 68, 89, 159, 163
change management, 54, 95
children's voice, xx, 16, 94–6, 107–9, 111–12, 118, 121–2, 125, 132
coaching, 7, 87, 88
collaboration
 co-construction, xvii, 74, 100, 150
 interagency, xxvii–xxviii, 11, 27–9, 88, 93, 111, 120, 159
 professional, xiv, xvi, xxi–xxii, 3, 14, 24, 45, 156
 research, 4, 9, 11, 28, 88, 93, 104, 110
collegiality, 81, 84, 120
colonial theories, xiv, xvi, xx, 14, 22, 24–6, 31, 107–8, 110
communication, 3, 5, 74, 89, 116, 124, 163
communities of learners, xix, 1, 51, 155, 163
communities of practice, xix, xxvii, 9, 10, 51, 57, 69, 163
complexity of change, xx, 2, 4, 5, 12, 16–19, 24, 28, 64, 68, 75, 82–3, 93, 155, 161–4

conflict, 11, 12, 22, 98, 99, 120, 121, 127, 162
connections
  relational, xvii, 3, 14, 21, 22, 36, 67, 101, 103, 106, 107
  between research and practice, 88, 93, 145, 146, 159
consciousness, 3, 6, 23, 34, 35, 38, 40, 45, 80, 88, 108, 137, 142, 144, 146
Consortium on Chicago School Research (CCSR), 53–4
contextual influences
  cultural context, 6–7, 31, 55, 62, 108, 152, 163
  curriculum context, 13, 30, 38, 41, 54
  evidence-based, 33, 56, 160
  political context, xiii, 9, 14, 86, 160, 165
  situational, 4, 14, 17, 21, 29, 30, 37, 52, 57, 58, 116, 154, 159, 164
  social context, xxvi, 37, 40, 54, 56, 61, 86, 156, 161, 163
control group, 7, 58, 76, 79, 84, 85
co-theorizing, 7, 94
critical reflection, 7, 75, 119, 137, 138, 150
critical theories, xvi, 31
cultural awareness, v, 119
cultural histories, xiii, 21, 23, 37, 160, 163
curriculum, xv, xvi, xix, xxvii, 5, 6, 24, 26, 28, 29, 30, 32, 33, 41, 42, 61, 71, 72, 73, 74, 75, 76, 80, 84, 85, 90, 95, 106, 107, 110, 111, 112, 119, 129, 133, 150, 155, 157, 160

Davydov, 28, 36, 37, 42, 44
Deleuze, xiv, xxi, xxii, 12, 14, 18, 24, 25, 100, 112, 113, 121, 133, 135, 136, 139, 142, 146, 148, 149
Developmentally Appropriate Practice (DAP), 38, 40, 42, 44
developmental theory, 30–4, 37, 42, 45, 46, 47, 80, 119

dialogic (approaches and encounters), xx, 46, 98, 99, 106, 132, 133
dialogue, xxviii, xx, xxi, 9, 24, 35, 45, 98, 99, 106, 111, 113, 119, 122, 125–9, 131, 132, 137–8, 156, 163
differential artifactualism, 12, 13, 20
distributed practice, 20, 32, 34, 36, 38, 43, 98
diversity, 32, 69, 75, 98, 109

Early Years Learning Framework (EYLF), 30, 32, 41
ecological sustainability, xxvi, 95, 105, 106
empathy, 89, 108, 121, 125, 163
empowerment, xvi, xvii, xx, xxii, 4, 7, 35, 106, 163
enablers
  professional practices, 4, 7, 28, 43, 96, 98, 142, 162
  relationships, xvii, 4, 11, 28, 40, 83–5, 94, 100–1, 104, 160
  research, xvi, 39–40, 66, 157, 159
equity, xxviii, 16, 50, 143, 145
ethics
  ethical action/ responses, xx, xxviii, 4, 7, 14, 26, 55, 64, 65, 100, 103, 110, 124–5, 127
  ethical questions/dilemmas, xiv, 5, 7, 20, 22, 23, 115, 118, 121, 126, 129, 131, 133
  research, 2, 4, 22, 96, 104, 105, 109, 112–13
expectations, 8, 73, 97, 136, 147, 151, 158
expertise
  adaptive, 4, 55, 63, 64
  complimentary, xviii, 4, 29, 30, 34, 39, 61, 137, 154, 158, 160
  developing, 4, 20, 39, 43, 126, 159
  distributed, xviii, xix, 29, 32, 34, 36, 38, 43
  relational, 3–7, 9, 45, 88, 163

INDEX

families (whānau), xiii, xxvi, xxvii, 7, 29, 32–5, 38, 40, 44–7, 102, 104, 107, 120, 121, 128–9, 157
First Nations, 20, 21, 160
Foucault, xxi, xxii, 9, 25, 43, 133, 135, 139, 142–6, 148–52
funding, 8, 27, 41, 53, 63, 88, 110, 136, 149, 156, 161

gender, xx, 31, 58, 118, 119, 125, 127, 132
goals, 5, 15–17, 23, 28, 30, 33, 39, 41, 43, 51, 54–6, 63–5, 88, 119, 120, 130, 160
Guattari, xxi, xxii, 12, 15, 18, 24, 100, 112, 135, 136, 139, 142, 146, 148–50, 152, 161, 164, 165

Hedegaard, 40–2, 46

identity, xxii, xxiii, 10, 17, 18, 64, 69, 79, 82, 123, 124, 133, 146
implications
  for policy, 67
  for practice, 8, 13, 44, 45, 71, 84, 89
  for research, xvi, 66
improving teaching and learning, xiii, xxvii, xxviii, 1, 6, 7, 9, 13, 16, 30, 41, 43, 54, 56–69, 73, 76, 79, 84, 105, 138, 140, 149–51, 159, 162
inclusion, xx, 26, 75, 132, 139
indigenous, xix, 51, 57–9, 69, 94, 103, 104, 107, 109, 112, 160
inequities, xx, 59, 108, 160
insights, xvi, xxviii, 1–3, 35, 36, 37, 39, 40, 75, 85, 86, 95, 106, 141, 155
intentions, xvii, 8, 22, 24, 28, 43, 100, 131, 160
intervention, xiii, xix, 2, 5, 6–9, 13, 44, 46, 49–54, 56–68, 72, 75–80, 84–90, 118
intra-action, 2, 17, 19
Investigating Quality (IQ), xxv, xxviii, 7, 115

Kaitiakitanga (ecological sustainability), xxviii, 105
Karakia (Māori spiritual invocation), 104
Kaumātua, 103, 104, 110
Kaupapa Māori, xiv, 55, 65, 108, 109, 110
Kei tua o te pae (NZ ECE assessment explemars), 74, 90
kindergarten, xxv, xxvii, xxix, 67, 72, 74, 80, 82, 84, 85, 87, 88, 90, 94, 103, 108, 125, 139, 140, 148, 150, 151, 157
knowledge
  gaining expertise, xvii, 4, 20, 39, 43, 49, 74, 76, 81, 112, 126, 159
  generating knowledge, xv, xix, 1, 10, 13, 16, 30–4, 40, 43, 90, 94, 96, 110, 154–7, 165
  indigenous, 24, 106
  knowledge systems, xvi, xxi, 1, 12, 28, 29, 37, 103, 154
Kuia (Māori female elder), 103, 108, 110

Lacan, xvi
language
  explicit use of language for learning, 17, 71, 73, 78, 80, 91
  importance in establishing relationships, 34, 107
  importance for group discussions, 26, 34, 39, 99, 130, 147
Learning Schools Model (LSM), 54, 58, 63, 66
learning stories, 74, 95
limitations, 8, 31, 75, 102, 129, 142
lines of flight, 14, 15, 100
literacy development
  phonological awareness, 71–3, 75–8, 83, 86, 87, 88–90
  reading, 6, 46, 50, 52, 57, 59, 60, 65, 67–8, 71, 73, 76–9, 82, 83, 87, 89–91

INDEX

Mana (prestige, integrity), 105, 106, 108
Manaaki (support), 105
Manaakitanga (caring, generosity, hospitality), 105
Māori children, 51, 66, 68
Māori worldview, xx, 103, 105

narrative, xiv–xvii, xx–xxiii, 7, 8, 12, 28, 37, 42, 97, 99–100, 102, 106–8, 113, 116–17, 123–31
National Early Literacy Panel (NELP), 71, 78
naturecultures, 12
negotiations, 99, 106, 158, 160
New Zealand, xiii, xv, xix, xxv–xxvix, 6–8, 10, 50, 52, 55, 64–8, 71–4, 76, 78, 81, 86, 87, 89, 91, 104, 106, 107, 110–12, 135–7, 139, 140, 149, 152, 156, 158, 160, 165
norms, xviii, xx, xxvii, 17, 32, 65, 68, 124, 143–6, 148–9, 155, 163
numeracy development, xviii, 32–6, 38, 40, 45, 81, 85, 89

opportunities, xiii, xv, xvi, 1, 2, 4, 5, 7, 8, 19, 36, 39, 46, 52, 73, 74, 77, 79, 80, 83–7, 94, 95, 96, 100, 102, 106, 126, 130, 132, 155, 159, 162, 163
outcomes
  longer term, 1, 7, 29, 64, 80, 159
  successful, 2, 8, 16, 27, 29, 41, 55, 87, 88, 157, 159
  unanticipated, 2, 59, 87, 159

partnerships
  complicity, 2, 5, 7
  enablers, xvii, 4, 11, 28, 40, 83, 85, 94, 100, 101, 104, 160
  establishing, xix, 6, 28, 65, 104, 109, 139, 140, 161
  importance of collaboration, xiv, xvi, xxi–xxii, 3, 4, 9, 11, 14, 24, 28, 45, 88, 93, 104, 110, 156
  obligations, 6, 55, 65
Pasifika children, 51, 66, 68

pedagogical issues
  conceptual development, xiv, 1, 14, 35–40, 45, 97, 146, 163
  pedagogical narrations, 14, 19, 24, 133
  place-based, 12, 20–2, 128, 159, 160, 162
  play, 5, 34, 43, 44–6, 108, 116–27, 130–3, 140
  responsibilities, 1, 23, 30, 105, 126, 130, 156, 158
pedagogy of uncertainty, xx, 9, 116, 119, 163
planning, 31, 44, 80, 141, 161
plurality, 17
politics, xx, 12, 25, 26, 89, 90, 119
positivism, 97
power, xxii, 8, 9, 13, 16, 21, 22, 31, 32, 42, 65, 96, 98, 101, 108, 109, 110, 111, 112, 117, 119, 121, 123–7, 132, 142, 143, 146, 147, 150, 151, 155, 156, 162, 163, 165
practice
  assumptions, 8, 75, 115, 148
  negotiating, xviii, xix, 1, 2, 14, 15, 31, 85, 100, 115, 126
  quality, xvii, xix, 106, 118, 128, 141, 153
  reflective, see reflective practice
  risks, 1, 4, 30, 56, 138
practitioners, xiii, xix–xxii, 1, 3, 5, 6, 54, 59, 88, 94, 110, 118, 119, 127, 152, 155, 158, 165
precocious methodologies, 94, 109, 111
priorities, 6, 110
professional development, xiii, xix, xxii, 2, 4, 8, 9, 13, 16–19, 25, 26, 33, 45–7, 51, 60, 61, 66, 67, 73, 75, 76, 78, 79, 83–6, 89, 98, 151, 154, 155, 162, 165
professional learning, xv, xxvii–xxviii, 1, 7, 8, 41, 44, 45, 51, 53, 57, 60, 69, 72, 74, 75, 81, 85, 86–90, 103, 104, 163

professional practice, xviii, 2, 30, 47, 84, 101, 157
protocols, 6, 55, 60, 109

qualitative research, xxvi, 13, 23, 25, 95, 110, 111, 156
quantitative research, 57–8
quasi-experimental, xiv, 50, 56–8, 76

reconceptualizing, v, xiv, xxii, xxviii, 1, 4, 14, 17, 26, 97, 110, 163
reflective journals, 135, 136, 141, 143, 149
reflective practice, xiv, xxi, 1, 14, 19, 50, 81, 84, 116, 119, 128, 136–8
regeneration, 5, 12, 23, 25
relationality, xviii, 11, 12, 13, 19, 20, 21, 22, 23, 93, 104, 107, 162, 163, 164
relationships
  agency, xx, 83–6, 93, 106, 163
  co-constructive, 19, 81, 102, 104, 130, 146, 157
  with early years centres, 16, 28, 81, 101, 104, 107, 139, 163, 165
  regeneration of relationships, xviii, 12, 47
  with schools, xx, 50, 75, 156
  tensions, 7, 94, 100, 129, 149
research
  capacity, 3, 106, 122, 160
  control, 7, 58, 63, 75, 76, 77, 79, 80, 83–5
  data gathering, xix, xxix, 7, 42, 54, 56, 76, 81–5, 88, 95, 96, 107, 135, 138, 141, 146, 149, 158, 162
  design, 2, 6–9, 16, 50–61, 64, 66, 67–9, 76, 78, 80, 81, 85, 86, 95, 105, 106, 109, 143, 154
  evidence-based, xxvii, 6, 8, 24, 27–8, 33, 41, 49, 53, 56, 58, 59, 60, 62, 67–9, 74, 84, 86, 89, 91, 118, 138, 144, 153, 164
  funding, 8, 27, 41, 53, 65, 88, 110, 136, 149, 156, 161
  interpretivist, 12, 18, 39, 74, 108, 111, 155

  issues, 59, 62, 94, 116
  narrative, xiv–xxiii, 7, 8, 12, 28, 37, 42, 97, 99, 100, 102, 106–8, 113, 116, 117, 123, 124, 127–33
  self-study, 8, 9, 138, 139, 151, 152, 154, 155
  use of journals, 8, 136, 139, 141, 143, 145–7, 149
researchers
  associates, 158
  changing dynamics, xiv, xx, xxiv, 94
  co-researchers, 94, 95, 105–10
  gaining expertise, 4, 20, 39, 43, 126, 159
  teachers as researchers, 1, 9, 164
roles
  academics, 8, 64, 85, 97, 103, 105, 110, 154
  collaborations, xxi, 8, 27, 55, 65, 85, 156–8
  educators, 8, 34, 36, 38, 119, 124, 129, 132, 141, 147, 158
  ethical, xx, 85
routines, 16, 82, 119

Schön, 137, 152
self study, 8, 9, 138, 139, 151, 152, 154, 155
sharing circle, 116, 127, 131, 132, 163
skill development, 6, 61, 77, 86
social histories, 23
social justice, xxviii, xxix, 16, 87, 109
social relations, 13, 23, 37
stories, xvii, xx, 12–15, 19–23, 25, 74, 83, 95, 97, 99, 107, 110, 116, 117, 122, 123, 127, 129, 130, 132, 149
Strategic Education Research Partnership (SERP), 54, 56, 69
surveillance, xv, xxi, xxii, 139, 140, 143, 144, 145, 146, 149
sustainability of partnerships, 23, 51, 65, 95
institutional strategies, 52, 53

Tamariki (Māori term for child), xxviii, 3, 93, 94, 104, 105, 106, 107, 109

Tangata Whenua (Indigenous), 104
Taonga (treasure), 103, 109
teacher education, xv, xvi, xvii, xxv, xxix, 2, 13, 18, 74, 75, 98, 131, 138, 155, 157
teacher researchers, 10, 50, 51, 65, 66, 90, 94, 100, 103, 104, 107, 110, 111, 112, 138, 149, 151, 152, 157–9, 164, 165
Teaching and Learning Research Initiative (TLRI), xxviii, 6, 8, 50, 51, 65, 66, 94, 100, 103, 104, 107, 110, 138, 149, 157, 158, 159
teaching practices, xix, 3, 51, 57–8, 61, 64, 66, 67, 86, 95, 149
Te Ao Māori, 103, 105, 106
Te Tiriti o Waitangi (Treaty of Waitangi), xxviii, 7, 95, 104, 106, 107, 110
Te Whāriki (NZ early childhood curriculum), 72–4, 80, 90, 107, 109, 112
theories of
　child development, xviii, 10, 30, 31, 32, 33, 34, 37, 38, 41, 42, 68, 69, 112, 119
　colonialism, xiv, xx, 14, 21, 22, 23, 24, 31, 108, 160
　cultural-historical, xiv, 5, 28, 31–4, 36–9, 44, 45, 47, 163
　feminist, 12, 14, 25, 111, 118
　maturation, 31, 33, 34, 37, 39
　postcolonial, xvi, 14, 25, 26, 108
　post-developmental, 31, 39
　post-humanist, 9, 14, 24
　postmodern, xvi, 24, 96, 165

post-structural, xiv, 9, 14, 25, 31, 43, 94, 95, 133, 163
queer, 14
Tikanga, 103
Tino Rangatiratanga (self determination), 108
transformation, 11, 17, 24, 36, 37, 40, 42, 43, 94, 154
transformative thinking, 87, 93, 161
transience, 17, 57
trust, xx, 35, 50, 69, 89, 100, 101, 104, 119, 123, 125–7, 128–30, 163

uncertainty, xiv, xvi, 9, 18, 24, 115, 116–19, 126, 128–30, 148, 154, 163, 164
urban communities, 6, 49

Victoria Investigating Quality Group (IQ), xxv, xxviii, 7, 115, 119, 123, 126, 127, 129
vision, xiv, 11–13, 15, 23, 43, 148
vulnerability, xxi, 102, 119, 124, 126, 140
Vygotsky, 5, 10, 28, 32, 35, 42, 47, 60, 69

Wairuatanga (spiritual interconnectedness), 104, 105
Whakapapa (origins, genealogy), 105
Whakatau (Māori greeting ceremony), 104
Whānau (family, extended family), xiii, xxvi, xxvii, 7, 29, 32–5, 38, 40, 44–7, 102, 104, 107, 120, 121, 128–9, 157
Whānaungatanga (relationships), xx, 106

GPSR Compliance
The European Union's (EU) General Product Safety Regulation (GPSR) is a set of rules that requires consumer products to be safe and our obligations to ensure this.

If you have any concerns about our products, you can contact us on

ProductSafety@springernature.com

In case Publisher is established outside the EU, the EU authorized representative is:

Springer Nature Customer Service Center GmbH
Europaplatz 3
69115 Heidelberg, Germany

www.ingramcontent.com/pod-product-compliance
Lightning Source LLC
LaVergne TN
LVHW051912060526
838200LV00004B/101